Written and Compiled by

**Dave Kemper, Patrick Sebranek,
and Verne Meyer**

Illustrated by

Chris Krenzke

WRITE SOURCE®

GREAT SOURCE EDUCATION GROUP
a division of Houghton Mifflin Company
Wilmington, Massachusetts

Reviewers

Genevieve M. Bodnar
Youngstown City
  School District
Youngstown, Ohio

Joan Chiodo
Patricia Di Chiaro
  Elementary
Yonkers, New York

Kay Dooley
Naperville Community USD
Naperville, Illinois

Jean Evans
Jenks Southeast
  School District
Tulsa, Oklahoma

Paula Denise Findley
White Hall, Arkansas

Mary Fischer
Arlington Public Schools
Arlington, Massachusetts

Cullen Hemstreet
Jefferson Parish
  School District
Metairie, Louisiana

Elma G. Jones
Wallingford-Swarthmore
  School District
Swarthmore, Pennsylvania

Marilyn LeRud
Tucson Unified
  School District
Tucson, Arizona

Mary Osborne
Pinellas County
  School District
Largo, Florida

Amy Stenger
Millard Public Schools
Omaha, Nebraska

Pamela J. Strain
Rosemead School District
Rosemead, California

Technology Connections for *Write Source*

This series is supported by two Web sites:

The **Great Source iwrite** site is a writing resource that supports students, teachers, and parents. You'll find tutorials about the forms and traits of writing, as well as the latest articles, features, tips, and contests. Go to **www.greatsource.com/iwrite**.

The **Write Source** site features all the materials available from Write Source, as well as handy writing topics, student models, and help with research. You can even read about the history of Write Source. Go to **www.thewritesource.com**.

Printed in the United States of America

International Standard Book Number: 978-0-669-00663-6 (hardcover)
2 3 4 5 6 7 8 9 10 -RRDC- 15 14 13 12 11 10 09

International Standard Book Number: 978-0-669-00896-8 (softcover)
2 3 4 5 6 7 8 9 10 -RRDC- 15 14 13 12 11 10 09

Using the *Write Source* Book

Your *Write Source* book is loaded with information to help you learn about writing. One section that will be especially helpful is the "Proofreader's Guide" at the back of the book. This section covers all of the rules for capitalization, punctuation, spelling, and grammar.

The book also includes four main units covering the types of writing that you may have to complete on district or state writing tests. At the end of each unit, there are samples and tips for writing in science, in social studies, and in practical writing.

The *Write Source* book will help you with other learning skills such as speaking, listening, and test taking. This makes the *Write Source* book a valuable learning guide in all your subjects.

Your *Write Source* guide . . .

With practice, you will be able to find information in this book quickly using the guides explained below.

- The **CONTENTS** lists the six major sections in the book and the chapters found in each section.

- The **INDEX** (starting on page 560) lists every topic covered in the book in alphabetical order.

- The **COLOR CODING** used for "Basic Grammar and Writing," "A Writer's Resource," and the "Proofreader's Guide" make these important sections easy to find.

- The green **PAGE NUMBERS** send you to other pages in the book for additional information.

The Writing Process

Why Write? 1

USING THE WRITING PROCESS

Using the Writing Process 2

Understanding the Writing Process 4

    Connecting with the Traits   5
    Using the Writing Process   6
    Becoming a Writer   8

One Writer's Process 10

    Prewriting Selecting a Topic   11
                   Gathering Details
    Writing Developing a First Draft   12
    Revising Improving the Writing   13
    Editing Checking for Conventions   14
    Publishing Sharing Your Writing   15
    STUDENT MODEL "Special Storytellers"   15

Working with Partners 16

    Helping One Another   17
    Reviewing with Partners   18
    Using a Response Sheet   19

Traits of Good Writing 20

    ■ **Ideas**   21
    ■ **Organization**   22
    ■ **Voice**   23
    ■ **Word Choice**   24
    ■ **Sentence Fluency**   24
    ■ **Conventions**   25

contents

Contents

Using a Rubric 26

Understanding Rubrics 27

Getting Started with a Rubric 28

Understanding Your Goal 29

Assessing with a Rubric 30

Assessing an Expository Essay 32

STUDENT MODEL "Taking Care of a Dog" 32

Sample Assessment 33

Publishing and Portfolios 34

Publishing Your Writing 35

Writing a Neat Final Copy 36

STUDENT MODEL "When I Grow Up" 36

Using a Portfolio 38

Creating a Portfolio 40

Sample Portfolio Introductions 41

The Forms of Writing

DESCRIPTIVE WRITING

Writing a Descriptive Paragraph **44**

    STUDENT MODEL "The Fire-Breathing Truck"   45

Writing a Descriptive Essay **50**

    Understanding Your Goal   51

    STUDENT MODEL "Seashells by the Seashore"   52

    Prewriting   54

    Writing   56

    Revising   62

    Editing   64

    Publishing   66

    STUDENT MODEL "Locket in My Pocket"   66

    Reflecting on Your Writing   67

★ **Writing for Assessment** **68**

    STUDENT MODEL "Powwow Jingle Dress"   69

NARRATIVE WRITING

Writing a Narrative Paragraph 74
STUDENT MODEL "The Mountain Climber"   75

Writing a Narrative Essay 80
Understanding Your Goal   81
STUDENT MODEL "Mrs. Rios"   82
Prewriting   84
Writing   86
Revising   92
  ■ **Ideas:** Connecting with Your Reader   94
  ■ **Organization:** Using Time Order   96
  ■ **Voice:** Making Your Voice Sound Like You   98
  ■ **Word Choice:** Choosing Action Verbs   100
  ■ **Sentence Fluency:** Combining Sentences   102
Editing   105
  ■ **Conventions:** Checking for the Right Words   105
Assessing: Using a Rubric   108
Publishing   110
STUDENT MODEL "Skateboard Emergency 9-1-1"   110
Reflecting on Your Writing   111

★ Writing Across the Curriculum 112
Social Studies: Biographical Narrative   113
STUDENT MODEL "Chocolate in His Pocket"   113
Art: A Personal Art Story   116
STUDENT MODEL "Texture Detectives"   116
Practical Writing: Friendly Letter   118
STUDENT MODEL "Dear Damitria"   118

★ Writing for Assessment 120
STUDENT MODEL "Dancing Drums"   121

EXPOSITORY WRITING

Writing an Expository Paragraph **126**
STUDENT MODEL "The Great Thing About My Bike" **127**

Writing an Expository Essay **132**
Understanding Your Goal **133**
STUDENT MODEL "The Home on My Back" **134**
Prewriting **136**
Writing **138**
Revising **144**
◼ **Ideas:** Showing Details **146**
◼ **Organization:** Checking the Parts **148**
◼ **Voice:** Sounding Interested **150**
◼ **Word Choice:** Using Specific Nouns **152**
◼ **Sentence Fluency:** Fixing Run-On Sentences **154**
Editing **157**
◼ **Conventions:** Using Commas in a Series **157**
Assessing: Using a Rubric **160**
Publishing **162**
STUDENT MODEL "All Right, an Overnight!" **162**
Reflecting on Your Writing **163**

★ **Writing Across the Curriculum** **164**
Social Studies: News Report **165**
STUDENT MODEL "Kids in China" **165**
Music: Report **168**
STUDENT MODEL "Boom-Whack-a-Boom" **168**
Practical Writing: How-To Essay **170**
STUDENT MODEL "Growing, Growing, Gone!" **170**

★ **Writing for Assessment** **172**
STUDENT MODEL "Learning by Doing and Going" **173**

PERSUASIVE WRITING

Writing a Persuasive Paragraph **178**
STUDENT MODEL "Who Gets to Talk?" **179**

Writing a Persuasive Letter **184**
Understanding Your Goal **185**
STUDENT MODEL "Dear Mr. Greer" **186**
Prewriting **188**
Writing **190**
Revising **192**
■ **Ideas:** Using Good Reasons **194**
■ **Organization:** Including All the Parts **196**
■ **Voice:** Sounding Convincing **198**
■ **Word Choice:** Choosing Helping Verbs **200**
■ **Sentence Fluency:** Fixing Short Sentences **202**
Editing **205**
■ **Conventions:** Checking Capitalization **206**
Assessing: Using a Rubric **208**
Publishing **211**
STUDENT MODEL "Dear Mrs. Lincoln" **211**
Reflecting on Your Writing **213**

★ **Writing Across the Curriculum** **214**
Science: Persuasive Poster **215**
STUDENT MODEL "Come to the Science Fair" **215**
Health: An Important Issue **218**
STUDENT MODEL "Look Out!" **218**
Practical Writing: E-Mail Message **220**
STUDENT MODEL "Library Story Hour" **220**

★ **Writing for Assessment** **222**
STUDENT MODEL "Save Our Recess" **223**

RESPONDING TO LITERATURE

Writing a Response Paragraph **228**
STUDENT MODEL "Keeping Friends"   229

Writing a Book Review for Fiction **234**
STUDENT MODEL "Freckle Juice"   235
Prewriting   236
Writing   238
Revising   242
Editing   243
Publishing   244
STUDENT MODEL "Stone Fox"   244
Reflecting on Your Writing   245

Writing a Book Review for Nonfiction **246**
STUDENT MODEL "To Fly"   247
STUDENT MODEL "Snakes"   251

Comparing a Fiction and a Nonfiction Book **252**
STUDENT MODEL "The Wright Brothers"   253
STUDENT MODEL "Snakes or Verdi?"   257

Responding to a Poem **258**
STUDENT MODEL "A Braggin' Dragon"   259
STUDENT MODEL "A Big Adventure"   263

★ **Writing for Assessment** **264**
STUDENT MODEL "Watch Out for Mountain Lions"   265

CREATIVE WRITING

Writing Imaginative Stories **270**

  Understanding Stories   **271**

    STUDENT MODEL "Sailing on a Paper Dream"   **272**

    Prewriting   **274**

    Writing   **276**

    Revising   **277**

    Editing   **277**

  Creating a Play   **278**

    STUDENT MODEL "Sailing on a Paper Dream"   **278**

  Learning Elements of Fiction   **280**

  Understanding a Plot Line   **281**

Writing Poems **282**

  Rhyming Poem   **283**

    STUDENT MODEL "Jump to It!"   **283**

    Prewriting   **284**

    Writing   **288**

    Revising   **289**

    Editing   **289**

  Writing a Limerick   **290**

    STUDENT MODEL "Pete, the Fat Cat"   **290**

  Writing a Clerihew   **291**

    STUDENT MODEL "Ms. Doud" and "My Dog Sasha"   **291**

  Writing a 5 W's Poem   **292**

    STUDENT MODEL "My Bunny Helicopter"   **292**

  Writing an Alphabet Poem   **293**

    STUDENT MODEL "Parrot Music" and "Bear Cubs"   **293**

RESEARCH WRITING

Finding Information **296**
    Using the Library   297
    Using the Internet   307

Writing a Summary Paragraph **308**
    STUDENT MODEL "*Messenger* Goes to Mercury"   309

Writing a Research Report **312**
    STUDENT MODEL "Exploring Mercury"   313

    Prewriting
    Planning Your Report   316
    Gathering Information   318
    Planning an Interview   320
    Making an Outline   322

    Writing
    Starting Your Report   324
    Developing Your Middle Paragraphs   326
    Ending Your Report   328

    Revising
    Using a Response Sheet   330
    Improving Your Ideas   332

    Editing   334

    Publishing
    Presentation: Sharing Your Report   336
    Reflecting on Your Writing   337

Creating a Multimedia Presentation **338**
    Selecting a Topic and Details   339
    Making a Storyboard   340
    STUDENT MODEL "Exploring Mercury"   340
    Improving Your Presentation   341

The Tools of Learning

Giving Speeches **344**

Planning Your Speech   **345**

Writing Your Speech   **347**

Giving Your Speech   **348**

STUDENT MODEL "Skunks"   **349**

Writing in Journals and Learning Logs **350**

Keeping a Personal Journal   **351**

Writing in a Reading Journal   **352**

Writing in a Learning Log   **354**

Viewing and Listening Skills **356**

Viewing News Programs   **357**

Viewing TV Programs   **358**

STUDENT MODEL "Zebras on the Open Plains"   **359**

Understanding Commercials   **360**

Evaluating Web Sites   **361**

Learning to Listen   **362**

Taking Tests **364**

Studying for a Test   **365**

Understanding Types of Tests   **366**

Responding to Writing Prompts   **370**

STUDENT MODEL

"One-Room School"   **370**

Remembering for Tests   **371**

Basic Grammar and Writing

WORKING WITH WORDS

Using Nouns **375**

  Singular, Plural, and Possessive Nouns 376

  Choose Specific Nouns 378

Using Pronouns **379**

  Possessive Pronouns 380

  Check for Pronoun-Antecedent Agreement 381

  Check Your Plural Pronouns 382

Choosing Verbs **383**

  Linking and Helping Verbs 384

  Use the Proper Verb Tenses 386

  Check for Subject-Verb Agreement 388

Selecting Adjectives **389**

  Check the Form of Each Adjective 390

Selecting Adverbs **391**

  Make the Sentence Clearer 392

Using Prepositions **393**

Connecting with Conjunctions **394**

  Combine Ideas 395

WRITING SENTENCES

Writing Complete Sentences **397**

  Find the Complete Subject and Predicate 398

  Identify Simple Subjects and Predicates 400

  Identify Compound Subjects and Predicates 401

  Use Correct Capitalization and Punctuation 402

Fixing Sentence Problems 403

Correct Run-On and Rambling Sentences   **404**

Check for Subject-Verb Agreement   **406**

Improving Sentence Style 407

Combine with Key Words or a Series   **408**

Combine with Compound Subjects
and Compound Predicates   **409**

Use Compound Sentences   **410**

Use Different Kinds of Sentences   **411**

Try Sentence Modeling   **412**

Preparing for Tests 414

Checking Sentences   **414**

Answering Questions with Sentences   **415**

BUILDING PARAGRAPHS

Parts of a Paragraph 416

STUDENT MODEL "My Little Brother Roy"   **417**

Writing Strong Topic Sentences   **418**

Writing Closing Sentences   **419**

Using Details   **420**

Organizing Paragraphs   **422**

    Time Order   **422**

    Order of Location   **422**

    Order of Importance   **422**

Writing Guidelines   **424**

Marking Paragraphs   **426**

STUDENT MODEL "Grow It Again"   **427**

Preparing for Tests   **428**

STUDENT MODEL "Mini Horses to the Rescue"   **429**

A Writer's Resource

Selecting Ideas 432

How can I find a good topic to write about?

Ideas

Keep a Writer's Notebook   432

Look at a List of Topics   434

Consider Topics for Each Form of Writing   435

How can I start learning about a topic?

Start Thinking   436

How can I write good topic sentences?

Check Your Purpose First   437

Improving Organization 438

Which graphic organizers should I use?

Organization

Try a Venn Diagram to Compare Subjects   438

Make a Time Line to Put Events in Order   439

Use a Story Map to Make a Plan   440

Draw a Life Map to Remember Events   441

Make a 5 W's Chart to List Ideas   442

Make a Sensory Chart to Find Details   443

Make an Outline to Organize Details   444

How do I organize a friendly letter?

Sample Friendly Letter   445

Discovering Your Writing Voice 446

How can I find the right writing voice?

Voice

Make Your Voice Fit Your Purpose   446

What forms of writing can I try?

Try These Forms of Writing   448

Building Word Choice 449

How can I learn new words?

Word Choice

Keep a New-Word Notebook	**449**
Use a Dictionary	**450**
Use a Thesaurus	**452**

How can I figure out what a new word means?

Divide the Word into Parts	**453**
Learn Prefixes	**453**
Study Suffixes	**454**
Remember Root Words	**456**

Improving Sentence Fluency 458

How can I make my sentences easy to follow?

Sentence Fluency

Use Transitions	**458**

Polishing Your Presentation 460

How can I make my writing look better?

Conventions

Add Graphs to Your Writing	**460**
Make Tables to Share Information	**461**

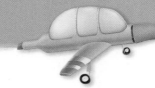

Proofreader's Guide

Marking Punctuation **463**

Periods   463

Question Marks, Exclamation Points   464

Commas   466

Apostrophes   472

Quotation Marks   476

Underlining and Italics   478

Colons   480

Hyphens, Parentheses   482

Editing for Mechanics **486**

Capitalization   486

Plurals   492

Numbers   494

Abbreviations   496

Improving Spelling **502**

Spelling Words   503

Using the Right Word **510**

Understanding Sentences **526**

Using the Parts of Speech **532**

Nouns   532

Pronouns   536

Verbs   538

Adjectives   546

Adverbs   550

Prepositions   552

Conjunctions, Interjections   554

Test Prep!
The "Proofreader's Guide" includes test-prep pages to help you practice taking standardized tests on punctuation, mechanics, usage, sentences, and the parts of speech.

1

Why Write?

When you write, you move your pencil, but you also move your mind. That's why writing helps you in so many ways.

Writing will help you . . .

- **learn more.** When you write something down in your own words, you remember it.

- **explore your mind.** Writing shows you thoughts and feelings you didn't even know you had.

- **share with others.** Letters and e-mail messages let you share your life with those you care about.

- **have fun.** In stories, poems, and plays, you can do amazing things like fly on a cloud or have a picnic on the moon.

Remember . . .

The best way to become a better writer is to write every day. Soon writing will be as natural as walking, and it will take you even farther!

Using the Writing Process

Cassie does a lot of daydreaming and thinking before she puts any words on paper. Gene likes to talk about a story idea with friends before he writes anything. Aaron likes to draw a few pictures before he adds his words.

Writers have many different ways of starting out. However, they all follow the same steps during **the writing process**.

The chapters in this section talk about this process. Following the steps in the writing process will help you keep on track with your writing.

What's Ahead

- Understanding the Writing Process
- One Writer's Process
- Working with Partners
- Traits of Good Writing
- Using a Rubric
- Publishing and Portfolios

Understanding the Writing Process

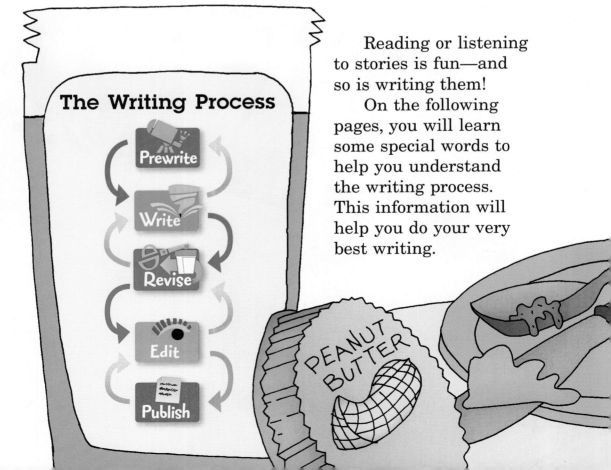

The Writing Process

Prewrite

Write

Revise

Edit

Publish

Reading or listening to stories is fun—and so is writing them!

On the following pages, you will learn some special words to help you understand the writing process. This information will help you do your very best writing.

Connecting with the Traits

Do you know what can happen if you write too fast? You might leave out some important ideas or you might put ideas in the wrong order. Then again, you might use boring words. You might even forget to put periods at the end of your sentences!

When these things happen, the **writing process** gives you time to fix them. It gives you time to make each writing **trait**—and each part of your writing—the best it can be.

Writing Traits

- Ideas
- Organization
- Voice
- Word Choice
- Sentence Fluency
- Conventions

JELLY

Using the Writing Process

Even your favorite authors follow the steps in the writing process. You should, too.

Prewriting

- **Select** a topic that truly interests you.
- **Gather** details about the topic.
- **Plan** what you want to say.

Writing a First Draft

- **Introduce** your topic.
- **Get** all your ideas on paper.

Revising

- **Read over** your first draft.
- **Share** your draft with another person.
- **Make changes** to improve your writing.

Edit

Editing and Proofreading

- **Check** your spelling, capitalization, and punctuation.
- **Write** a neat final copy of your work.
- **Check** one last time for errors.

Publishing

- **Share** your writing.
- **Display** it in class.
- **See pages** 34-41 for other ideas.

Publish

Talk it over . . .

1. What is the easiest part of the writing process for you?
2. What is the hardest part?
3. Do you like to write? Explain your answer.

Becoming a Writer

Guess what? Anyone can become a great writer, including you! Here are six ideas that can help you become a great writer.

Read a lot.

Read fat books and skinny books, short books and tall books. Reading shows you how authors put together their best stories. Also, it can give you great ideas for your own writing!

Write a lot.

Try to write something every day, even on weekends. All of your practice will make you a better writer.

Try different forms.

Writing comes in many shapes and sizes. There are stories, poems, plays, letters, journals, and reports. Try writing in all these different ways.

Talk it over . . .

1. **Name your two favorite books.**
2. **What do you like best about these books?**
3. **What do you like to write—stories, poems, reports, or plays? Why?**

Be alert for writing ideas.

Good story ideas are just waiting to be found—on the bus, in the cafeteria, and everywhere in between. Many of the best stories are written about things you see and hear in real life.

Try different things.

Play sports. Visit museums. Help your neighbors. The more new things you try, the more you have to write about.

Celebrate words.

Collect words that are fun to say, like *caboose* and *cocoon*, *giggle* and *gooey*. Keep your new words in a notebook and use them in your writing!

Practice

1. Write down two things that happened to you before school today.

2. Also list two things that you like to do on weekends.

3. Which idea could you write a story about?

One Writer's Process

Nikki Wilson's class studied stories and songs from different cultures around the world. Their teacher, Ms. Lee, asked the students to write a story about something they learned.

Nikki likes to write, so she was excited to get started. This chapter shows you how she used the writing process to complete her story.

Prewriting Selecting a Topic

Nikki's teacher talked with the class about different topics they had studied. Afterward, Nikki decided to write about griots (GREE-ohs). Griots are special storytellers.

Gathering Details

Ms. Lee showed Nikki an interesting book about griots. Nikki read the book. When she finished, she listed the important details she had learned on a 5 W's chart.

5 W's Chart

5 W's Chart	
Who?	storytellers called griots
What?	tell stories about important events
When?	a long time ago and now
Where?	in Africa
Why?	to honor people

Tip Use a 5 W's chart the next time you have to list the important details about a writing topic.

 # Writing Developing a First Draft

In her first draft, Nikki put all of her ideas on paper. She didn't worry about making a few mistakes. She'd fix them later.

Special Storytellers

My grandpa tells grate stories. He is so good that he could be a griot. A griot is a special storyteller in Africa.

His job was to remember important events. A griot worked for a ruler or a cheif. He also sings songs to honor people

A griot learned from his parents. They would teach him how to sing and to play musical instruments. he would also have to remember many things. When a griot got older, he helped out at festivals.

Talk it over . . .

What details does Nikki's first draft include from her 5 W's chart on page 11?

Revising Improving the Writing

Nikki read her first draft to herself. She read it to a partner, too. Then she made her story better by revising it.

Special Storytellers

Nikki added important information.

My grandpa tells grate stories. He is so good that
(GREE-oh)
he could be a griot. A griot is a storyteller in Africa.

She moved an idea.

→ His job was to remember important events.

A griot worked for a ruler or a cheif. He also sings

songs to honor people

She changed an idea and started a new paragraph.

A griot learned from his parents. They would

teach him how to sing and to play musical instruments.
stories and songs
he would also have to remember many things. When a

griot got older, he helped out at festivals. Sometimes

he also studied with a master storyteller.

Talk it over . . .

1. What is one other thing that Nikki could have changed?
2. Did you wonder about any idea in Nikki's story?

Edit **Editing** Checking for Conventions

Next, Nikki edited her writing. She checked for mistakes in capitalization, punctuation, spelling, and grammar.

Nikki corrected misspelled words.

She changed a verb tense.

She added punctuation.

She added a capital letter.

Special Storytellers

My grandpa tells ~~grate~~ *great* stories. He is so good

that he could be a griot. A griot (GREE-oh) is a

special storyteller in Africa.

A griot worked for a ruler or a ~~cheif~~ *chief*. His job

was to remember important events. He also ~~sings~~ *sang*

songs to honor people⊙

A griot learned from his parents. They would

teach him how to sing and to play musical

instruments. <u>H</u>he would also have to remember

many stories and songs .

When a griot got older, he helped out at

festivals. Sometimes he also studied with a master

storyteller.

Publish **Publishing** Sharing Your Writing

When Nikki finished, she couldn't wait to share her final essay with her classmates . . . and her grandfather.

Special Storytellers

My grandpa tells great stories. He is so good that he could be a griot. A griot (GREE-oh) is a special storyteller in Africa.

A griot worked for a ruler or a chief. His job was to remember important events. He also sang songs to honor people.

A griot learned from his parents. They would teach him how to sing and to play musical instruments. He would also have to remember many stories and songs.

When a griot got older, he helped out at festivals. Sometimes he also studied with a master storyteller.

I'm going to tell my grandpa about griots. Then maybe I'll ask him to sing me a story.

Talk it over . . .

What do you like best about Nikki's story?

Working with Partners

Toshi likes writing-workshop time in her class. She gets to work on her stories and reports, and she also gets to work with her friends.

Toshi's friends help her improve her writing. Sometimes they help her think of a good writing topic. Other times they help her find ways to improve a first draft. They even help her find mistakes before she makes a final copy.

Sharing your writing will help you learn a lot about the writing process.

Helping One Another

You can work with writing partners throughout the writing process, from prewriting to proofreading.

During Prewriting

Partners can help you . . .
- brainstorm topics to write about and
- find information about your topic.

As You Review Your First Draft

Partners can tell you . . .
- what they like and
- what parts they have questions about.

As You Revise

Partners can tell you if . . .
- the beginning gets their interest,
- the middle part sticks to the topic, and
- the ending is strong.

As You Edit and Proofread

Partners can help you . . .
- check your capitalization,
- check your punctuation, and
- check your spelling.

Talk it over . . .

1. Has a partner ever helped you with your writing? How?
2. Tell your classmates about a time you worked with a partner.

Reviewing with Partners

Use the guidelines below when you and a partner are ready to review a piece of writing.

When You're the Writer

- **Be ready to share your writing.**
  You can share your first draft, and you can share your changed writing.
- **Tell why you wrote this piece.**
  Tell just a little about it.
- **Read your writing aloud.**
- **Listen to your partner's comments.**
  They will help you improve your writing.

When You're the Listener

- **Listen carefully to the writer.**
- **Jot down a few notes to help you remember ideas.**
- **Tell the writer something you like about the writing.** "I like the way . . . "
- **Ask about things you don't understand.** "What do you mean when you say . . . ?"
- **Be positive, kind, and helpful.**

Practice

Share a first draft with a partner. Make sure to follow the guidelines listed above.

Using a Response Sheet

A response sheet like this one can help you when you make comments about a classmate's writing.

Response Sheet

Writer: _____ Responder: _____

Title: _____

What I like:

_____

_____

_____

_____

Questions I have:

_____

_____

_____

_____

Traits of Good Writing

To do your best writing, use the six traits listed below as a guide. You will learn all about these traits in this chapter.

Ideas — Start with good ideas!

Organization — Make your writing clear and easy to follow.

Voice — Sound interested or excited about your topic.

Word Choice — Use specific, strong words.

Sentence Fluency — Write different kinds of sentences.

Conventions — Follow the rules for capitalization, punctuation, spelling, and grammar.

Ideas

Rachel likes collecting ideas for her stories and reports. Having plenty of information helps her to do her best writing.

First, Rachel selects a **writing topic**.

Next, she gathers many **details** about her topic.

Writing topic

My cat, Henry

Details

– weighs 16 pounds!

– has bright green eyes

– hides in many places

– loves to eat people food

– sneaks outside sometimes

– sits on my lap during meals

Practice

1. Think of a topic you would like to write about.

2. List at least five details about this topic.

3. Share your ideas with the class.

Organization

Ernesto always tries to begin his stories in an interesting or exciting way. He also tries to connect the middle and ending parts to the beginning.

Beginning

The **first part** should introduce your topic in an interesting way.

Middle

The **middle part** should tell all about your topic.

Ending

The **last part** should share a final thought about the topic.

My Special Partner

Uncle Hector is a carpenter. He knows everything about building and remodeling. Some day I want to be a carpenter, too.

Last summer, my uncle and I built a tree fort in my grandma's backyard. I measured the lumber and nailed some of the boards together. It took us all day, but it sure was fun!

Uncle Hector has all kinds of power tools. I can't use any of them now. But when I grow up, my uncle says that I can be his partner. Then I can use all the tools!

Voice

Tara likes to write about the people in her family. Her stories sound like she is telling them to a friend—that's Tara's *voice*. Writing that sounds like the writer, and no one else, has a voice.

Super Saturdays

Aunt Amita and I have great Saturdays together. We start by making blueberry pancakes. Yummy! Then we go to a store that sells used books. Amita always lets me buy two books, but I have to promise to read them.

Next, my aunt always takes me to a new place. Once she took me to a shelter for injured animals that is right in the city. I donated a dollar to help feed the animals.

At the end of our day, we always have a treat like frozen yogurt. Aunt Amita is so much fun that I never want our Saturdays to end.

Practice

Write a story about someone or something that you really like. Remember to be yourself so your reader can hear your voice.

Word Choice

Theo has learned an important lesson about writing: *Always use specific words.* Specific words help give the reader clear pictures and ideas.

General words (not clear)
The boy ate a big breakfast.

Specific words (clear)
Jamal gobbled up scrambled eggs and bacon.

Sentence Fluency

Mori always reads over her stories before she shares them. She wants all of her sentences to be easy to read.

Smooth sentences
Max is my brother's new retriever. This crazy dog loves to chew on everything. He even chews on the remote control! Max loves to play, too. He is so big that he can knock me down.

Practice

1. Read over a story or report you have written.
2. Circle two words that could be more specific.
3. Write a specific word (or words) for each circled word.
4. Underline any sentences that are hard to read.

Conventions

At the end of every writing assignment, Ravi checks his writing for capital letters and for end punctuation. Then he checks his work for any spelling and grammar errors.

Conventions

Punctuation

____ **1.** Did I use end punctuation after my sentences?

____ **2.** Did I use commas for a series of words (red, white, and blue)?

Capitalization

____ **3.** Did I start every sentence with a capital letter?

____ **4.** Did I capitalize names?

Spelling

____ **5.** Have I checked my spelling?

Grammar

____ **6.** Did I use the right words (*one* instead of *won*)?

Using a Rubric

Have you ever watched figure skating in the Olympics? The judges have a list of things to look for in the skater's performance, like difficulty and variety. That's how they come up with a score for the skater.

Writing can be judged, too, with a **rubric**. A rubric is a chart of the traits of good writing. There are different rubrics for different types of writing. This chapter shows you how to use a rubric to judge an expository essay.

Learning how to use a rubric will help you write better!

Understanding Rubrics

This page will tell you more about rubrics and how to use them to improve your writing.

What do the rubrics cover?

The rubrics used in this book cover the traits of writing—*ideas, organization, voice, word choice, sentence fluency,* and *conventions.*

How can I use a rubric?

During prewriting, a rubric helps you to plan your writing. During revising and editing, it can guide the changes you make. After you finish your writing, the rubric can help you judge your final copy.

How do I judge my writing with the rubric?

Each trait of your writing can be scored. A **6** is the highest score, and a **1** is the lowest score. For example, if the ideas in your essay are *strong*, you would get a **5** for ideas.

6	5	4	3	2	1
Amazing	Strong	Good	Okay	Poor	Incomplete

Should I score all of the traits in my writing?

Your teacher will tell you how many writing traits to judge. You may be told to score only one or two of the six traits.

Getting Started with a Rubric

At the beginning of each main writing unit, you will see a chart like the one on page **29**. It shows you what to include in your writing. At each step in the writing process, certain traits are more important than others.

The traits of writing are very important in the writing process. For example, in prewriting, you are focusing on your <u>ideas</u>.

Read the entire chart before you start your writing.

Study *ideas*. This is the most important trait when you begin your writing.

Learn what you need to do. For example, when you focus on ideas, you should do two things.

- Choose an interesting topic.
- Explain it with details.

Ideas Choose an interesting topic and explain it with details.

Sample Goals Page

Understanding Your Goal

Your goal in this chapter is to write an essay that explains something that is important to you. The six traits below and the expository revising lessons (pages 146–156) will help you reach your writing goal.

Your goal is to . . .

Traits on this side

Goals on this side

Ideas
Choose an interesting topic and explain it with details.

Organization
Put the parts of your essay in the right order.

Voice
Show your interest and excitement.

Word Choice
Use specific nouns to help make your ideas clear.

Sentence Fluency
Write complete sentences that are easy to read.

Conventions
Check your punctuation, capitalization, spelling, and grammar.

Assessing with a Rubric

Follow three steps when you use a rubric like the one on these two pages to judge a piece of your writing.

1 Make an assessment sheet. (See the sample below.)

2 Read the final copy carefully.

3 Score the writing for each trait.

Assessment Sheet

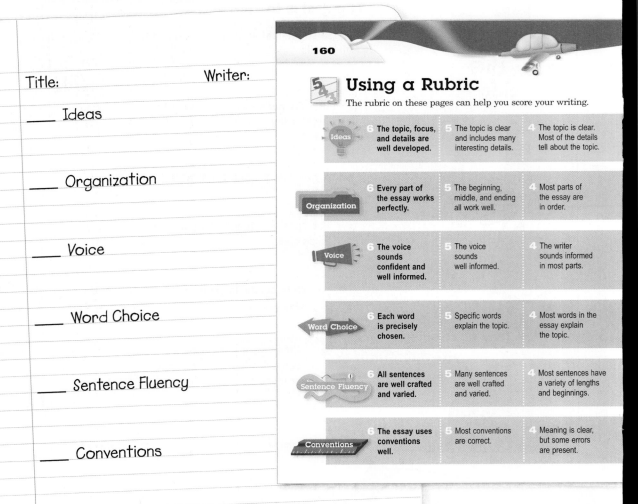

Title: _____ Writer: _____

____ Ideas

____ Organization

____ Voice

____ Word Choice

____ Sentence Fluency

____ Conventions

160

Using a Rubric

The rubric on these pages can help you score your writing.

	6	5	4
Ideas	The topic, focus, and details are well developed.	The topic is clear and includes many interesting details.	The topic is clear. Most of the details tell about the topic.
Organization	Every part of the essay works perfectly.	The beginning, middle, and ending all work well.	Most parts of the essay are in order.
Voice	The voice sounds confident and well informed.	The voice sounds well informed.	The writer sounds informed in most parts.
Word Choice	Each word is precisely chosen.	Specific words explain the topic.	Most words in the essay explain the topic.
Sentence Fluency	All sentences are well crafted and varied.	Many sentences are well crafted and varied.	Most sentences have a variety of lengths and beginnings.
Conventions	The essay uses conventions well.	Most conventions are correct.	Meaning is clear, but some errors are present.

Each rubric helps you judge a final copy for the traits of writing. A **6** is the highest score. A **1** is the lowest score.

Writing an Expository Essay 161

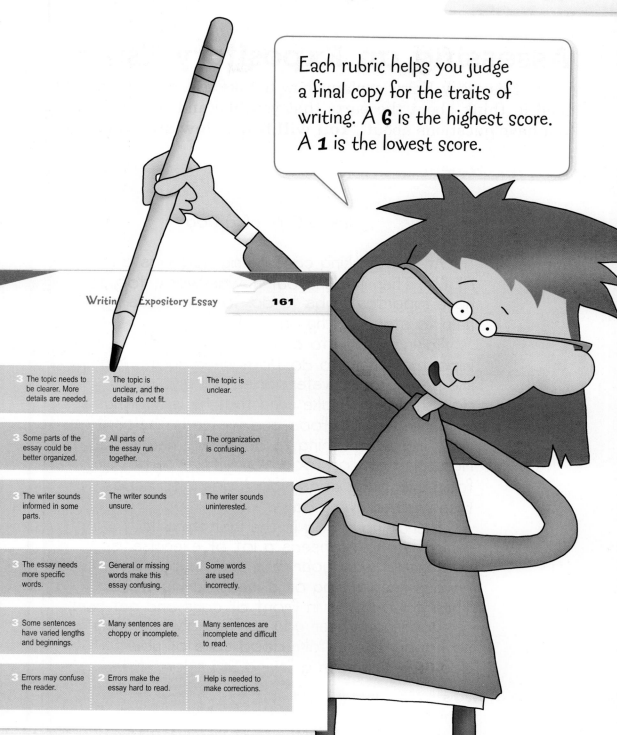

3 The topic needs to be clearer. More details are needed.

2 The topic is unclear, and the details do not fit.

1 The topic is unclear.

3 Some parts of the essay could be better organized.

2 All parts of the essay run together.

1 The organization is confusing.

3 The writer sounds informed in some parts.

2 The writer sounds unsure.

1 The writer sounds uninterested.

3 The essay needs more specific words.

2 General or missing words make this essay confusing.

1 Some words are used incorrectly.

3 Some sentences have varied lengths and beginnings.

2 Many sentences are choppy or incomplete.

1 Many sentences are incomplete and difficult to read.

3 Errors may confuse the reader.

2 Errors make the essay hard to read.

1 Help is needed to make corrections.

Assessing an Expository Essay

In this essay, Kerry explains how to take care of a dog. As you read it, think about the parts that you like and the parts that you have questions about. (**You will find a few mistakes.**)

Taking Care of a Dog

At first, taking care of my dog was a lot of fun. Then I found out it was work, too. I have important jobs to do. Topper needs my help to stay healthy and safe.

Taking a dog to a veterinarien is the most important thing to do. Dogs need shots, just like people do. A veterinarien will give your dog shots and make sure that he is healthy.

Giving a dog food and water is the next most important thing to do. A dog needs the right kind of dog food. Some kinds of people food can make dogs sick. A dog also needs fresh water every day.

Exercising a dog is the last thing to remember. A dog needs a lot of exercise, so you should walk your dog and play with it. Always keep a dog on a leesh during walks. Then it won't run in front of cars and get hurt.

Dogs can cheer you up. They always seem so happy. If you take good care of your dog, you will have a friend for a long time.

Sample Assessment

Kerry used the rubric on pages **30–31** to judge his essay. His teacher told him to score *ideas*, *organization*, and *conventions*. In addition to the numbers, Kerry wrote comments. He wrote about what he liked in his writing, as well as what he would change.

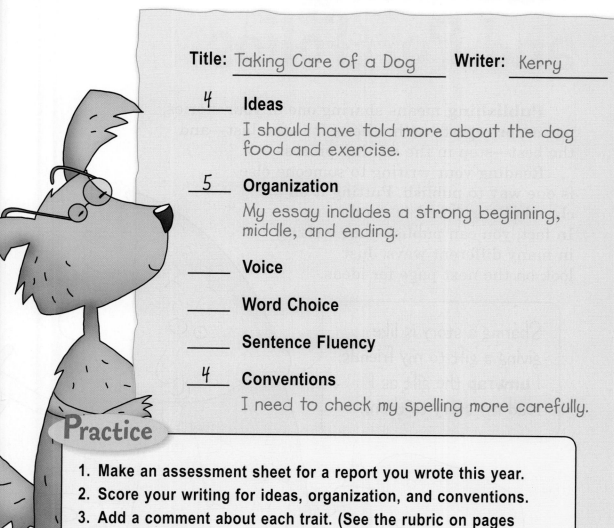

Title: Taking Care of a Dog   **Writer:** Kerry

__4__   **Ideas**
I should have told more about the dog food and exercise.

__5__   **Organization**
My essay includes a strong beginning, middle, and ending.

_____   **Voice**

_____   **Word Choice**

_____   **Sentence Fluency**

__4__   **Conventions**
I need to check my spelling more carefully.

Practice

1. Make an assessment sheet for a report you wrote this year.
2. Score your writing for ideas, organization, and conventions.
3. Add a comment about each trait. (See the rubric on pages 160–161.)

Publishing and Portfolios

Publishing means sharing one of your stories, poems, or reports with others. It is the last—and the best—step in the writing process.

Reading your writing to someone else is one way to publish. Putting it on a class bulletin board is another way. In fact, you can publish your writing in many different ways. Just look on the next page for ideas.

> Sharing a story is like giving a gift to my friends. I **unwrap** the gift as I read my story to them.

Publishing Your Writing

Print it!
Put together a book of your stories or poems, or make a book with your classmates.

Send it!
Send a family story or a special poem to a relative who lives far away.

Submit it!
Send one of your stories or poems to the editor of a magazine. Wait to see if he or she will publish it.

Post it!
Post your writing on a class Web site.

Act it out!
Act out one of your stories or plays with the help of your classmates.

Talk it over . . .

1. Have you ever tried one of the publishing ideas listed above? Tell the class about it.

2. Which new publishing idea would you like to try?

Writing a Neat Final Copy

A neat final copy shows that you care about your writing. It also makes your writing easy to read. Follow these guidelines when you write a final copy by hand.

Handwritten Copy

Use one side of the paper.

Indent the first line of each paragraph.

Use your best penmanship.

When I Grow Up

When I grow up, I want to be a doctor. I am not going to be an ordinary doctor. I want to be a traveling doctor.

First, I will travel to Africa. On television, I saw pictures of many people who are suffering there. That's why I want to be a doctor!

When I'm in Africa, I will do three things. I will help sick children. I will also show them how to stay healthy. Then I will get other doctors to join me.

After I go to Africa, I will travel all around the world to help other sick children. I will go to places like India, China, and Haiti.

I will have to go to school for a long time to be a doctor. My dad says that I will be 28 by the time I get out of school! That's okay. By then, I will be old enough to travel all by myself.

Using a Computer

Follow these guidelines when you use a computer to print out a final copy.

Computer Copy

↑
1"
↓

Mansi Patel

When I Grow Up

Use a font that is easy to read.

When I grow up, I want to be a doctor. I am not going to be an ordinary doctor. I want to be a traveling doctor.

First, I will travel to Africa. On television, I saw pictures of many people who are suffering there. That's why I want to be a doctor!

When I'm in Africa I will do three things.

Try to use a list, chart, or picture.

1. I will help sick children.
2. I will also show them how to stay healthy.
3. Then I will get other doctors to join me.

After I go to Africa, I will travel all around the world to help other sick children. I will go to places like India, China, and Haiti.

Indent the first line of each paragraph.

I will have to go to school for a long time to be a doctor. My dad says that I will be 28 by the time I get out of school! That's okay. By then, I will be old enough to travel all by myself.

Practice

Compare one of your final copies to the example above or the one on page 36. How are they alike? How are they different?

Using a Portfolio

Juan likes collecting pictures of horses. He keeps his pictures in a special album. Juan also collects his stories and poems. He puts them in a **portfolio**, a special place to gather your writing. When you keep a portfolio, you can look over your work and enjoy all the types of writing you have done.

Making a Personal Portfolio

A **personal portfolio** is just for you. You can use a three-ring binder, a pocket folder, a gift box, or you can make your very own portfolio. In your portfolio, you can save everything from topic ideas to finished stories. Here is one way to plan your portfolio.

Collect ideas for new stories and poems.

Store writing that you are still changing.

Save the final copies of your writing.

Making a Classroom Portfolio

Your teacher may ask you to make a **classroom portfolio**. There are two main types of classroom portfolios: a showcase portfolio and a growth portfolio.

Showcase Portfolio

In a **showcase portfolio**, you show your best writing. Here are some ideas for choosing your best work. Your teacher will help you decide which pieces of writing to include.

- Choose writing you really like.
- Pick a piece you worked hard on.
- Select something that shares your feelings.
- Include writing that you're proud of.

Growth Portfolio

In a **growth portfolio**, you save writing that helps you and your teacher see how you are growing as a writer. You may save something you wrote in September, in October, in November, and so on. It's amazing how your writing skills can improve by the end of the school year!

Here are some of the skills you'll want to keep track of.

- Using specific details
- Organizing your ideas
- Writing clear sentences

Practice

1. Think of one thing you wrote from this year or last year that you would include in a showcase portfolio.
2. List the title of your writing and tell why you would include it.

Creating a Portfolio

When you put together a classroom portfolio, use these guidelines.

Follow your teacher's directions.

- Know what your portfolio should look like. You may get special instructions for making a folder.
- Know what kind of writing and how many pieces you need to include. Is any other information needed?

Be organized.

- Save all your work whenever you write.
- Sometimes you may be asked to include all of your prewriting notes and revisions for a piece of writing.

Take pride in your work.

- Finish each writing assignment on time.
- Do your best work. Keep your final copy neat and clean.

Remember: A portfolio is the story of you as a writer. Make sure that you are proud of that story.

Sample Portfolio Introductions

Your teacher may ask you to introduce each piece of writing in your portfolio. You can say why you like the piece or where you got the idea for it. Here are some sample introductions.

Two Authors' Introductions

"I started writing *Trouble River* after our family returned from a trip west. Out there, it was easy enough to imagine pioneer days."

—Betsy Byers

"I took my dad's corny joke, and combined it with a few corny jokes of my own, and created the story, *Dog Breath: The Horrible Trouble With Hally Tosis*"

—Dav Pilkey

A Student's Introduction

My best story is "My Friend Paulo." It was fun writing about Paulo. I had so much to say about him.

—Michael

Practice

1. Write an introduction to something you wrote earlier this year.
2. Tell why you like what you wrote or where you got the idea.

Descriptive Writing

Descriptive writing uses details to help the reader clearly imagine a certain person, place, thing, or idea. Sensory details help someone *see, hear, feel, smell,* and *taste* what you are describing. These details also keep the reader interested in what you have to say. Whenever you write, remember to describe people, places, and things in order to make your writing clear and interesting.

What's Ahead

- **Writing a Descriptive Paragraph**
- **Writing a Descriptive Essay**
- Writing for Assessment

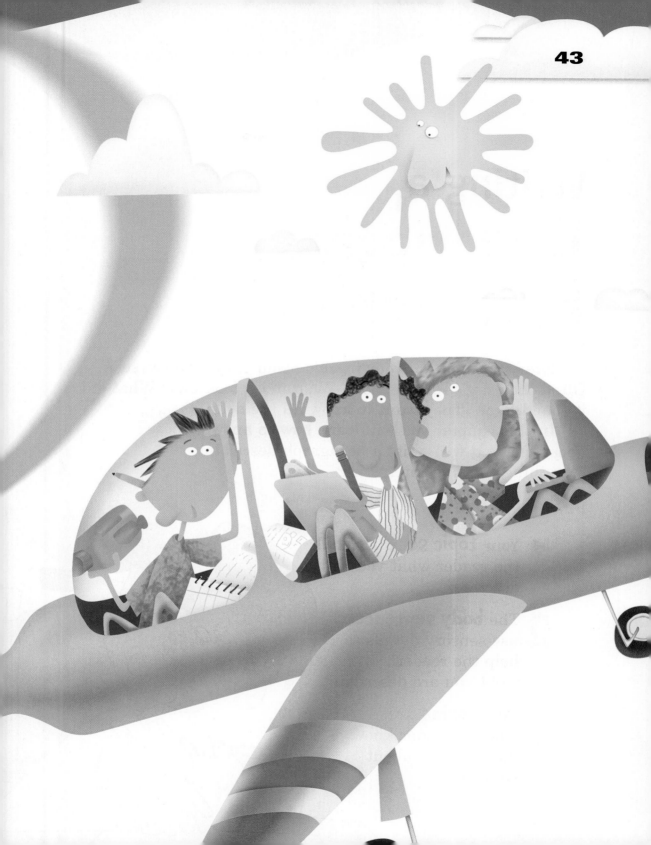

Writing a
Descriptive
Paragraph

Every day you tell your friends about things you've seen. Often they say, "Tell me more. What did it look like? What did it sound like?" They want to know all the details.

In this chapter you will learn how to answer those questions. You will write a paragraph describing something you find interesting.

Paragraph Parts

1 Your **topic sentence** tells the reader what you will describe.

2 The **body sentences** use sensory details to help the reader *see* what you are describing.

3 The **closing sentence** lets the reader know how you feel about your topic.

Descriptive Paragraph

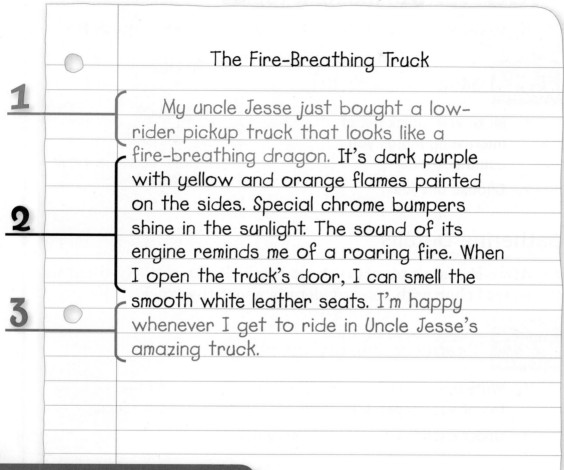

The Fire-Breathing Truck

1 My uncle Jesse just bought a low-rider pickup truck that looks like a fire-breathing dragon. It's dark purple with yellow and orange flames painted on the sides. Special chrome bumpers shine in the sunlight. The sound of its engine reminds me of a roaring fire. When I open the truck's door, I can smell the smooth white leather seats. I'm happy whenever I get to ride in Uncle Jesse's amazing truck.

2

3

After you read . . .

- **Ideas** (1) Find two sensory details that help you see the truck.

- **Organization** (2) What order does the writer use to describe the truck (top to bottom, front to back, outside to inside)?

- **Voice** (3) What words in the closing sentence show how the writer feels about the truck?

Prewriting Finding a Topic

Ky wondered what he could describe. He made a quick list.

 Make a quick list.

1. Make your quick list of interesting things you could describe.

2. Choose one idea.

Quick List

- -baseball
- -chess set
- -Uncle Jesse's new pickup truck

Gathering Details

After choosing to write about the pickup truck, Ky filled in the chart below with sensory details about the truck.

 Create a sensory chart.

1. Write the words *See, Hear, Feel,* and *Smell* across the top of your paper. List *Taste* if those details fit your topic.

2. Under each heading, list sensory details.

Sensory Chart

See	Hear	Feel	Smell
dark purple yellow and orange flames shiny bumpers	loud radio engine like a roaring fire	smooth seats hard chrome bumpers	leather seats plastic mats

Writing Creating your Paragraph

Every paragraph has three basic parts: a topic sentence, body sentences, and a closing sentence.

Topic Sentence

A good topic sentence states your topic and the main idea.

Topic   **Main Idea (or Focus)**

Uncle Jesse's pickup truck looks like a dragon.

Body Sentences

The body of your paragraph includes sensory details that help the reader *see, hear, feel, smell,* or *taste* the topic.

Closing Sentence

The closing sentence tells how you feel about your topic.

 Create your paragraph.

1. Write a topic sentence that tells what you will describe.

2. Write body sentences using details from your sensory chart.

3. Write a closing sentence that shows your feelings about your topic.

My Uncle Jesse's new pickup truck looks like a dragon. It's purple with yellow flames. It has shiny bumpers.

Revising Improving Your Paragraph

When you revise, you look over your paragraph and try to make it sound even better. Sometimes you may need to add more sensory details. Other times you may cut a detail that doesn't belong. After you try the minilesson below, check your own paragraph.

Revise Check your details.

■ Read your paragraph carefully. Then try one or more of the following revising ideas:

● Add at least one more sensory detail to help your reader imagine your topic even better.

● Cut a detail that doesn't belong.

● Move any details that seem out of place.

Practice

Read the following paragraph. List one detail that does not belong. Then think about and write down another sensory detail you could add. Tell how it would help the reader.

Cheese dogs cooked on a campfire are great. I like the way they look and smell. When I bite into one, I can see the melted yellow cheese. My brother doesn't like them if they are burned. Roasted cheese dogs feel crunchy on the outside and creamy in the middle. I like them with lots of catsup or just plain.

Editing Checking for  Conventions

When you edit your paragraph for conventions, you check your capital letters, punctuation, spelling, and grammar. Then you correct any errors that you find.

Conventions

Punctuation

_____ **1.** Did I end each sentence with the correct punctuation?

Capitalization

_____ **2.** Did I begin each sentence with a capital letter?
_____ **3.** Did I use capital letters for the names of people and places?

Spelling

_____ **4.** Did I check the spelling of words I'm not sure of?

Grammar

_____ **5.** Did I indent the first line of my paragraph?

Practice

Tell which end punctuation each sentence needs (. period, ? question mark, ! exclamation point). Explain your answers. See pages 463–464 for help.

1. Did you ever see a kaleidoscope
2. There's one in the school library
3. Look through the kaleidoscope's eyepiece
4. Wow, I love the red, green, and blue designs

Writing a Descriptive Essay

Think about something that is special to you. Do you have a great pair of shoes, a special collection, or a favorite book? It could be just about anything.

In this chapter, you will describe your special object for your classmates. Instead of just telling them about it, you will use words to help them "see" what you are describing.

Understanding Your Goal

Your goal in this chapter is to write a descriptive essay. The essay will describe an object that is special to you.

Your goal is to . . .

Ideas   Describe an object so that your reader can imagine it.

Organization   Create a strong beginning, middle, and ending.

Voice   Use a voice that shows you are excited about the object.

Word Choice   Choose nouns and adjectives that let the reader picture your object.

Sentence Fluency   Write complete sentences that flow smoothly.

Conventions   Use correct capitalization, punctuation, spelling, and grammar.

Descriptive Essay

A descriptive essay should describe something so clearly that the reader can imagine it. You could say that a descriptive essay paints a picture with words. Lebron wrote the essay below. His focus sentence is underlined.

Lebron's Essay

Seashells by the Seashore

Every summer my family goes to the beach. I dig in the sand and look for seashells. Last year, my sister helped me glue some of my shells in a shadow box. <u>I'm very proud of my seashell collection.</u>

In the top part of the box, I put common shells. On the left, I put shiny orange, silver, and gray "jingle" shells. They are the size of nickels and dimes. They jingle just like money! In the top right part, I put bear-paw shells that have some purple color inside and tiny white spikes on the outside.

In the bottom part of the shadow box, I put my rare shells. The left side holds my shark's eyes. Each one looks like a snail shell with a swirly gray eye on one side. My Florida augers are on the right. They remind me of long, skinny ice-cream cones.

On the corners of my shadow box, I glued brown, orange, purple, and white-striped calico scallops. Having a collection is fun. When I look at my shadow box, the shells remind me of the fun I have at the beach.

Parts of a Descriptive Essay

A descriptive essay has a beginning, a middle, and an ending. These three parts work together to make your essay clear and interesting for the reader.

Beginning
Middle
Ending

Beginning

The **beginning paragraph** gets the reader's attention and names the topic. It also includes the main idea of the essay in a focus sentence.

Middle

Each **middle paragraph** begins with a topic sentence. Details in the rest of the paragraph explain the topic sentence.

Ending

The **ending paragraph** shares one final thought about the topic.

After you read . . .

- **Ideas** (1) What object is the writer describing?
- **Organization** (2) How does the writer organize the two middle paragraphs? (Think about the shadow box.)
- **Voice** & **Word Choice** (3) Find words or phrases that show the writer cares about his topic.

Prewriting Selecting a Topic

When you select a topic, you need to think about objects that are special to you. Amy made a list of her special objects. Then she chose the one that she wanted to write about.

 Prewrite **List all of your ideas.**

1. Write "Special Objects" on the top of a piece of paper.

2. List things that are special to you.

3. Mark (*) the one that you would like to write about.

4. Write a focus sentence that names your special object and tells how you feel about it.

Ideas List

<u>Special Objects</u>

skates   science kit

fuzzy sweater   stretchy
                       bracelet

art supplies   my locket *

<u>Focus sentence:</u>

My locket is very special to me.

Gathering Details

One way to gather details about your object is to draw a picture of it and label its parts. This is called a **picture diagram**. Use words that tell about the color, shape, size, special details, and maybe even sounds of your object.

 Prewrite   **Make a picture diagram.**

1. Draw the object you want to describe.
2. Label your drawing with words that describe your object.

Picture Diagram

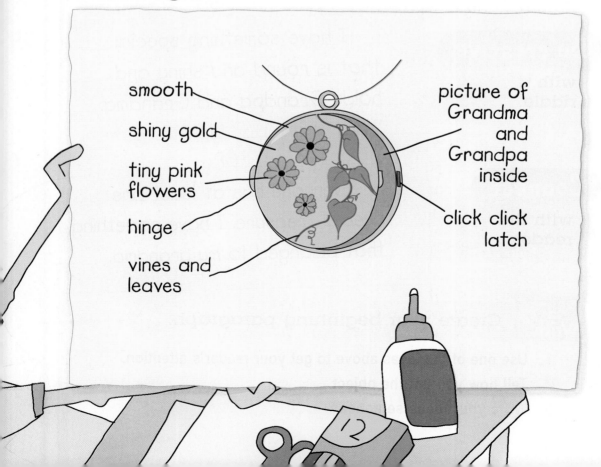

smooth

shiny gold

tiny pink flowers

hinge

vines and leaves

picture of Grandma and Grandpa inside

click click latch

Writing Beginning Your Essay

Beginning
Middle
Ending

The beginning paragraph in your essay should get your reader's attention. Then it should tell how you got the object. Finally, your focus sentence should tell how you feel about your object.

You could try one of the "ABC's of beginnings" shown below to get your reader's attention.

Ask
a question.

> Do you know what a locket is?
>
> OR
>
> I have something special that is round and shiny and holds Grandpa and Grandma. What is it?
>
> OR
>
> Everyone has at least one special treasure. I have something that belonged to my grandma.

Be creative
with a riddle.

Connect
with the reader.

Write Create your beginning paragraph.

1. Use one of the ideas above to get your reader's attention.
2. Tell how you got the object.
3. Write your focus sentence.

Amy's Beginning Paragraph

When Amy started writing her descriptive essay, she did not worry about making a few mistakes. Instead, she worked to get all of her ideas on paper.

Beginning
. . . .
A question gets the reader's attention.

Do you know what a locket is? Well, it's a little case that hangs on a neckless. A locket opens and has pictures inside. I

Details tell how the writer got this object.

have one thats been in our family for a realy long time. My grandpa gave it to my grandma before they were married. many years later, Grandma gave it to my mom,

The focus sentence (underlined) tells the writer's feelings.

and now it's mine. <u>My locket is very special to me.</u>

Writing Developing the Middle

Each of your middle paragraphs should begin with a topic sentence and tell about a certain part of your topic. Use **order of location** by describing your topic in one of three ways shown below.

Beginning
Middle
Ending

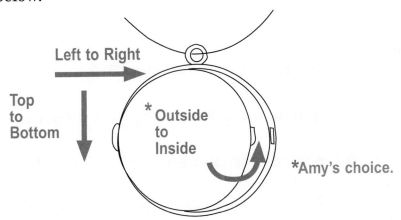

Left to Right

Top to Bottom

* Outside to Inside

*Amy's choice.

Write

Write your middle paragraphs.

1. Choose one way to describe your object (left to right, top to bottom, outside to inside).

2. Look at your picture diagram again. Now write two topic sentences that describe the main parts of your object—the left and right parts, for example.

3. Write two body paragraphs by adding more sentences after each topic sentence. Include details from your picture diagram to support each topic sentence.

Amy's Middle Paragraphs

In her middle paragraphs, Amy described her locket. She still didn't worry about making a few mistakes.

it to my mom, and now it's mine. My locket is very special to me.

Topic Sentence

The writer describes the outside of the locket.

Many lockets are shapped like a valentine heart, but not mine. Its shiny gold and hangs on a long chain The outside has vines and flowers carved in it. Some of the vines are smooth from mom and grandma rubbing it with there fingers. My brother wouldn't wear it for a million dollars.

Topic Sentence

Then she describes the inside of the locket.

Inside my locket, there are pictures of my grandma and grandpa when they were young. grandma was pretty. She had curly blonde hair. He had dark hair and didn't wear Glasses as he does now. Grandpa looked so different.

Writing Ending Your Essay

Your ending paragraph should give your reader one final thought about the topic. Here are some ways to create a strong ending.

Beginning

Middle

▶ Ending

Remind

your reader about your beginning.

> Now you know what a locket is. Maybe the next time you see one, you'll ask about the pictures inside of it.

OR

Show

your feelings about your topic.

> I'm so glad the locket is finally mine. I always feel special when I wear it.

OR

Tie

the special object to your life.

> Someday, I can pass down this beautiful locket to my daughter, so she can enjoy it as much as I do.

Write Create your ending paragraph.

1. Try one of the ideas above to write your ending.

2. If none of these work, try your own idea.

Amy's Ending Paragraph

In Amy's first draft of her ending, she didn't worry about making a few mistakes. She just got all of her ideas on paper.

didn't wear Glasses as he does now.

Grandpa looked so different.

I open and close my locket over and

over again. I like to feel it in my hand and

here the click, click it makes. My mom says

I shouldnt do it so much. I might ware it

out. She says I should be careful with

Ending

The writer connects the special object to her life.

it. Someday, I can pass it down to my

daughter, so she can enjoy it as much as

I do

Revising Improving Your Essay

Revising is one of the most important steps in the writing process. It is your chance to make changes to your description. You can add, cut, or move details, depending on how you want to improve your essay.

 Check your details.

1. Look for places where you could add, cut, or move details.

2. How could you make your description even better?

When should I add details?

You should **add** details to make your description clearer and more exciting. Use a caret ∧ to show where you want to put the new detail.

When should I cut a detail?

You should **cut** any detail that does not belong in your description. Use a delete mark ⌒ to show what you want to cut.

When should I move details?

You should **move** details that are out of order. Circle any idea that you want to move. Then draw an arrow ⟶ to show where you want to put it.

Amy's Revising

Here are the changes Amy made as she revised her two middle paragraphs. She added, cut, and moved some words and sentences. By doing this, she improved her ideas and organization.

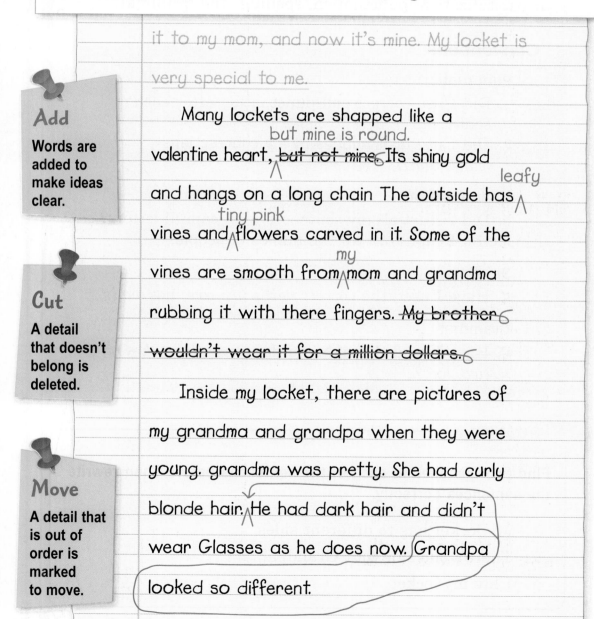

it to my mom, and now it's mine. My locket is

very special to me.

Add

Words are added to make ideas clear.

Many lockets are shapped like a

but mine is round.

valentine heart, ~~but not mine.~~ Its shiny gold

leafy

and hangs on a long chain The outside has

tiny pink

vines and ^flowers carved in it. Some of the

my

vines are smooth from ^mom and grandma

rubbing it with there fingers. ~~My brother~~

Cut

A detail that doesn't belong is deleted.

~~wouldn't wear it for a million dollars.~~

Inside my locket, there are pictures of

my grandma and grandpa when they were

young. grandma was pretty. She had curly

Move

A detail that is out of order is marked to move.

blonde hair. He had dark hair and didn't

wear Glasses as he does now. Grandpa

looked so different.

Editing Checking for Conventions

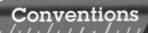

Now it's time to edit your essay. When you edit, you check your capitalization, punctuation, spelling, and grammar.

Conventions

Punctuation

____ **1.** Did I use correct end punctuation after each sentence?

____ **2.** Did I use apostrophes in my contractions (*can't, don't*)?

Capitalization

____ **3.** Did I start all my sentences with capital letters?

____ **4.** Did I capitalize all the names of people?

Spelling

____ **5.** Have I used the correct verbs (*we **are**, not we **is***)?

Grammar

____ **6.** Have I used the right words (*there, their, they're; to, two, too*)?

Practice

Find two mistakes in each of the sentences below. Then rewrite the sentences correctly.

1. My locket has to different sides

2. There's one side four Grandpa?

3. I luv my locket

Amy's Editing

When she edited her essay, Amy carefully checked for errors.

Amy corrects a spelling error.

it to my mom, and now it's mine. My locket is

very special to me.

shaped
Many lockets are ~~shapped~~ like a

valentine heart, but mine is round. It's shiny

She adds punctuation.

gold and hangs on a long chain. The outside

has leafy vines and tiny pink flowers carved

in it. Some of the vines are smooth from

She corrects a wrong word.

their
my mom and grandma rubbing it with ~~there~~

fingers.

Inside my locket, there are pictures of

my grandma and grandpa when they were

She fixes two capitalization errors.

young. grandma was pretty. She had curly

blonde hair. Grandpa looked so different. He

had dark hair and didn't wear Glasses as

he does now.

Publishing Sharing Your Essay

After you have corrected any mistakes, it is time to write a final copy of your descriptive essay.

Publish **Make a final copy.**

1. Follow your teacher's instructions, or use the model below. (For computer papers, see page 37.)

2. Carefully write a clean final copy and proofread it.

Locket in My Pocket

Do you know what a locket is? Well, it's a little case that hangs on a necklace. A locket opens and has pictures inside. I have one that's been in our family for a really long time. My grandpa gave it to my grandma before they were married. Many years later, Grandma gave it to my mom, and now it's mine. My locket is very special to me.

Many lockets are shaped like a valentine heart, but mine is round. It's shiny gold and hangs on a long chain. The front has leafy vines and tiny pink flowers carved in it. Some of the vines are smooth from my mom and grandma rubbing it with their fingers.

Inside my locket, there are pictures of my grandma and grandpa when they were young. Grandma was pretty. She had curly blonde hair. Grandpa looked so different. He had dark hair and didn't wear glasses like he does now.

I open and close my locket over and over again just to feel it in my hand and hear the

...ays I might wear
...areful with it. Then,
...his beautiful locket
...njoy it as much as

Reflecting on Your Writing

Congratulations! You have finished your descriptive essay. Take a little time to think about what you have learned. Here are Amy's thoughts about her essay.

Thinking About Your Writing

Name: _Amy McKekkin_

Title: _Locket in My Pocket_

1. The best part of my essay is . . .

   telling everyone how special my locket

   _is to me._

2. The part of my essay that sill needs work is . . .

   the part where I describe the chain.

3. The main thing I learned about descriptive writing is . . .

   how to use a picture diagram. That helped me

   think about all of the details.

Descriptive Writing
Writing for Assessment

When you take a writing test, you may be given a descriptive writing prompt. It may ask you to write an essay that describes a person, a place, or a thing, using sensory details. On page **69**, you can read Tola Moonbird's response to the prompt below.

Descriptive Prompt

What is your most interesting item of clothing? Write an essay in which you describe the item of clothing and how you feel when you wear it.

Sketch

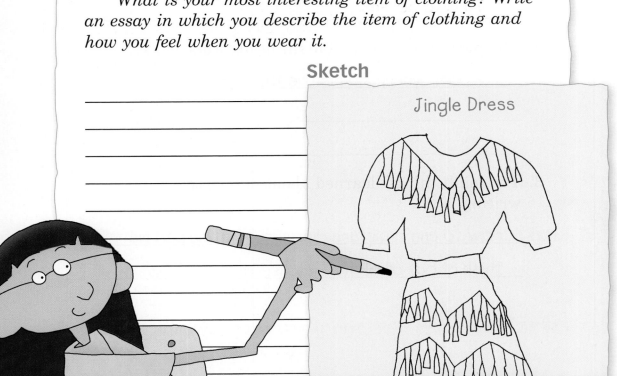

Jingle Dress

Powwow Jingle Dress

The beginning gives the focus sentence (underlined).

Some girls have fancy party dresses. I have a very special dress that my aunt helped me sew. It's for a festival called a powwow. My jingle dress is the best piece of clothing I have.

The top part of my jingle dress is called the yoke. Aunt Isa and I made it out of red satin. We sewed red and yellow ribbons in a V across the front of the yoke. Jingles hang from the ribbons. We made all the jingles by bending tin into long cones. They ring like little bells when I dance to the drums.

The middle gives details by order of location.

In the middle of my dress, I wear a wide leather belt. I sewed tiny white beads in the center. Then I used brown beads to make two running horses.

The blue skirt of my dress has ribbons and jingles. We sewed red and yellow ribbons in zigzags across the front and back. The jingles hang below the ribbons in two rows.

The ending tells why the object is special.

My jingle dress looks great and sounds even better! It makes me think of my tribe. I loved sewing it with my aunt, and I love wearing it when I dance at powwows!

After you read . . .

- **Ideas** (1) How does the writer's dress make her feel? Why?
- **Organization** (2) How are the paragraphs organized?
- **Word Choice** (3) Find two interesting sensory words.

Writing Tips

Before you write . . .

- Read the prompt carefully.
- Look for words that tell you what the prompt is asking you to do.
- Choose a topic you know well.
- Use a picture diagram to help you remember important details.

During your writing . . .

- Use key words from the prompt in your beginning paragraph.
- Be sure you write a clear beginning, middle, and ending.
- Include sensory details to describe your topic.

After you've written your first draft . . .

- Be sure your focus sentence clearly states your topic for the essay.
- Take time to correct mistakes in capitalization, punctuation, spelling, and grammar.

Descriptive Prompt

Is your favorite object a toy, a game, a picture, a football? It could be anything. Write an essay in which you describe your favorite object.

Descriptive Writing in Review

In descriptive writing, you use sensory details. Sensory details help your reader *see, feel, smell, taste,* and *hear* what you are writing about. These guidelines can help you.

Select a topic that interests you. (See page 54.)

Gather and organize sensory details about your topic. (See page 55.)

Write a focus sentence that introduces your topic. (See page 54.)

In the beginning part, introduce your topic in an interesting way. (See page 56.)

In the middle part, use sensory details to help the reader *see, hear, feel, smell,* and *taste* your topic. (See pages 55 and 58–59.)

In the ending part, share one final thought or feeling about your topic. (See pages 60–61.)

Review your essay for ideas and organization. Be sure you've included the right details. Make changes to improve your writing. (See pages 62–63.)

Check your writing for conventions and correct any errors you find. (See pages 64–65.)

Make a final copy. Proofread it again for errors. Share your final copy with classmates. (See page 66.)

Narrative Writing

"What did you do today?" Whenever you answer that question, you are creating a very short narrative. A narrative is simply a true story about something that has happened.

Narratives come in all shapes and sizes. You can write a narrative in one sentence: "We went to the Milwaukee Art Museum and saw the ballerina sculptures." You can write a narrative in a paragraph, or a narrative that includes many paragraphs. This section will help you begin your adventures in narratives.

What's Ahead

- **Writing a Narrative Paragraph**
- **Writing a Narrative Essay**
- Narrative Writing Across the Curriculum
- Writing for Assessment

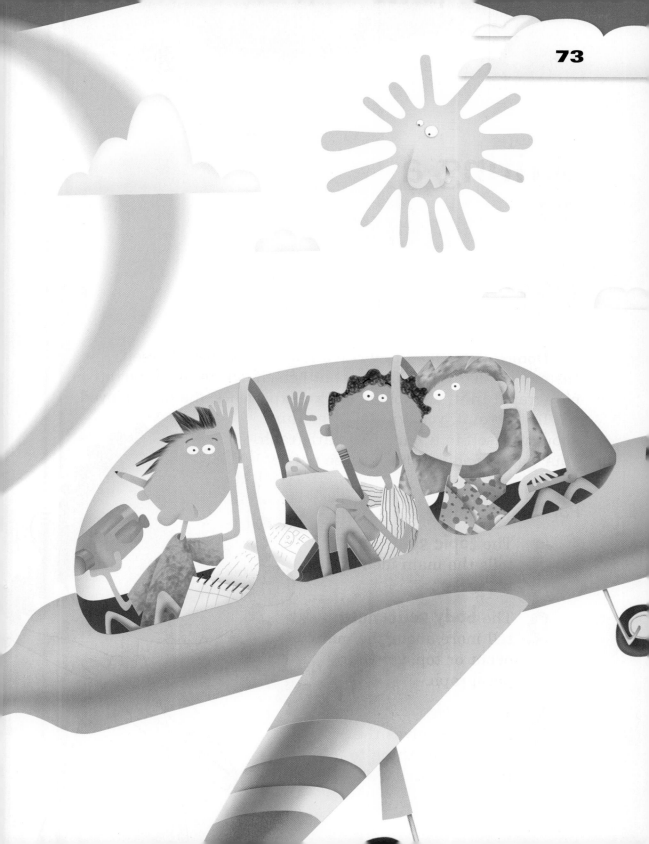

Writing a Narrative Paragraph

Donica was asked to write a few things about herself. Instead of just telling facts about herself, she wrote a narrative paragraph! In it, she told about an experience she had enjoyed.

In this unit, you will tell something about yourself in a narrative paragraph. Your paragraph will have three parts.

Paragraph Parts

1 The **topic sentence** tells the main idea of the paragraph.

2 The **body sentences** tell more about the main event or topic of your paragraph.

3 The **closing sentence** gives the reader something to think about.

Narrative Paragraph

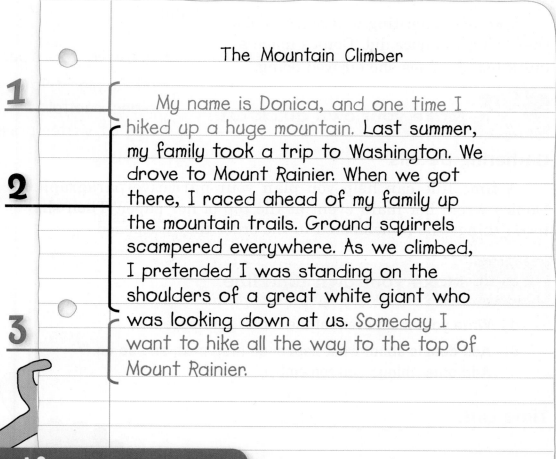

The Mountain Climber

1

My name is Donica, and one time I hiked up a huge mountain. Last summer, my family took a trip to Washington. We drove to Mount Rainier. When we got there, I raced ahead of my family up the mountain trails. Ground squirrels scampered everywhere. As we climbed, I pretended I was standing on the shoulders of a great white giant who was looking down at us. Someday I want to hike all the way to the top of Mount Rainier.

2

3

After you read . . .

Answer these questions about Donica's paragraph.

- **Ideas** (1) What is the main idea or event of this paragraph?

- **Organization** (2) What part of the paragraph tells all about the main event?

- **Word Choice** (3) What words and phrases do you like best in the paragraph? Explain why.

Prewriting Finding an Idea

You will be writing a paragraph about something you once did. Donica made a quick list of things she enjoyed doing.

Make your own quick list.

Gathering Details

A time line can help you plan your narrative paragraph. Donica wrote her main event at the top of her paper. Then she listed things she remembered in the order they happened.

Make your own time line.

1. Write your main event at the top of your paper.
2. Add details about what happened first, next, and so on. Add other things you remember.

Time Line

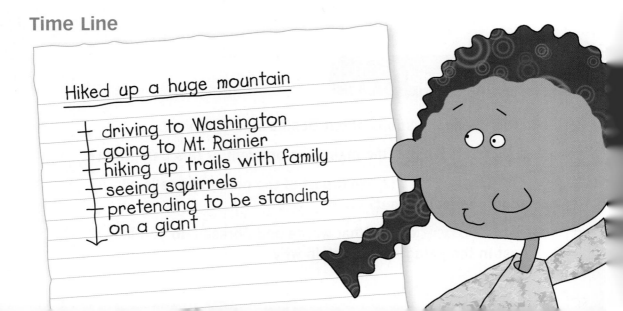

Hiked up a huge mountain

- driving to Washington
- going to Mt. Rainier
- hiking up trails with family
- seeing squirrels
- pretending to be standing on a giant

Writing **Beginning Your First Draft**

Each part of your narrative paragraph has a special job to do.

- Your **topic sentence** names the topic (you) and tells what event you will talk about.
- The **body sentences** tell interesting details about the event.
- Your **closing sentence** leaves your reader with a final thought about the topic.

Begin your paragraph.

1. First write your topic sentence.
   "My name is _____, and I _____(event)_____."

2. Then write at least three body sentences that tell some interesting details about your event.

3. Write a closing sentence that leaves the reader with a final thought about the topic.

First Draft

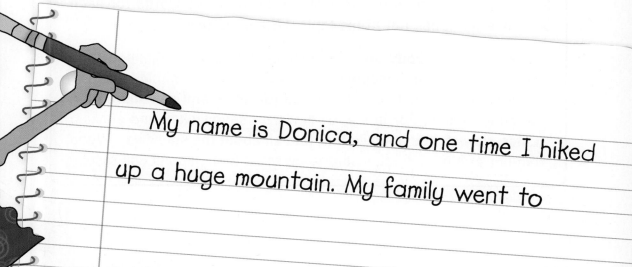

My name is Donica, and one time I hiked up a huge mountain. My family went to

Revising Improving Your Paragraph

Now it's time for you to revise your paragraph. Remember that all of your body sentences should include interesting details about your topic. If they don't, you can add some now.

Check your details.

Ask yourself the following questions about your paragraph.

1. Does each body sentence include an interesting detail about my topic?

2. Are there any sentences that do not tell about my topic? (If you find a sentence that doesn't fit, cross it out.)

3. Are my sentences in the order that the event happened? (If not, move your sentences around.)

4. Does my paragraph have at least three body sentences? (If it doesn't, add details in one or two new sentences.)

Practice

Read Cody's paragraph below. Write the first two words for each sentence that does not fit his topic. (There are two.)

My name is Cody, and I like race cars. Last year, my uncle took me down to the Indianapolis Speedway Hall of Fame. My uncle is a senior in high school. We walked for miles and saw more than 50 famous cars. For lunch, we had sub sandwiches and shakes. Later, we watched a movie that told all about the speedway. When I'm out of high school, I want to go to an Indianapolis 500 race.

Editing Checking for Conventions

When you've finished revising, you are ready to edit. Be sure you have used the right words. Words like *to*, *two*, and *too* are easy to confuse because they sound the same.

A computer's spell-checker won't point out a word that is spelled correctly when it is the wrong word for your sentence. It is important that you check these words yourself.

Frank has two brothers.	**Two** means the numeral "2."
I have two brothers, too.	**Too** means "also."
We all walk to the park together.	**To** means "toward."

Edit

Check your work.

1. Did I indent the first line of the paragraph?

2. Did I start each sentence with a capital letter?

3. Did I punctuate the end of each sentence?

4. Have I used the right words, like *their*, *they're*, and *there*? (See pages **510–522** for tips on using the right word.)

Practice

Change the incorrect word or words in each sentence below.

1. I was born right hear in California.
2. I road my bike in the holiday parade.
3. I like to swim, to.
4. At the science fare, I one a blue ribbon.
5. Every summer, I visit my grandma for a hole week.

Writing a Narrative Essay

Helpful people are all around us! They can be family members, friends, teachers, and even community people, like police officers and firefighters.

Cara decided to write a narrative essay about Mrs. Rios, a person who helped her in first grade. You will read Cara's essay and learn to write one of your own.

Texas
first grad
English
Mrs. Rios

Understanding Your Goal

Your goal in this chapter is to write a personal narrative about someone who has helped you. The six traits below and the narrative revising lessons (pages 92–104) will help you reach your goal.

Your goal is to . . .

Ideas — Use interesting details to write about a helpful person.

Organization — Put the parts of your essay in an order that makes sense.

Voice — Write as if you are talking to a classmate.

Word Choice — Use action verbs to keep your story moving.

Sentence Fluency — Use a variety of sentence lengths.

Conventions — Check your capitalization, punctuation, spelling, and grammar.

Narrative Essay

A personal narrative tells a true story about you. This narrative tells about an important helper in Cara's life.

Mrs. Rios

When I was in first grade, I met Mrs. Rios. She speaks Spanish and English, and she helped me learn English.

My family moved to Texas when I was five years old. Before that, we lived in Mexico. No one in my family spoke any English when we came to the United States.

When I started school, I met Mrs. Rios. She sat with me in class and told me what the teacher was saying. She taught me simple English words. She was always there to help me.

"You can do it, Cara," Mrs. Rios said.

Soon, I could understand my classmates. I began to speak and read English, too. Today, I know English very well.

Mrs. Rios helps new first graders every year. She made learning English fun and easy. Now I'm even helping my family learn English. When I saw Mrs. Rios in the hall last week, I thanked her for all her help.

Parts of a Personal Narrative

A narrative essay has three parts.

Beginning

The **beginning paragraph** names your topic and makes the reader want to keep reading.

Middle

The **middle paragraphs** tell more about the topic. They include details that make the story sound real.

Ending

The **ending paragraph** wraps things up. It tells how you felt and what was important to you.

Beginning

Middle

Ending

After you read . . .

- **Ideas** (1) What is the topic (or focus) of the essay?
- **Organization** (2) How does Cara organize her narrative in a way that makes sense?
- **Word Choice** (3) What words and phrases make Mrs. Rios seem real to the reader?

Prewriting Selecting a Topic

The topic of your essay will be a person who has helped you. Taylor used a gathering wheel to list the names of his helpers.

 Make a gathering wheel.

1. On your own paper, make a wheel like the one below.

2. Write the words "Helpful People" in the center of the wheel.

3. In the spaces around the center, write the names of people who have helped you.

4. Put a star (✳) next to the person you want to write about.

Gathering Wheel

Dr. Green | Mr. Chua
Officer Cruz | Helpful People | Aunt Sue
my sister Morgan | my friend Brandon ✳ | my teacher

Putting Your Details in Order

Narratives are organized by time. First, one event happens, then the next event, and so on. Using a time line can help you put your events in order. You can see the time line Taylor created below.

Make a time line.

1. Draw an arrow going down the left side of your paper.

2. Next to the arrow, write a few words about the times when your helper helped you.

3. Make sure to write down the events in the right order.

Time Line

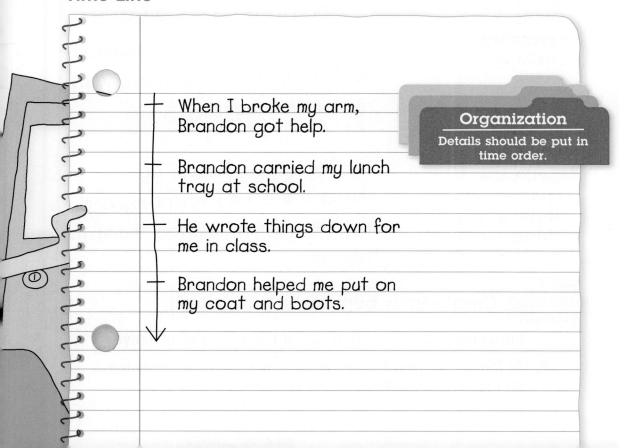

When I broke my arm, Brandon got help.

Brandon carried my lunch tray at school.

He wrote things down for me in class.

Brandon helped me put on my coat and boots.

Organization

Details should be put in time order.

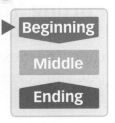

Writing **Beginning Your Essay**

▶ Beginning

Middle

Ending

Your beginning paragraph introduces the topic (your helper). Here are three ways to begin the first paragraph of your essay.

Ask
a question.

> Have you ever had a terrible day? On my terrible day, I hurt my arm. Luckily, Brandon was with me.

OR

Begin
with someone talking.

> "Don't worry. I will help you." That's what my friend Brandon told me when I came home with my arm in a cast.

OR

Connect
with the reader by telling a little story.

> One day, I fell off my skateboard, and I hurt my arm. My friend Brandon was there to help me.

Write **Create your beginning paragraph.**

1. Introduce your topic using one of the ways shown above.
2. At the end of your first paragraph, write a focus sentence that tells how you feel about your helper.

Taylor's Beginning Paragraph

Taylor began his narrative essay by asking a question. In his first draft, he just wanted to get his ideas down on paper. He didn't worry about errors.

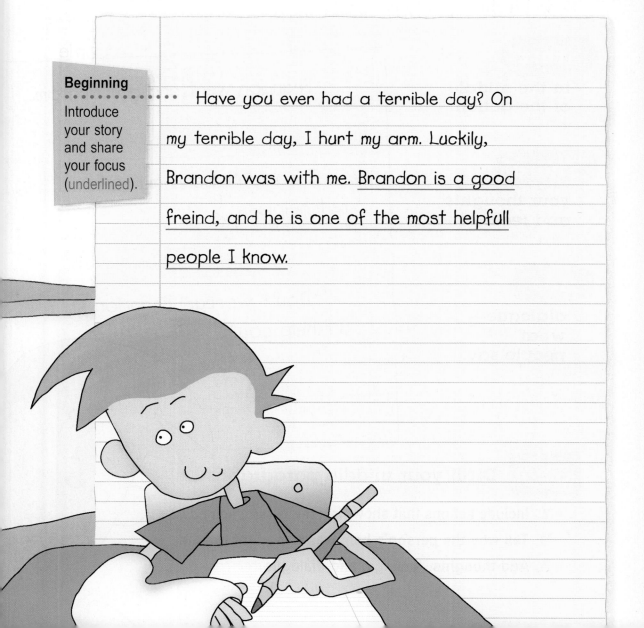

Beginning
....
Introduce your story and share your focus (underlined).

Have you ever had a terrible day? On my terrible day, I hurt my arm. Luckily, Brandon was with me. Brandon is a good freind, and he is one of the most helpfull people I know.

Writing Developing the Middle

In the middle part of your essay, you show how the person helped you and why that help was important. Use your *time line* from page 85 and include plenty of details.

> Beginning
> ▶ Middle
> Ending

Start

in the middle of the action.

> Brandon went and got my mom.

Share

your thoughts and feelings.

> I couldn't bend my elbow. I felt helpless.

Add

dialogue— what people say.

> "Don't worry," Brandon said. "I'll help you."

 Draft your middle paragraphs.

1. Include actions that show how the person helped you.
2. Tell why the person's help was important to you.
3. Add thoughts, feelings, and dialogue.

Taylor's Middle Paragraphs

Here are Taylor's middle paragraphs. He continues to tell what happened and adds details that show how Brandon helped him.

Brandon is a good freind, and he is one of the most helpfull people I know.

Middle
Use actions and details.

One Saturday, Brandon and I was skateboarding. I fell. I got hurt. Brandon went and got my mom. I came back from the hospital with a plaster cast on my write arm. that's the arm I use the most. I couldn't bend my elbow. I felt helpless.

Share thoughts and feelings.

"Don't worry about it," Brandon said. "I'll help you.

Tell what someone said (dialogue).

At school, he carried my lunch tray. We had pizza. Whenever there was something I couldn't do, Brandon was there to help me. Brandon wrote things down for me. He even helped me put on my coat and boots.

Writing Ending Your Essay

In your ending paragraph, you tell why the person's help was important to you. Here are some ideas for ending your essay.

Beginning

Middle

▶ **Ending**

Restate

why the person's help was important.

Share

your feelings about the person.

Talk

with your reader.

> Without Brandon's help, I don't know what I would've done.
>
> OR
>
> I'll never forget what Brandon did for me.
>
> OR
>
> Have you ever needed help? That's when you know how great it is to have a friend to help you.

 Complete your ending paragraph.

1. Use one or more of the ways above to write an interesting ending.

2. Try one of your own. Use the ending you like best.

Taylor's Ending Paragraph

Here is Taylor's final paragraph. He told why the help was important and shared his feelings about Brandon.

helped me put on my coat and boots.

Ending

The writer combines two ways of ending the essay.

The day I broke my arm was terrible, but I had a great helper. Now my arm is okay. I'll never forget what Brandon did for me.

Revising Improving Your Essay

When you finish your first draft, you are ready to make changes to improve your writing. Begin the revising part of the writing process by reading your narrative to yourself.

Then read your essay out loud to a partner. You may ask your partner the following questions that are based on your writing goals (see page 81).

Ideas
- Did I use interesting ideas to write about a helpful person?

Organization
- Did I put the parts of my essay in an order that makes sense?

Voice
- Did I write as if I am talking to a classmate?

Word Choice
- Did I use action verbs to keep my story going?

Sentence Fluency
- Did I use a variety of sentence lengths?

Getting a Partner's Response

Here is another way a partner can help you decide how to improve your writing. This is a partner's response to Taylor's essay (pages 87–91).

Response Sheet

Writer: Taylor   Responder: Antonio

Title: Skateboard Emergency 9–1–1

What I like:

I was happy Brandon went to get your mom.

That detail shows how Brandon helped you.

_____

I liked it when Brandon said, "Don't worry."

Questions I have:

Was the cast heavy?

How did your arm feel?

_____

 Tip Be sure to ask a classmate to read your work and fill out a response sheet.

Revising for

Ideas

Strong ideas and details will help the reader connect with your experience.

Q. How can I connect with my reader?

You can connect by helping your reader to see and feel what you experienced. Use a T-chart like the one below to collect these kinds of details for your reader.

See . . .	Feel . . .
people waving their arms	chugging, slow start
hair flying everywhere	scary drops and loops
the giant roller coaster	shaking side to side
red and yellow cars	wind and speed

Practice

Make a T-chart like the one above. Fill it in with details about what you want your reader to see and feel when reading your essay.

Revising in Action

Here are some of the changes Taylor made to improve the ideas in a middle paragraph in his first draft. He added a detail to one sentence and specific details to another sentence.

> One Saturday, Brandon and I was
>
> skateboarding. I fell. I got hurt. Brandon went
>
> and got my mom. I came back from the hospital
>
> heavy
> with a ∧ plaster cast on my write arm. That's the
>
> my arm felt hot and itchy, and
> arm I use the most. ∧ I couldn't bend my elbow.
>
> I felt helpless.

Revise — Check your ideas.

1. Read your work carefully.
2. Find places to add details that connect with your reader.
   - **Add** details. Use a caret ∧ to show where you want to add words.
3. Remove details that don't connect with the reader.
   - **Cut** unnecessary details. Use a delete mark ℓ to show what you want to remove.

Revising for

Organization

In narrative writing, you should organize your details in time order.

Q. How can I put details in time order?

You can put details in **time order** (in the order they happened) by using words like *first, second, next,* and *finally*.

First, I made sure my aunt was ready. Then I called my mom. As soon as I did, I hid with my cousins. Mom brought Grandma in from the yard. We were all ready to celebrate Grandma's surprise party.

Tip Transition words (words that show time) help connect events in your writing.

first	soon	after
second	later	before
next	as soon as	tomorrow
then	finally	suddenly

Practice

Add one more sentence to the paragraph about Grandma's surprise party. Use one of the transitions listed above.

Revising in Action

Here are some of the changes Taylor made to improve the organization of his first draft. He added a transition word, punctuation, and other words as needed.

One Saturday, Brandon and I was

skateboarding. I fell. I got hurt. Brandon went

When
and got my mom. ∧ I came back from the hospital ∧,
I had   heavy
∧ with a plaster cast on my write arm. That's the
∧
                    My arm felt hot and itchy, and
arm I use the most. ∧ I couldn't bend my elbow.

I felt helpless.

Revise — Check your organization.

1. Be sure that you've used transition words to show time order and to keep your narrative moving.
   - Add transition words and phrases.
2. Check your essay to be sure all the events are in the order they happened.
   - Move any details or sentences that are not in the best order.

Revising for

Voice

Your writer's voice is the special way you express your ideas. In narrative writing, your writer's voice should sound like you.

Q. What makes my voice sound like me?

Your writing voice sounds like you if you tell your story using your own words–the way you would tell it to a friend.

> The parade was almost over. *Suddenly,* the girl *sitting on the curb next to me* darted into the street. Her *big yellow balloon sailed away,* and *her cowboy hat flew off.*

Practice

Read the following list. Then use these events to "tell the story" to a classmate. Be sure to use lots of details in your own words.

- little girl running into street
- horses coming toward them
- boy shouting and running
- boy pulling the girl to safety
- the parents thanking him

Revising in Action

Here are some of the changes Taylor made to improve the voice of his first draft. He added a detail that makes him sound like he's talking to a friend.

> One Saturday, Brandon and I was
>
> skateboarding. I fell. I got hurt. Brandon went
>
> When
> and got my mom. I came back from the hospital
>
> I had   heavy
> with a plaster cast on my write arm. That's the
>
> my arm felt hot and itchy, and
> arm I use the most. I couldn't bend my elbow.
>
> as   as a baby
> I felt helpless.

Revise
Check your writing voice.

1. Read your essay and imagine that you are telling a friend what happened.

2. Rewrite any parts of your essay that don't sound like you.

   - **Add** words to make your writing sound like you are talking to a friend.

   - **Cut** any words that sound boring or uninteresting.

Revising for

Action verbs can help your writing come alive.

Q. How should I choose action verbs?

Choose action verbs that make pictures for the reader to imagine. An **action verb** tells what the subject is doing.

Angela tripped over the old, rotten log.
The kite dipped in the wind.
Martin slams the ball into the basket.

Practice

On your own paper, write the stronger action verb for each sentence below. The choices are shown in parentheses.

1. My dad (*went, biked*) to Mexico City.
2. Todd (*moved, raced*) toward the end zone.
3. I (*painted, made*) a picture in art class.
4. "Be quiet," Zoe (*whispered, said*).
5. The horse (*hurried, galloped*) around the track.

Revising in Action

Here are some changes Taylor made to improve the word choice in his narrative. He used better action verbs.

One Saturday, Brandon and I was

skateboarding. I ~~fell~~. I got hurt. Brandon, ~~went~~ ran

found When

and ~~got~~ my mom. I came back from the hospital

I had heavy

with a plaster cast on my write arm. That's the

my arm felt hot and itchy, and

arm I use the most. I couldn't bend my elbow.

as as a baby

I felt helpless.

Revise **Check your word choice.**

1. Read your essay and underline the action verbs.
2. Be sure you have chosen action verbs that make word pictures for the reader.
   - **Add** better action verbs wherever you can.
   - **Replace** general words with specific words.

Revising for

Sentence Fluency

Sometimes combining sentences can make your writing smoother.

Q. How can I combine sentences?

Here are three ways to combine short sentences into one longer sentence.

Use a series. Combine short sentences that tell different things about the same subject.

Cole is smart. Cole is funny. Cole is strong.
Cole is smart, funny, and strong.

Use compound subjects. Combine two or more subjects into the compound subject of one sentence.

My friend plays soccer. I play soccer.
My friend and I play soccer.

Use compound verbs. Combine two or more verbs into the compound verb of one sentence.

Rico wrote his essay. Rico published his essay.
Rico wrote and published his essay.

Practice

Combine these two sentences using a compound verb.

Nigel swam at the lake. He fished there, too.

Revising in Action

Here are some changes Taylor made to improve the flow of his writing in his first draft. He combined two short sentences by using a compound verb.

One Saturday, Brandon and I was

~~and~~   ran

skateboarding. I fell~~,~~ ~~I~~ got hurt. Brandon went

found   When

and got my mom. I came back from the hospital

I had   heavy

with a plaster cast on my write arm. That's the

my arm felt hot and itchy, and

arm I use the most. I couldn't bend my elbow.

as   as a baby

I felt helpless.

Revise ## Check your sentence lengths.

1. Make sure your essay has both long and short sentences.

2. If you find too many short sentences, combine some of them. Use the three suggestions on page 102.

   - Cut words, add punctuation, and add a conjunction to combine two sentences using a compound verb.

Revising Using a Checklist

 Check your revising.

Number your paper from 1 to 9. Read each question and put a check mark after the number if the answer to a question is "yes." Otherwise, continue to work with that part of your essay.

Ideas

_____ **1.** Do I tell about one helpful person?
_____ **2.** Do I include sensory details?

Organization

_____ **3.** Do my beginning, middle, and ending work well?
_____ **4.** Are my details in time order?

Voice

_____ **5.** Does my voice sound like me?
_____ **6.** Do I use transitions to move the story along?

Word Choice

_____ **7.** Have I used action verbs?

Sentence Fluency

_____ **8.** Have I varied my sentence beginnings?
_____ **9.** Have I varied the lengths of my sentences?

 Make a clean copy.

After revising your narrative, make a clean copy for editing.

Editing for

Conventions

When you edit for conventions, check your spelling, capitalization, punctuation, and grammar.

Q. How can I check for the right words?

Watch for words that sound the same but have different spellings and meanings. Such words are called *homophones*.

When you use a homophone, check a dictionary to make sure you have used the right one.

are, our	rode, road
buy, by	there, their, they're
for, four	to, two, too
its, it's	you're, your

Practice

On your own paper, write the correct word or words for each sentence below. The choices are shown in parentheses.

1. We *(rode, road)* *(are, our)* bikes to the park.
2. *(There, They're, Their)* coming *(to, too, two)* my house later.
3. Mrs. King said *(its, it's)* fine for me to come, *(to, too, two)*.
4. *(You're, Your)* mom is looking *(for, four)* you.
5. Would you *(buy, by)* a dozen eggs and *(to, too, two)* loaves of bread?

Editing Checking for  Conventions

A checklist like the one below can help you find errors in capitalization, punctuation, spelling, and grammar.

Conventions

Punctuation

_____ **1.** Did I use end punctuation after all my sentences?

_____ **2.** Did I put quotation marks around words people said?

Capitalization

_____ **3.** Did I start all my sentences with capital letters?

_____ **4.** Did I correctly capitalize proper nouns?

Spelling

_____ **5.** Have I carefully checked my spelling?

Grammar

_____ **6.** Did I use correct verbs (he **plays**, not he **play**)?

_____ **7.** Did I make sure to use the right word (to, too, two)?

Practice

Find the place where you should indent for a new paragraph.

I told everyone that I didn't like roller coasters. They scared me. People always were screaming on the rides, and my stomach got queasy thinking about all the dips and loops and turns. Then one day, my friend Danny talked me into trying a small roller coaster with him. My stomach started doing cartwheels. I grabbed the safety bar as we chugged up the first steep climb. When we shot down the steep track, I began screaming and then laughing. I never had so much fun!

Editing in Action

Here are the changes Taylor made to the first several paragraphs of his revised draft.

Taylor corrected a misspelled word.

Have you ever had a terrible day? On my terrible day, I broke my arm. Luckily, my good friend Brandon was with me. he is one of the

helpful

most (helpfull) people I know.

A verb is corrected.

were

One Saturday, Brandon and I was skate-boarding, and I fell and got hurt. Brandon ran home and found my mom. When I came back

He replaced a wrong word.

from the hospital, I had a heavy plaster cast

right

on my write arm. That's the arm I use the

He added a capital letter.

most. my arm felt hot and itchy, and I couldn't bend my elbow. I felt as helpless as a baby.

He added quotation marks.

"Don't worry," Brandon said. "I'll help you.

Edit

Check for conventions in your essay.

 # Using a Rubric

The rubric on these pages can help you rate your writing.

 Ideas

6 Rich ideas and details make an unforgettable essay!

5 The experience and the details are interesting.

4 The experience is interesting, but it needs more details.

 **Organization**

6 The narrative is arranged superbly!

5 The writing is well organized from beginning to end.

4 Most of the narrative works well.

Voice

6 The voice is original and exciting!

5 The voice sounds exactly like the writer.

4 The voice sounds like the writer most of the time.

Word Choice

6 The word choice makes a vivid picture!

5 Strong nouns and verbs make clear pictures.

4 Some strong nouns and verbs are used.

Sentence Fluency

6 The sentences are a joy to read!

5 The sentences are clear and varied.

4 Most sentences are clear.

Conventions

6 Conventions are correct.

5 Most conventions are correct.

4 Some errors appear.

3 The experience isn't clear, and some details don't belong.

2 The narrative should focus on one experience.

1 A new experience or suitable details should be found.

3 Parts (beginning, middle, or ending) should be stronger.

2 All parts of the essay run together.

1 The narrative needs to be organized.

3 Sometimes the voice sounds like the writer.

2 The writing does not sound like the writer.

1 The writing has no real voice.

3 Many strong words are needed.

2 Some words are overused.

1 Some words make the essay confusing.

3 Many sentences are choppy.

2 Many sentences are choppy or incomplete.

1 Many sentences are incomplete.

3 Errors may confuse the reader.

2 Errors make the writing hard to read.

1 Help is needed to make corrections.

Publishing Sharing Your Essay

After editing, it's time to write a neat copy of your essay to share with your classmates. If you want to, you may add an illustration.

 Make a final copy.

1. Follow your teacher's instructions, or use the model below. (For computer papers, see page 37.)
2. Create a clean final copy and proofread it.

Skateboard Emergency 9-1-1

Have you ever had a terrible day? On my terrible day, I broke my arm. Luckily, my good friend Brandon was with me. He is one of the most helpful people I know.

One Saturday, Brandon and I were skateboarding. I fell and got hurt. Brandon ran and found my mom. When I came back from the hospital, I had a heavy plaster cast on my right arm. That's the arm I use the most. My arm felt hot and itchy, and I couldn't bend my elbow. I felt as helpless as a baby.

"Don't worry," Brandon said, "I'll help you." At school, he carried my lunch tray. He wrote things down for me in class. After school, he helped me put on my coat and boots. Whenever there was something I couldn't do, Brandon was there to help me.

The day I broke my arm was terrible, but I had a great helper. Now my arm is fine. Brandon and I play ball and go skateboarding just like before. I'll never forget what Brandon did for me when I needed a helping hand.

Reflecting on Your Writing

Congratulations! You have finished your narrative essay. Now it's time to think about what you have learned. Here are Taylor's thoughts about his essay.

Thinking About Your Writing

Name: _Taylor Matelski_

Title: _Skateboard Emergency 9-1-1_

1. The best part of my essay is . . .

   telling about my good friend and how he

   really helped me.

2. The part that sill needs work is . . .

   the second paragraph. I could have used

   more action and dialogue.

3. The main thing I learned about narrative writing is . . .

   how to tell what happened in the

   right order.

Narrative Writing

Across the Curriculum

"What happened?" One way to answer that question is to write a narrative. Sometimes the narrative tells about an experience in your own life. Sometimes it tells about an experience in the life of someone else.

On the following pages, you'll learn how to write both types of narratives. You'll also learn how to respond to a narrative prompt on a writing test.

Social Studies:
Biographical Narrative

For social studies, Tony needed to write a narrative about an inventor. He chose a person whose invention is used in millions of homes every day.

Beginning

The beginning gives the focus statement (underlined).

Middle

The middle tells what happened.

Ending

The ending tells how the inventor's work made a difference.

Chocolate in His Pocket

One day, Percy L. Spencer was working with a radar power tube. He worked at a company in Massachusetts. Suddenly, the chocolate bar in his pocket melted! Percy wasn't mad, though. Percy's accident gave him an idea for a new kind of oven.

Percy tested another food. He put some popcorn in front of the power tube. Pop! Pop! Pop! The kernels popped into popcorn! Microwaves had cooked it.

Percy decided to make an oven that would use microwaves. He finished his first microwave oven in 1945. It was 5 1/2 feet tall and weighed 750 pounds.

Today microwave ovens are much smaller. People still use them to pop popcorn!

Prewriting Selecting a Topic

Your biographical narrative will be about an inventor. Tony looked at some Web sites and some library books about inventors. He wrote down people and inventions that interested him.

Prewrite Create a topic chart.

1. Write "Inventors" and "Inventions" at the top of your paper.

2. Check a book or Web site and list your ideas.

3. Put a star (✳) next to the inventor you choose.

Inventors	Inventions
Thomas Edison	lightbulb
George Washington Carver	bleach
Percy L. Spencer ✳	microwave oven

Gathering Details

Questions help you gather facts. See Tony's notes below.

Prewrite Answer these questions about your topic.

<u>Who is the inventor?</u> Percy L. Spencer
<u>What was the invention?</u> The microwave oven
<u>How was it invented?</u> Chocolate in his pocket melted near a power tube.
<u>When was it invented?</u> 1945

Writing Creating a First Draft

Use these guidelines to write your biographical narrative.

Write your narrative.

1. Include a focus sentence in the beginning.
2. Tell the story of the inventor in the middle.
3. Share a final thought in the ending.

Revising Improving Your Writing

The following questions can help you revise your first draft.

Improve your work.

Ask yourself the following questions about your narrative.

■ Did I include enough details?
■ Did I put the events in the order they happened?
■ Did I use a writing voice that sounds interested?

Editing Checking for Conventions

Check capitalization, punctuation, spelling, and grammar.

Check your work.

■ Did I end each sentence with correct punctuation?
■ Did I look up any difficult spelling words?
■ Did I use the right words (*it's/its, you're/your*)?

Art: A Personal Art Story

Texture Detectives

One day in art, Mr. Morehead had us make rubbings. We put plain paper on top of an object. Then we rubbed the side of a crayon over it. The texture of the object left a pattern on the paper.

We didn't want to stop. Mr. Morehead said, "Rub things in nature and at home. Then bring back your rubbings for a guessing game." Wow, I wanted my rubbing to be the biggest mystery.

First, I rubbed my jean jacket. That was boring. Big leaves from my backyard made awesome patterns, but looked just like leaves. My last rubbing looked like alligator skin and felt bumpy. My dad's metal watchband stumped everybody.

Writing Tips

Before you write . . .

- Think about an art experience that you could share.
- Make a time line to tell you story in the order it happened.

During your writing . . .

- Get the reader's attention in the beginning of your story.
- Then write about each part of the story in one paragraph.
- Write the way you would tell the story to a friend.

After you've written a first draft . . .

- Read your story and see if any important details are missing.
- Give your story an interesting title.
- Check capitalization, punctuation, spelling, and grammar.

Practical Writing:
Friendly Letter

A narrative letter lets you share your life with people who live far away. Kerri wrote this letter to a friend who had moved to another town.

April 23, 2009

Dear Damitria,

> **The beginning** tells about one event.

There was a circus at our school this week! Two real circus performers came and taught each class a circus trick. My class learned how to make balloon animals.

> **The middle** shares more about a specific part of the event.

I made a funny blue poodle. The first time I tried, my balloon popped. The next time, I made the little head and legs just right. I named my poodle Tria because I miss you.

On Friday, the whole school put on a circus in the gym. Mrs. Mancini played piano music. There were kids being clowns, juggling, and doing face painting. We even had popcorn. I wish you could have been here!

> **The ending** wraps up the narrative.

Your friend,
Kerri

Writing Tips

Before you write . . .
- Think about a recent experience you could share.
- List things you remember seeing, hearing, smelling, tasting, and touching (sensory details).

During your writing . . .
- Introduce the topic in the body of your letter.
- Write the body of your letter in paragraphs.
- Write about events in the order they happened.
- Share your thoughts and feelings.

After you've written a first draft . . .
- Read over your letter and add missing details.
- Make sure you used the correct form for a friendly letter.
- Check capitalization, punctuation, spelling, and grammar.

Think about the experience you want to share with someone who wasn't there. Then write your friendly letter.

Narrative Writing

Writing for Assessment

Some writing tests have narrative prompts. A narrative prompt asks you to remember an experience and write about it. Devin made a quick time line to plan his response.

Narrative Prompt

Think about one experience that you will never forget. Why is it unforgettable? Write a narrative about the experience. Tell what happened in time order and include plenty of sensory details.

Time Line

African Festival

— Class field trip to a festival

— Saw banners

— Listened to drums

— Kids learned dancing

— Now I take dance

Dancing Drums

The **beginning** gives the focus sentence (underlined).

My class took a field trip to an African festival. I was excited because my ancestors are from Africa. <u>I'll never forget that day because that's when I learned African dance.</u>

At first, we all sat on the wood floor and looked at the bright banners on the walls. Tall drums stood in the corner.

The **middle** tells about the experience.

Then a drum teacher named Kaleem took half the class over to the drums. He taught them how to make a beat. I could feel the drum beats in my chest.

Next, a dance teacher came to the rest of us. Her name was Dakima. She showed us some dance moves and told us to take off our shoes and socks. We danced barefoot while the others beat the drums!

The **ending** adds a thought about what happened.

I loved dancing. Now I take African dance lessons every week. I'll always remember the first time I danced to the drums.

After you read . . .

- **Ideas** (1) What is the topic of the story?

- **Organization** (2) How does Devin organize his experience?

- **Word Choice** (3) What words show Devin's excitement?

Writing Tips

Before you write . . .

- Read the prompt and underline the key words such as *one experience, unforgettable,* and *narrative.*
- Use a time line to list events.

During your writing . . .

- Write a focus sentence about your topic.
- Write events in time order.
- Add important details.
- Be sure to answer any question in the prompt.

After you've written your narrative . . .

- Make sure you have a clear focus and enough details.
- Check capitalization, punctuation, spelling, and grammar.

Respond to this narrative prompt. Finish your essay in the amount of time that your teacher gives you.

Narrative Prompt

Think about a time when you were surprised. How did you react? Write a narrative about the experience.

Narrative Writing in Review

In narrative writing, you tell about something that has happened in your own life or the life of another person.

Select a topic that will interest your reader. (See pages 84–85.)

Gather important details about the people and events in your narrative. Use a graphic organizer. (See pages 84–85.)

In the beginning part, give background information and introduce your topic. (See pages 86–87.)

In the middle part, tell about the events and people, using dialogue and specific details. (See pages 88–89.)

In the ending part, tell why the experience was important. (See pages 90–91.)

Review your ideas, organization, and **voice** first. Then review for **word choice** and **sentence fluency.** (See pages 92–104.)

Check your writing for conventions. Also have a classmate look at your writing for errors you may have missed. (See pages 105–109.)

Make a final copy and proofread it for errors before sharing it. (See page 110.)

Expository Writing

"What is the world's tallest mountain?"
"What is the deepest ocean?"
The world is full of questions. Writing that provides answers to these questions is called expository writing. Expository writing explains or informs.

In this section, you'll learn how to write an expository paragraph, an expository essay, and a few other forms. The world is full of questions, and here's your chance to provide some answers!

What's Ahead

- **Writing an Expository Paragraph**
- **Writing an Expository Essay**
- Expository Writing Across the Curriculum
- Writing for Assessment

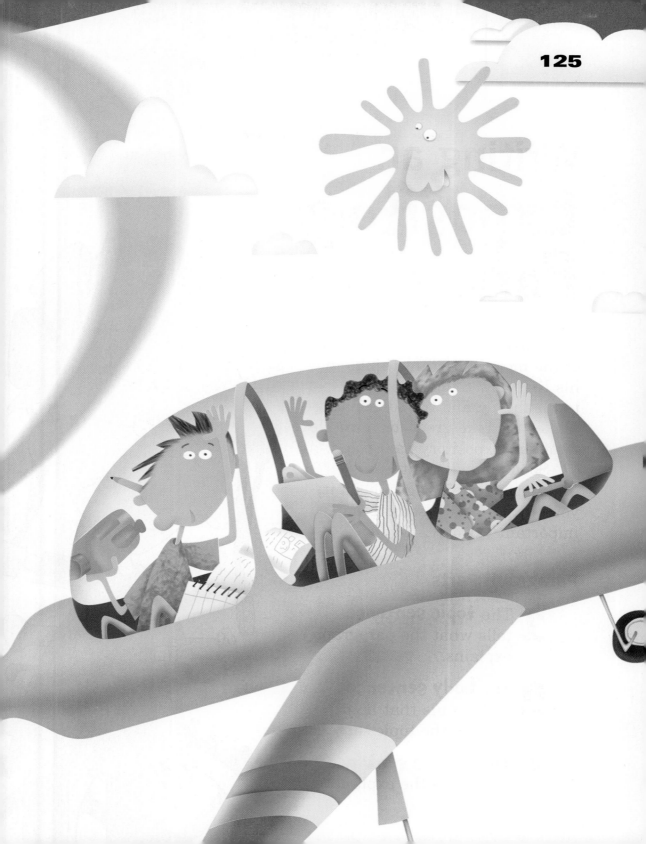

Writing an Expository Paragraph

Elijah had a bike. It was one of the most important things in his life. How could he explain to his family and friends what makes his bike great for him? He wrote an expository paragraph.

Soon you will write your own expository paragraph. In it, you'll explain why something is important to you.

Paragraph Parts

1 The **topic sentence** tells what the paragraph explains.

2 The **body sentences** add details that help explain the topic sentence.

3 The **closing sentence** completes the explanation.

Expository Paragraph

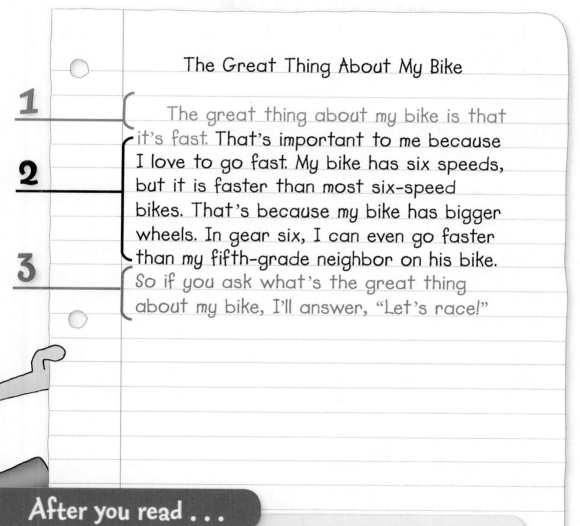

The Great Thing About My Bike

1

    The great thing about my bike is that

2

it's fast. That's important to me because I love to go fast. My bike has six speeds, but it is faster than most six-speed bikes. That's because my bike has bigger wheels. In gear six, I can even go faster than my fifth-grade neighbor on his bike.

3

So if you ask what's the great thing about my bike, I'll answer, "Let's race!"

After you read . . .

- **Ideas** (1) What details help explain the topic?
- **Organization** (2) What are the three parts of this paragraph?
- **Word Choice** (3) What three words or phrases show the writer's excitement about the topic?

Prewriting Selecting a Topic

An ideas cluster can help you think of the important things in your life. Elijah made the cluster below. He focused on objects that he could write a paragraph about.

 Prewrite Create an ideas cluster.

1. Write "Important Things" in the middle of your paper.

2. Around it, write the names of objects you like. Connect them.

3. Put a star (*) next to the idea you want to write about.

Ideas Cluster

piggy bank

bike*

baseball cards

Important Things

my art books

piano

video game

Writing Creating Your First Draft

As you write your paragraph, remember that each part has a special job to do.

- Your **topic sentence** names the topic and tells what's great about it.
- Each **body sentence** explains your topic sentence by answering the question *why?* or *how?*
- Your **closing sentence** completes your explanation.

 Develop your paragraph.

1. Write your topic sentence using this form:
   "The great thing about _____ is _____."

2. Write sentences that answer *why?* or *how?* about the topic sentence.

3. Write a closing sentence that completes your explanation.

First Draft

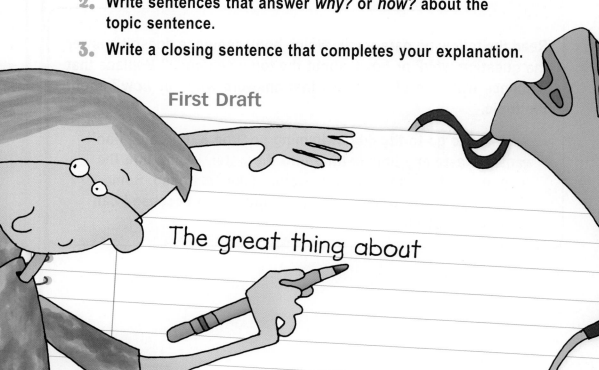

The great thing about

Revising Improving Your Paragraph

When you revise your paragraph, make sure your body sentences explain your topic sentence.

 Check your body sentences.

1. Underline your topic sentence.
2. Check each body sentence to make sure it answers *why?* or *how?* about your topic sentence.
3. Cross out any sentence that does not explain the topic.
4. If you need to, add one or two sentences to explain your topic better.

Practice

Read the following paragraph. Which body sentence doesn't answer the question *why?* or *how?* about the topic sentence? Replace that sentence with one of your own that answers *why?* or *how?* about the topic.

    I like to go to the city swimming pool on a hot day. I don't want to waste any time getting into the water. I jump into the deep end of the pool. The cool water makes me gasp. Some of my friends like to fish. I enjoy the high slide because I can make a big splash!

Editing Checking for Conventions

When you edit your paragraph, make sure you have included the right punctuation after each sentence.

- Most sentences end with a period.
- Questions end with a question mark.
- Exciting sentences end with an exclamation point.

Check your work.

1. Did I indent the first line of my paragraph?
2. Did I begin each sentence with a capital letter?
3. Did I end each sentence with the correct punctuation mark?
4. Have I checked my spelling?
5. Have I used the right words, like *there, their,* or *they're*?

Tell what the correct end punctuation mark would be for each sentence below.

1. How much money do you think I have in my piggy bank__
2. I wish I had a million dollars__
3. I will count my money tonight when I get home__

Writing an
Expository
Essay

What is important to you? Everyone has a different answer. For a student named Gabrielle, having friends stay overnight for her birthday was very important.

In this chapter, you'll write about something important to you. First, you'll need to show what is important to you, and then you'll tell the reader why it's important.

Understanding Your Goal

Your goal in this chapter is to write an essay that explains something that is important to you. The six traits below and the expository revising lessons (pages 146–156) will help you reach your writing goal.

Your goal is to . . .

Ideas
Choose an interesting topic and explain it with details.

Organization
Put the parts of your essay in the right order.

Voice
Show your interest and excitement.

Word Choice
Use specific nouns to help make your ideas clear.

Sentence Fluency
Write complete sentences that are easy to read.

Conventions
Check your punctuation, capitalization, spelling, and grammar.

Expository Essay

An expository essay gives information to the reader. This essay explains why Aidan's backpack is important to him.

The Home on My Back

Some kids can't stand their backpacks. A backpack makes them think of books and homework. My backpack is different. It is important to me because it holds everything I need.

I love books, and my backpack keeps them with me. I don't mean just schoolbooks. I mean my reading books, too. Right now, I'm reading *Ribsy* by Beverly Cleary. Next, I'll read *Henry Huggins*.

Another reason my backpack is important is that it holds my lunch box. Dad always packs a good lunch for me, with a snack. Sometimes he even puts a note in. That way, my dad visits me in the middle of the day! Thanks to my backpack, that's possible.

Sometimes my backpack gets heavy to carry, but I don't mind. It has everything I need. It's like a home I carry on my back.

Parts of an Expository Essay

An expository essay has three parts.

Beginning

The **beginning paragraph** names the topic and gives the focus sentence.

Middle

Each **middle paragraph** starts with a topic sentence. Details in the other sentences explain the topic sentence.

Ending

The **ending paragraph** tells how the writer feels about the topic.

After you read . . .

- **Ideas** (1) What does the writer think is important about his backpack?

- **Organization** (2) How does the writer introduce his topic?

- **Word Choice** (3) What words or phrases help show the writer's feelings about his backpack?

Prewriting Selecting a Topic

Your essay should be about something that means a lot to you. Gabrielle used a T-chart to think about things that were important to her.

 Make a T-chart.

1. Write "Important Things" at the top of your paper.
2. Write "At Home" and "At School" underneath.
3. List important things under each heading.
4. Put a star (✲) next to the thing you want to write about.

T-Chart

Important Things

At Home	At School
family	the tetherball court
my bedroom	recess
overnights*	art class
my pastels set	

Thinking About the Topic

(1) *What is most important about your topic?*
(2) *Why is that important?*
(3) *How is that important?*

Gabrielle answered these questions about her topic. Her first answer is her **focus sentence**. It tells *what* her essay will be about. The other two answers are the **topic sentences** for the body paragraphs. They will tell *why* and *how* about her topic.

 Answer these three questions.

1. Write "What's most important?"
   Answer this question by writing your focus sentence.
2. Write "Why?"
   Answer this question by writing your first topic sentence.
3. Write "How?"
   Answer this question by writing your second topic sentence.

Topic Questions

1. What's most important?
   An overnight is a special kind of party.
2. Why?
   Friends can be together all night at an overnight.
3. How?
   An overnight is full of fun activities.

Writing **Beginning Your Essay**

Your beginning paragraph introduces the topic. Here are three possible ways to introduce your topic.

▶ Beginning

Middle

Ending

Ask
a question.

> What could be better than an overnight with friends?
>
> *OR*
>
> At midnight, something tapped on the window, and I . . .
>
> *OR*
>
> When my sister Celia had an overnight, I listened through the wall to the spooky stories she told.

Be creative
and tell a little story.

Connect
with readers.

 Write **Create your beginning paragraph.**

1. Use one of the three ways above to introduce your topic.

2. Include your focus sentence. (See the bottom of page 137.)

Gabrielle's Beginning Paragraph

Gabrielle's beginning had some great ideas, and some errors. That's all right for a first draft.

Beginning

The topic is introduced.

The focus sentence is added. (underlined)

My sister had an overnight. I listened threw the wall to her spooky stories about voices sounds and shadows. The next day Mom asked me if I wanted to have my own overnight. <u>An overnight is a special kind of party.</u>

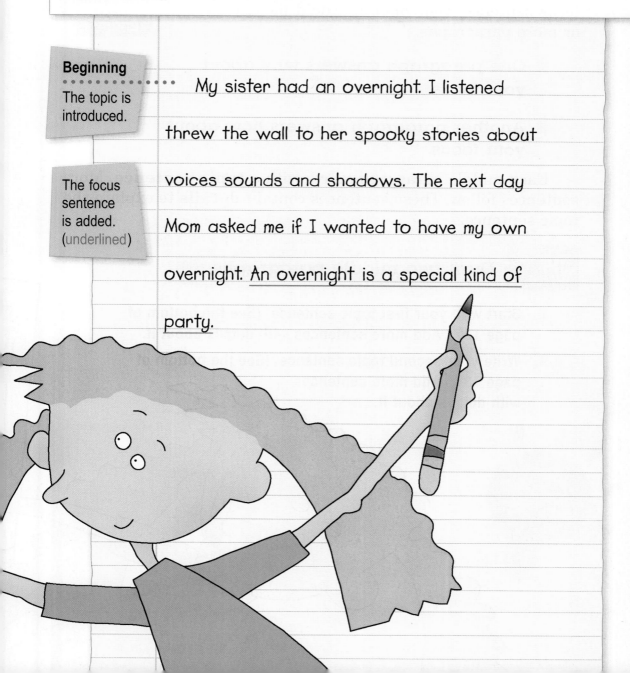

Writing Developing the Middle

Beginning
▶ **Middle**
Ending

The middle part of your essay explains your focus sentence. Your middle should include two or more paragraphs.

■ **One paragraph answers why about your focus.**

■ **Another paragraph answers how about your focus.**

Each middle paragraph starts with a **topic sentence**. More sentences follow. Those sentences contain **details** to explain the topic sentence.

Write **Draft two middle paragraphs.**

1. Start with your first topic sentence. (See the bottom of page 137.) Add more sentences with details about it.

2. Write your second topic sentence. (See the bottom of page 137.) Add more sentences with details about it.

Ideas
Gather details that "show."

Gabrielle's Middle Paragraphs

Gabrielle explained *why* and *how* about her focus sentence. Her writing has a few errors, as all first drafts do.

overnight of my own. An overnight is a

special kind of party.

Middle

A topic sentence begins the first paragraph.

Freinds can be together all night at an overnight. That's more fun than just seeing each other at school. It's great to stay up late with good freinds.

Details are added.

A topic sentence begins the second paragraph.

Another great thing about an overnight is that it is full of fun activities. Nighttime is perfect for telling spooky stories what could be better than a movie marathon, eating, board games, and sleeping on the floor in the living room.

Details are added.

101

Writing Ending Your Essay

Beginning

Middle

▶ Ending

Your ending paragraph completes your explanation. Here are three possible ways to end your essay.

Return to your beginning idea.

Share something funny.

Talk with the reader.

> Now Celia will have to listen to my spooky stories because my very first overnight will be next weekend.
>
> OR
>
> I'm so excited about my overnight, I can't sleep.
>
> OR
>
> If you're like me, you've been dreaming about having an overnight.

Write Create your ending.

1. Use one of the three ways above to write an ending for your essay.
2. Try a second way and choose the one you like best.

Gabrielle's Ending Paragraph

Gabrielle created a strong ending by going back to the beginning of her essay. Her first ending contains some errors.

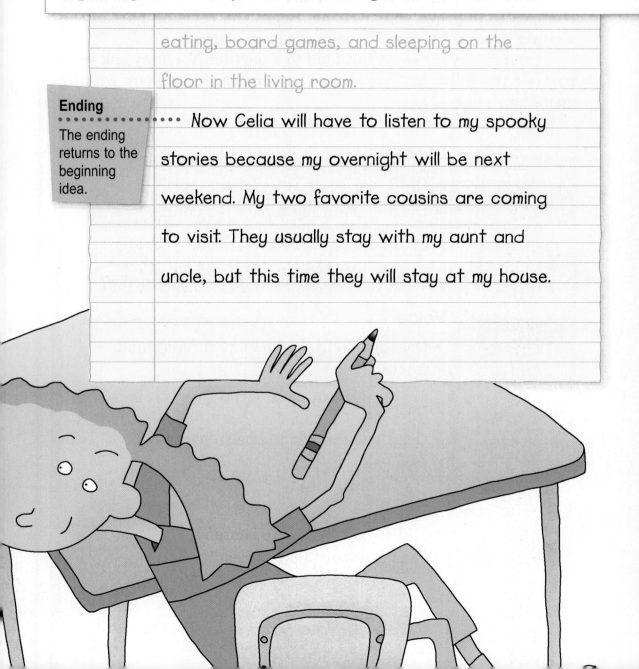

eating, board games, and sleeping on the

floor in the living room.

Ending
. . . .
The ending returns to the beginning idea.

Now Celia will have to listen to my spooky

stories because my overnight will be next

weekend. My two favorite cousins are coming

to visit. They usually stay with my aunt and

uncle, but this time they will stay at my house.

Revising Improving Your Essay

When you finish your first draft, you are ready to make changes to improve your writing. Begin the revising part of the writing process by reading your essay to yourself.

Then read your essay out loud to a partner. You may ask your partner the following questions that are based on your writing goals (see page 133).

Ideas

- Did I choose an interesting topic?
- Did I explain my topic with details?

Organization

- Did I put the parts of my essay in order?

Voice

- Does my writing show my interest and excitement?

Word Choice

- Did I use specific nouns to make my ideas clear?

Sentence Fluency

- Did I write complete sentences?
- Is my writing easy to read?

Getting a Partner's Response

A partner can help you find ways to improve your writing. Here is a partner's response to Gabrielle's essay on pages 139–143.

Response Sheet

Writer: __Gabrielle__   Responder: __Dario__

Title: __All Right, an Overnight!__

What I like:

__Everybody likes overnights!__

__The part about Celia was funny.__

Questions I have:

__What do you eat?__

__Where do your cousins live?__

Revising for

Strong writing "shows" readers what you mean rather than just "telling" them.

Q. How can I "show" instead of "tell"?

Here are three ways you can *show* instead of *tell*.

1 **Use sensory details:** Include things that can be seen, heard, smelled, tasted, or touched.

    Telling   Thanksgiving dinner is always good.

    Showing   Thanksgiving dinner means juicy turkey, hot rolls, and steaming stuffing.

2 **Use specific details:** Give exact information.

    Telling   I love going to baseball games.

    Showing   I love sitting in the bleachers, cheering for our team, and eating hot dogs.

3 **Use dialogue:** Let people speak for themselves.

    Telling   Mom said she was proud of me.

    Showing   Mom said, "No one works harder than you do."

Practice

Rewrite the telling sentence below. Use one of the three showing strategies above.

My pet is important to me.

Revising in Action

Here are some of the changes Gabrielle made to improve the ideas in the beginning paragraph of her first draft. She changed one telling sentence and put the idea into dialogue.

My sister had an overnight. I listened threw

the wall to her spooky stories about voices

sounds and shadows. The next day Mom asked

"Would you like   your

me ~~if I wanted~~ to have my own overnight. An

overnight is a special kind of party. Friends can

be together all night at an overnight.

Revise   **Check your ideas.**

Find at least one place in your writing to "show" instead of "tell" using details or dialogue.

- **Add** sensory and other specific details. Use a caret ∧ to show where you want to add words or punctuation.
- **Add** dialogue if it adds information.
- **Cut** words that tell instead of show. Use a delete mark ℓ to show what you want to remove.

Revising for

Organization

Your writing is well organized if it has all the parts it needs and each part is in the right place.

Q. How can I check my organization?

You can check the organization of your essay by doing the following scavenger hunt.

Organization Scavenger Hunt

1. Add a ¶ beside each paragraph indent.
2. Make a * next to your focus sentence in your beginning paragraph.
3. Put a ☺ next to the topic sentence in each middle paragraph.

Practice

Where would you place the above symbols in the passage below?

My brother and I have a tree house in a huge oak tree in the pasture. On a hot day, a breeze flows up from the valley like a cool clear stream. A tree house is a great place to play, read a book, or just be alone. Our tree house has two floors. Boards hammered into the tree make a ladder to the first floor. Then a trapdoor leads to the second level. Dad used wooden braces to make the floors and side rails strong. Our tree house even has a roof. Being up in a tree is fun. We pretend to be sailing on a ship or looking down at the world from space. We have many adventures in our treehouse.

Revising in Action

Gabrielle checked the organization of her first draft. She marked her focus sentence and paragraph indents. She needed to create one new paragraph.

¶ My sister had an overnight. I listened threw

the wall to her spooky stories about voices

sounds and shadows. The next day Mom asked

"Would you like   your
me if I wanted to have my own overnight.* An

¶ ☺
overnight is a special kind of party. Friends can

be together all night at an overnight.

Revise   Check your organization.

Mark your own essay for the scavenger hunt on page 148. You may need to write a focus sentence, indent a paragraph, or add a topic sentence.

Revising for

Your writing voice is your own special way of expressing yourself. For an expository essay, your voice should sound interested.

Q. How can I write with an interested voice?

Your voice will sound interested if your sentences aren't silly or boring. Use the ideas below to check your voice.

Silly · · · · · · · · · · ·
(Tone it down.)

> I'd like to jump over the moon.

Interested · · · · · ·

> I can see craters on the moon when I look through my telescope.

Boring · · · · · · · · ·
(Build it up.)

> I like to look at the moon at night.

Practice

Rewrite the boring sentence below so that you sound interested in the topic.

I have a red bicycle.

Revising in Action

Here is how Gabrielle changed her first paragraph to improve the voice in her first draft. She added interesting words to a sentence that sounded boring. She also added a sentence to show excitement.

¶ My sister had an overnight. I listened threw

the wall to her spooky stories about ∧ voices

growly

screechy   dark

∧ sounds and ∧ shadows. The next day Mom asked

"Would you like   your   ,"I can't wait

me if I wanted to have my own overnight. ∧ An

¶ ☺

overnight is a special kind of party. Friends can

be together all night at an overnight.

Check your writing for voice.

1. Read your essay and underline any sentences that sound silly or boring.

2. Rewrite underlined sentences so that you sound more interested.

- **Cut** words or sentences that sound silly or boring.
- **Add** words that make your writing more interesting.

Revising for

Word Choice

In an expository essay, your goal is to explain something. Specific nouns can make your explanations clearer.

Q. How can I use specific nouns?

You can use specific nouns to replace general nouns. A specific noun names an exact person, place, thing, or idea.

General Nouns:	car	brother	animal	tree
	↓	↓	↓	↓
Specific Nouns:	hot rod	Tyrone	manatee	weeping willow

Practice

Replace each underlined general noun with a specific noun.

1. Most of the time, we play <u>games</u>.
2. We stop playing long enough to eat <u>food</u>.
3. We also watch <u>movies</u>.
4. It is usually a movie about <u>something</u>.
5. On Saturday morning, we have to clean the <u>room</u>.

Revising in Action

Here is how Gabrielle changed her first paragraph to improve the word choice in her first draft. She added some specific nouns to make the words *sister* and *overnight* clearer.

¶ My sister had ~~an overnight~~. I listened threw
<u>Celia   her friends sleep over at our house</u>

the wall to her spooky stories about voices
<u>growly</u>

sounds and shadows. The next day Mom asked
<u>screechy   dark</u>

me if I wanted to have my own overnight. An
<u>"Would you like   your   I can't wait</u>

overnight is a special kind of party. Friends can

be together all night at an overnight.

Revise

Check your word choice.

1. Read you essay and underline all the nouns.
2. Replace any general nouns with specific nouns.
   - **Cut** any nouns that are general.
   - **Add** specific nouns to make your explanation clearer.

Revising for

Sentence Fluency

Your sentences won't flow smoothly if you have too many short, choppy sentences.

Q. How can I combine sentences?

You can combine two sentences with a comma and a conjunction.

- Combine two sentences by adding a comma and one of these conjunctions: *and, but, or, for, so,* or *yet.*

  Two Short Sentences
  The tree changes each season. It is always beautiful.

  One Compound Sentence
  The tree changes each season, but it is always beautiful.

Practice

Combine the following two sentences using a comma and a conjunction.

My granola is easy to make. It doesn't even need to be cooked.

Revising in Action

Here is how Gabrielle changed her first paragraph to improve the sentence fluency in her first draft. She combined the first two sentences.

¶ My sister had an overnight. ~~Celia~~ her friends sleep over at our house and I listened threw the wall to her spooky stories about growly voices screechy dark sounds and shadows. The next day Mom asked me if I wanted to have my own overnight. "Would you like your I can't wait An overnight is a special kind of party. ¶ ☺ Friends can be together all night at an overnight.

Revise · **Check for smooth sentences.**

1. Read your essay and look for places that you could combine two sentences.

2. Try to create at least one compound sentence.
   - **Add** a comma and a conjunction to combine two sentences.

Revising Using a Checklist

Check your revising.

Number your paper from 1 to 8. If you can answer "yes" to a question, put a check mark after that number. If not, continue to work on that part of your essay.

Ideas

_____ **1.** Have I used my sensory details to "show" instead of "tell"?

_____ **2.** Have I used enough specific details?

Organization

_____ **3.** Do I indent each new paragraph?

_____ **4.** Do I have a focus sentence in my beginning paragraph?

_____ **5.** Does each middle paragraph have a topic sentence?

Voice

_____ **6.** Have I used an interested voice?

Word Choice

_____ **7.** Have I used specific nouns that fit my topic?

Sentence Fluency

_____ **8.** Have I combined some short, choppy sentences?

Make a clean copy.

After revising your essay, make a clean copy for editing.

Editing for

Conventions

When you edit for conventions, you need to be sure you have used commas in a series.

Q. How do I use commas in a series?

When you have a series (a list) of three or more things, put commas between each one. A series can have single words or groups of words.

My town has a pool, a river, and a lake.

Practice

Rewrite each sentence below. Add commas between the three or more items in a series.

1. My town is fun in spring summer winter and fall.
2. I enjoy swimming fishing and boating.
3. I also ride my bike walk my dog and play football.
4. I live with my mom a brother a sister and a hamster.
5. My family enjoys working in the garden going to the park and playing board games together.

Editing Checking for Conventions

Check for capitalization, punctuation, spelling, and grammar errors in your essay.

Conventions

Punctuation

_____ **1.** Did I use end punctuation after all my sentences?

_____ **2.** Did I correctly use commas in a series?

Capitalization

_____ **3.** Did I start all my sentences with capital letters?

_____ **4.** Did I capitalize all proper names in my essay?

Spelling

_____ **5.** Have I carefully checked my spelling?

Grammar

_____ **6.** Have I used the right words (*to, two, too; there, their, they're*)?

Practice

Find two errors in each sentence. Then rewrite the sentences correctly.

1. the best thing about overnights is the fun?

2. Kids sure don't git much rest

3. I cant wait too have my own overnight!

4. my cousins from miami will come on Friday.

5. We laughed and played bored games

Editing in Action

Here are some of the editing changes Gabrielle made to the first two paragraphs of her essay. She replaced a wrong word, added punctuation, and corrected misspelled words.

Gabrielle corrected a word.	When my sister Celia had her friends sleep over at our house, and I listened ~~threw~~ _through_ the
She added commas in a series.	wall to her spooky stories about growly voices, screechy sounds, and dark shadows. The next
She added an apostrophe.	day Mom asked me, "Would you like to have your own overnight?" I can't wait! An overnight
She changed end punctuation.	is a special kind of party. _Friends_ ~~Freinds~~ can be together all night at an overnight. That's more exciting than just seeing
She corrected a misspelled word.	each other in school or on weekends. I love laughing and talking and staying up late with my _friends_ ~~freinds~~.

Edit **Check your essay for conventions.**

1. Read your own essay and look for items in a series.
2. Put commas between the items.

Using a Rubric

The rubric on these pages can help you score your writing.

Ideas

6 **The topic, focus, and details are well developed.**

5 The topic is clear and includes many interesting details.

4 The topic is clear. Most of the details tell about the topic.

Organization

6 **Every part of the essay works perfectly.**

5 The beginning, middle, and ending all work well.

4 Most parts of the essay are in order.

Voice

6 **The voice sounds confident and well informed.**

5 The voice sounds well informed.

4 The writer sounds informed in most parts.

Word Choice

6 **Each word is precisely chosen.**

5 Specific words explain the topic.

4 Most words in the essay explain the topic.

Sentence Fluency

6 **All sentences are well crafted and varied.**

5 Many sentences are well crafted and varied.

4 Most sentences have a variety of lengths and beginnings.

Conventions

6 **The essay uses conventions well.**

5 Most conventions are correct.

4 Meaning is clear, but some errors are present.

3 The topic needs to be clearer. More details are needed.

2 The topic is unclear, and the details do not fit.

1 The topic is unclear.

3 Some parts of the essay could be better organized.

2 All parts of the essay run together.

1 The organization is confusing.

3 The writer sounds informed in some parts.

2 The writer sounds unsure.

1 The writer sounds uninterested.

3 The essay needs more specific words.

2 General or missing words make this essay confusing.

1 Some words are used incorrectly.

3 Some sentences have varied lengths and beginnings.

2 Many sentences are choppy or incomplete.

1 Many sentences are incomplete and difficult to read.

3 Errors may confuse the reader.

2 Errors make the essay hard to read.

1 Help is needed to make corrections.

Publishing Sharing Your Essay

Finally, it's time to proofread your essay and make a neat copy to share. You can also illustrate your essay.

All Right, an Overnight!

When my sister Celia had her friends sleep over at our house, I listened through the wall to her spooky stories about growling voices, screechy sounds, and dark shadows. The next day Mom asked me, "Would you like to have your own overnight?" I can't wait! An overnight is a special kind of party.

Friends can be together all night at an overnight. That's more exciting than just seeing each other in school or on weekends. I love laughing and talking and staying up late with my friends.

An overnight also has fun activities. Nighttime is perfect for telling spooky stories. What could be better than watching movies, munching on popcorn, playing board games, and sleeping on the floor in the living room?

Now Celia will have to listen to my spooky stories because my very first overnight will be Friday night. My two favorite cousins Maria and Gina are coming to visit from Miami. They usually stay with my aunt and uncle, but this time they will stay at my house. I can't wait.

Publish

Make a final copy of your essay.

Reflecting on Your Writing

You're done! Take a moment to think about what you have learned. Here's what Gabrielle thought about her essay.

Thinking About Your Writing

Name: _Gabrielle McGraff_

Title: _All Right, an Overnight!_

1. The best part about my essay is . . .

   my topic. I can't wait for my first overnight!

2. The part that sill needs work is . . .

   the middle. I need more details.

3. The main thing I learned about expository writing is . . .

   it's about explaining things in my own words.

Expository Writing
Across the Curriculum

Expository writing explains or gives information about a topic. You can find expository writing just about everywhere. A news report in a magazine, a recipe in a cookbook, the instructions for a model airplane—these are all forms of expository writing.

Expository writing also shows up in all your subjects at school. Whether you're studying science, social studies, or math, expository writing can help you explain just about anything!

Social Studies:
News Report

News reports give readers information about an event. One day, Jeremy's class had a special visitor. Jeremy wrote the following report for his school newspaper.

Kids in China

Beginning

The beginning gives basic information.

On Tuesday, October 4, Mr. Goff visited our class. He is Karen's dad, and he just got back from a business trip to China. He has many pictures of busy cities and beautiful mountains. Mr. Goff came to our class to tell us what life is like in China.

Middle

The middle lists important details.

We learned that kids in China go to school six days a week! They write with 2,000 characters instead of 26 letters. Each character is a complete word. After school, kids play basketball and volleyball and ride bikes. Kids in China do the same kinds of things we do.

Ending

The ending gives a final thought.

Mr. Goff said a businessman from China would visit him soon. We will invite the man to our class. That way, he can tell kids in China about us!

Prewriting Selecting a Topic

News is about "new" events. To find a topic for his school news report, Jeremy listed important events from the last week or two.

 List topic ideas.

1. Write important events from the past week or two.
2. Put a star (✲) next to the event you want to write about.

Gathering Details

Next, Jeremy used the 5 W's questions to gather details.

 Fill in the 5 W's about your event.

Ideas List

Events
We got a new jungle gym on the playground.
Mr. Goff visited and told us about China.✲
We got a class hamster named Ziggy.

5 W's

Who?	What?	When?	Where?	Why?
Mr. Goff	class visitor	Tuesday, October 4	our classroom	to tell us about life in China

Writing Creating a First Draft

It's time to write your news story! Follow the steps below.

 Create your first draft.

1. In the beginning paragraph, answer the 5 W's (page 166).
2. In the middle paragraph, include other interesting details.
3. In the ending paragraph, give a final thought.

Revising Improving Your Writing

Jeremy used some questions to help him revise.

 Improve your news report.

Answer the following questions as you revise your report.

1. Have I included all my information and interesting details?
2. Do I sound excited about my topic?

Editing Checking Conventions

Jeremy used these questions to check his capitalization, punctuation, spelling, and grammar.

 Check your work.

1. Did I start all my sentences with capital letters?
2. Did I end all my sentences with correct punctuation?
3. Have I checked for spelling errors?

Music: A Report

Boom-Whack-a-Boom

In 1994, Craig Ramsell was cutting up a cardboard gift wrap tube. He whacked his leg with the tube and liked the sound it made. A shorter piece made a different sound. That gave him the idea for Boomwhackers.

Red, orange, yellow—each brightly colored plastic tube makes the sound of a note on the musical scale when it is whacked against a hand, a leg, or anything hard. In schools, students use sets of Boomwhackers as rhythm instruments and music makers. Color-coded songbooks make playing music easy.

By 2007, Whacky Music, Inc., had sold 5 million sets of tuned percussion tubes around the world. For many kids, Boomwhackers are the first instruments they learn to play!

Writing Tips

Before you write . . .

- Think of things about music that you know and care about.
- Make a cluster to gather details about your topic.

During your writing . . .

- Get the reader's attention in the beginning of your report.
- Share interesting details in the body paragraphs.
- Give readers something to think about in the ending.

After you've written a first draft . . .

- Read your report and see if any important details are missing.
- Give your report an interesting title.
- Check capitalization, punctuation, spelling, and grammar.

Practical Writing:
How-To Essay

Expository writing can help a reader learn how to do something. Hillary wrote about how to repot a plant.

Growing, Growing, Gone!

The beginning introduces the topic.

When I outgrow my clothes, I get new clothes from my sister. When my plants outgrow their pots, they get new pots from me. It's easy to repot a plant.

To get started, you need to set up a place to work. An old table outside is a good place. Spread out newspapers to help protect the table. Then get a bigger pot, some stones, potting soil, and the plant.

The middle lists the steps.

First, cover the bottom of the new pot with stones and spread some soil over them. Next, tip the plant over and gently pull it out of its old pot. Put the plant into the new pot and hold it straight. Then pour in some more soil and pat it down. Finally, water the plant and add more soil if there is room.

The ending includes a final thought.

Plants are nice to have around. If you give their roots enough room, you will have beautiful plants for a long time.

Writing Tips

Before you write . . .
- Choose something you enjoy making or doing.
- List the ingredients or equipment you need.
- List each step for completing the project or doing the activity.

During your writing . . .
- Introduce your topic.
- Write a paragraph about the ingredients or equipment.
- Write another paragraph giving the steps in order.
- End with a final thought.

After you've written a first draft . . .
- Make sure your steps are complete and clear and are in the right order.
- Edit your work and make a neat copy.

Write a how-to essay about something you enjoy doing like making s'mores! Follow the tips above to write your directions. Share your work with a friend.

Expository Writing

Writing for Assessment

Some writing tests give you an expository topic or prompt to write about. An expository prompt asks you to explain something. Ellie responded to the following prompt. She started planning her response by making a list like the one below.

Expository Prompt

What is your favorite school subject? Write an expository essay about your favorite subject and give details that explain why you like it.

Ideas List

Science

- making crystals

- chicks hatching

- museum field trip

- forest field trip

Learning by Doing and Going

The **beginning** gives the focus (underlined).

Some kids say their favorite school subject is recess. My favorite subject is science. <u>I like science because the projects and field trips are exciting.</u>

The **middle** uses details to explain the focus.

In science we do many exciting projects. One time we made crystals form in a jar by using salt in water. Another time we watched baby chicks hatch. They were slimy at first, but then the feathers dried, and we had fluffy yellow chicks.

We also take exciting field trips for science. We went to a museum and saw huge dinosaurs and tiny butterflies. On Arbor Day, we went to a forest and collected leaves. A guide told us about all kinds of trees.

The **ending** finishes the explanation.

Recess is fun, but I would rather do experiments and go on field trips. That's why science is my favorite subject.

After you read . . .

- **Ideas** (1) What favorite parts of science did the writer mention in the focus sentence?

- **Organization** (2) How many paragraphs did the writer use?

- **Word Choice** (3) What words from the prompt did the writer use in the first paragraph?

Writing Tips

Before you write . . .

- Read the prompt carefully.
- Watch for words like *define, explain,* and *compare.* They tell you what to do in your writing.
- Think about any questions the prompt asks.
- Use a list or graphic organizer to put your ideas in order.

During your writing . . .

- Use some main words from the prompt.
- Follow the directions. In this case, the directions said "write an essay."
- Leave time at the end to check your work.

After you've written a first draft . . .

- Check your focus sentence and details.
- Read your writing and correct any errors.

> Write an expository essay in the time your teacher gives you.

Expository Prompt

Imagine that a new student has come to your class. What rules does the student need to know? Write an essay explaining the two most important class rules.

Expository Writing in Review

In expository writing, you share information with your reader. You may also explain how to do something. These guidelines can help.

Select an interesting topic. (See page 136.)

Gather details about your topic. Use a graphic organizer. (See page 137.)

Write a focus sentence. Name an important part of the topic. (See page 137.)

In the beginning part, introduce your topic and state your focus. (See pages 138–139.)

In the middle part, give details that explain the focus. (See pages 140–141.)

In the ending part, make a final comment. (See pages 142–143.)

Review your essay for ideas and organization. Be sure you've included the right details. Make changes to improve your writing. (See pages 144–156.)

Check your writing for conventions. Ask a classmate or parent for help. (See pages 157–161.)

Make a final copy. Proofread it for errors before sharing it. (See page 162.)

Persuasive Writing

"I made my bed, so may I call Molly now?" "It's a beautiful day. Let's have a picnic in the park!" Every day, you try to convince people to think or act in a certain way. Writing that tries to convince is called persuasive writing.

In this section, you will try different forms of persuasive writing. Your goal is to convince your reader to agree with you or even to take action. If you are persuasive enough, you might even get that picnic in the park!

What's Ahead

- **Writing a Persuasive Paragraph**
- **Writing a Persuasive Letter**
- **Persuasive Workshop**
- Persuasive Writing Across the Curriculum
- Writing for Assessment

Writing a Persuasive Paragraph

What does your class need? More computers? What about a classroom pet or parent helpers?

Sarah had an idea about what her class needed. She wrote a persuasive paragraph to convince others to agree with her. You, too, can write about what you think your class needs.

Paragraph Parts

1 The **topic sentence** states the topic (opinion).

2 The **body sentences** give reasons to support the opinion.

3 The **closing sentence** tells why the reader should agree.

Persuasive Paragraph

Who Gets to Talk?

1

   Our class needs a card that says "Talk." Right now, kids keep interrupting class discussions. They forget to raise their hands and take turns.

2

If Mrs. Lazzaro had a talk card, she could give it to one person at a time. Then only that person could talk. Everyone else would have to listen.

3

A talk card would help make our class discussions more enjoyable.

After you read . . .

- **Ideas** (1) What does Sarah think her class needs?

- **Organization** (2) What are the three parts of the paragraph?

- **Word Choice** (3) In the last sentence, Sarah uses the word *would*. Why is that a better word than *could* in the same spot?

Prewriting Selecting a Topic

Before you can select a topic, you need to think about things your class needs. An ideas chart can help you organize your thoughts. Sarah created the ideas chart below.

 Prewrite **Create an ideas chart.**

1. Write "Supplies," "Rules," and "Fun Stuff" on your paper.
2. Under each heading, list three things your class needs.
3. Put a star (✷) next to the idea you want to write about.

Ideas Chart

Supplies	Rules	Fun Stuff
good scissors	allowing gum	hat day
Bill Nye video	no line cutting	zoo trip
new reading books	a talk card✷	longer recess

Writing Creating Your First Draft

As you write your paragraph, remember that each part has a special job.

- The **topic sentence** gives your opinion about what your class needs.
- The **body sentences** give two or three reasons for your opinion.
- The **closing sentence** restates your opinion and tells why the reader should agree.

 Begin your first draft.

1. Write your topic sentence: "Our class needs _____."
2. Give two or three reasons for your opinion.
3. Write a closing sentence that restates your opinion. Use the word *would* or *should*.

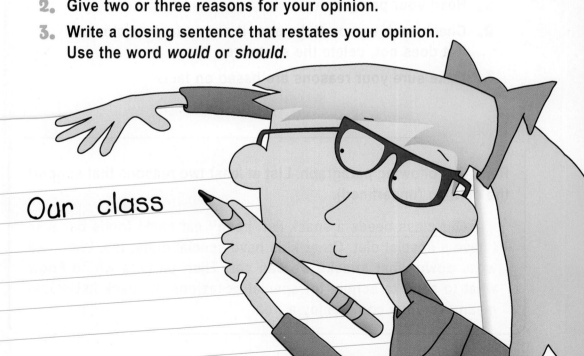

Our class

Revising Improving Your Paragraph

When you revise your paragraph, you make sure all your reasons are based on facts. A fact is different from an opinion.

An **opinion** is something you believe, think, or feel.

Our class needs a new seating order.

A **fact** is something you can prove.

Some kids talk during work time.
Other kids don't get along.
I can't see the chalkboard.

Revise — Check your facts.

1. Read your paragraph.

2. Check each reason to be sure it supports your opinion. If it does not, delete the sentence.

3. Make sure your reasons are based on facts.

Practice

Read the following paragraph. List at least two reasons that support the opinion (underlined).

Our class needs a snack list. I can't eat some foods because I have a special diet. Other kids have special diets, too. We could write down what snacks we can eat. Then parents would know what to send to school for special occasions. A snack list would mean everyone could enjoy a treat.

Editing Checking for Conventions

When you edit your paragraph, you need to check for proper capitalization, punctuation, and spelling.

Edit **Check your work.**

1. Did I indent the first line of my paragraph?
2. Did I begin each sentence with a capital letter?
3. Did I end each sentence with a punctuation mark?
4. Have I used words correctly?
5. Have I checked for spelling errors?

Practice

Learn to use these sets of words correctly.

to (toward)	there (in that place)
two (the number 2)	their (belonging to them)
too (very, also)	they're (they are)

For each sentence below, write the correct word from those in parentheses.

1. Our class needs lockers where kids can leave *(there, their)* things.
2. Sometimes *(to, two)* backpacks get mixed up.
3. It's *(to, too)* hard for kids to find their lunches.
4. We should put lockers next *(to, two)* the door.
5. If we put them *(their, there)*, the room will be neater.

Writing a
Persuasive
Letter

One way to make a positive change is to write a persuasive letter. A persuasive letter can convince someone to take action.

In this chapter, Brenda writes a persuasive letter about games needed for her third-grade class. Later, Roku writes about a new library checkout rule needed at his school.

Understanding Your Goal

Your goal in this chapter is to write a persuasive letter. The letter should give your opinion about something your school or community needs. The six traits below and the persuasive revising lessons (pages 192–203) will help you reach your goal.

Your goal is to . . .

Ideas — Convince the reader to agree with your opinion by sharing strong reasons.

Organization — Write a strong beginning, middle, and ending.

Voice — Use a polite, convincing voice.

Word Choice — Use words like *would* and *should* to express your opinion.

Sentence Fluency — Write sentences that flow smoothly.

Conventions — Use correct capitalization, punctuation, spelling, and grammar.

Persuasive Letter

A persuasive letter gives your opinion and tries to convince the reader to agree with you.

1592 Mertens Road
Renton, WA 98050
January 23, 2009

Mr. Greer, Principal
Eastside Elementary School
239 Jackson Road
Renton, WA 98050

Dear Mr. Greer:

I'm a third grader here at Eastside. I think our school needs new games for indoor recess. We could use board games, puzzles, and computer programs.

Many of our puzzles are old, and some of the pieces are missing. Also, there aren't enough games, so kids have to take turns playing them. New games would help kids and teachers on rainy days.

Please think about getting more games for indoor recess. Thank you for reading my letter.

Sincerely,

Brenda Davidson
Brenda Davidson

Parts of a Business Letter

Heading — The **heading** includes your address and the date.

Inside Address — The **inside address** includes the name and address of the person you are writing to.

Greeting — The **greeting** is a polite way of saying hello. It is followed by a colon (:).

Body — The **body** is the main part of the letter.

Closing — The **closing** is a polite way of saying good-bye.

Signature — The **signature** is your name at the end of the letter.

After you read . . .

- **Ideas** (1) What is the writer's opinion?
- **Organization** (2) What paragraph includes the reasons that explain Brenda's opinion?
- **Word Choice** (3) What words or phrases make the letter sound polite?

Prewriting Selecting a Topic

You can use a T-chart to help you choose your topic. (Look at Roku's T-chart below.)

 List topic ideas on a T-chart.

1. Write "School Needs" and "Community Needs" on your paper.

2. List three or four ideas under each heading.

3. Put a star (✱) next to the idea you want to write about.

4. Decide who should get your letter.

T-Chart

School Needs	Community Needs
bigger lunchroom	a park to walk dogs
more jump ropes	more sidewalks
new checkout rule ✱ for the library	Ha-P Charl-E's Pizza

Writing an Opinion Sentence

Think about the idea you chose and your opinion about it.

 Write your opinion sentence.

■ Use the following form to write your opinion sentence:

I think our _____(place)_____ needs _____(what is needed)_____.

Opinion Sentence

> I think our <u>school library</u> needs <u>a new checkout rule</u>.
>   (place)   (what is needed)

Gathering Reasons

An opinion sentence should be supported by strong reasons.

 Gather reasons for your opinion.

■ Write at least two or three reasons that answer this question: Why is my opinion a good idea?

Reasons List

> Why is my opinion a good idea?
>
> 1. Fast readers finish their books early.
>
> 2. Then they have to wait to get other books.
>
> 3. Some kids don't get to read as much as they want.

Voice
A persuasive voice is convincing.

Writing Starting Your First Draft

The Beginning Paragraph

The beginning paragraph should tell the reader who you are and what your opinion is.

 Draft your beginning paragraph.

1. Remember to include your opinion sentence from page 189.

2. You should also write a sentence that tells a little more about you or your idea.

The Middle Paragraph

The middle paragraph should give two or three reasons that explain your opinion.

 Create your middle paragraph.

■ Include the reasons that explain your opinion. Look at the list you wrote for page 189.

The Ending Paragraph

The final paragraph of a persuasive letter has two jobs to do: (1) It should politely ask the reader to do something. (2) It should thank the reader for reading the letter.

 Create your ending paragraph.

1. Write a sentence that asks the reader to do something.

2. Then politely thank the reader.

Roku's First Draft

Here is Roku's first draft, including errors. Notice how he wrote on every other line to leave room for his revisions.

Dear Mrs. Lincoln,

Beginning
• • • • • • • • • • •
Give your
opinion.

I'm a student who loves to read. I could

eat books for breakfast, lunch, and dinner.

I'm writing to you because I think our school

libary needs a new checkout rule.

students must be able to check out more

Middle
Use reasons
to explain
your opinion.

books. Kids can check out only a few books.

That means fast readers have to wait. They

have to wait forever for the next library day.

Everybody likes library day.

Ending
• • • • • • • • • • • •
Use polite
words such
as "thank
you."

Other kids like me who want to gobble

up all the books they can. Think about a new

checkout rule. I'm begging you. Thank you.

Sincerely,

Roku Hitsuki

Revising Improving Your Persuasive Letter

When you finish your first draft, you are ready to make changes to improve your writing. Begin the revising part of the writing process by reading your letter to yourself.

Then read a your letter out loud to a partner. You may ask your partner the following questions that are based on your writing goals (see page 185).

Ideas

- Did I convince you to agree with my opinion by sharing strong reasons?

Organization

- Did I write a strong beginning, middle, and ending?

Voice

- Did I use a polite and convincing voice?

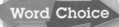

Word Choice

- Did I use the words *would* and *should* to express my opinion?

Sentence Fluency

- Do my sentences flow smoothly?

Getting a Partner's Response

A partner can help you find ways to improve your writing. Here is a partner's response to Roku's letter on page 191.

Response Sheet

Writer: _Roku_   Responder: _Linda_

Title: _Letter to Mrs. Lincoln_

What I like:

I like your idea about checking out

more books.

I'm glad you are writing about kids

reading more.

Questions I have:

How many books can kids check out now?

Could there be more library days?

Revising for

Ideas

Your writing will be convincing if your opinion is supported with good reasons.

Q. How do I know if my reasons are good?

Your reasons are good if they answer the question *why*.

Opinion: Our class should tour the Chicago Field Museum.

Why? The museum has the largest T. rex skeleton ever found.

Why? The museum has other dinosaurs, too.

Practice

Read the opinion above. Which of the following reasons answers *why* for that opinion?

1. We are studying dinosaurs.
2. The museum's founder owned a department store.
3. The Shedd Aquarium is another cool place.
4. It's fun to see what you read in books.
5. Chicago has some of the world's tallest buildings.

Revising in Action

Here is how Roku improved the first draft of his letter. He added an explanation so that his reason answers the question *why*. He also cut a reason that did not support his opinion.

I love to read. I could eat books for breakfast, lunch, and dinner. I'm writing to you because I think our school libary needs a new checkout rule.

 students must be able to check out more books. Kids can check out only a few books.

 <u>finish there books and</u>
That means fast readers ∧ have to wait. They have to wait forever for the next libary day.

~~Everybody likes libary day~~

 Other kids like me want to gobble up all the books they can. Think about a new checkout
 <u>or more library days</u>
rule ∧ I'm begging you. Thank you.

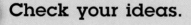

Revise **Check your ideas.**

Read your opinion and your supporting reasons.

- **Add** information so that your opinion is clear and all your reasons answer the question *why*.

- **Cut** any reasons that do not support your opinion.

Revising for

Organization

In persuasive writing, the beginning, middle, and ending parts work together.

Q. How can I check my organization?

The following checklist can help you review the organization of your writing.

Organization

Beginning

____ **1.** Did I make my beginning interesting for the reader?
____ **2.** Did I write a clear opinion sentence?

Middle

____ **3.** Did I include reasons that support my opinion?

Ending

____ **4.** Did I politely ask the reader to do something?

Practice

Which ending sentences below sound polite? Write a polite final sentence for an essay in support of a fund-raiser to buy a new tree for your school grounds.

1. Please help this worthy cause.
2. I'm asking you to vote "yes."
3. Act now or you'll be sorry.

Revising in Action

Here is how Roku improved the organization of the first draft of his letter. He moved his opinion to the end of his beginning paragraph. He added another polite word to his ending paragraph.

I love to read. I could eat books for breakfast, lunch, and dinner. I'm writing to you because I think our school libary needs a new checkout rule. ←

~~students must be able to check out more books.~~ Kids can check out only a few books. *finish there books and* That means fast readers ^ have to wait. They have to wait forever for the next libary day. ~~Everybody likes libary day.~~

Other kids like me want to gobble up all the
Pleese
books they can. ^ Think about a new checkout
or more library days
rule. ^ I'm begging you. Thank you.

Revise — Check your organization.

Use the organization checklist on page 196 as a guide.

- **Move** information as needed.

Revising for

Voice

Your writing voice is your own special way of expressing yourself. For persuasive writing, your voice should sound convincing.

Q. How can I make my voice convincing?

You can make your voice convincing by being accurate. If you exaggerate, your reader may not believe you.

Convincing: Kids have to line up outside even if it's really cold.

Exaggerating: Kids have to line up outside even if it's 50 degrees below zero!

Practice

Rewrite each exaggeration below so it sounds more convincing.

1. We get a snow day only if there's 70 feet of snow.
2. Kids have to play outside even in a hurricane.
3. The summer-school classrooms are 300 degrees.
4. This situation is hopeless.
5. When it rains, the playground turns into an ocean.

Revising in Action

Here is how Roku improved the voice in the first draft of his letter. He added words to make his information more accurate. He also cut an exaggeration.

I love to read. I could eat books for breakfast,

lunch, and dinner. I'm writing to you because I think

our school libary needs a new checkout rule.

students must be able to check out more

as many books as the number of their

books. Kids can check out only a few books grade.

finish there books and

That means fast readers have to wait. They

have to wait ~~forever~~ for the next libary day.

~~Everybody likes libary day.~~

Other kids like me want to gobble up all the

Pleese

books they can. Think about a new checkout

or more library days

rule. I'm begging you. Thank you.

Revise ## Check your voice.

Read your letter carefully.

- **Add** convincing words as needed.
- **Cut** any exaggerations.

Revising for

 Word Choice

When you make a suggestion, you need to choose the best words for your audience.

Q. Which helping verbs will fit my audience?

If your audience includes people who are older than you, use the helping verbs *could* and *should*, not *must*.

Could (an acceptable choice)
Teachers could remind us to walk in the hall.

Should (an acceptable choice)
Teachers should be fair to us.

Must (**not** an acceptable choice)
Teachers must make us obey class rules.

Practice

1. Write a polite sentence to someone older—the principal, your neighbor, or someone else. Use the word *could*.

2. Rewrite the sentence with the word *should*.

3. Rewrite the sentence again with the word *must*. How does each sentence sound?

Revising in Action

Here is how Roku improved the word choice in the first draft of his letter. He changed a helping verb that didn't fit his audience. He rewrote his final sentence to make it more polite.

I love to read. I could eat books for breakfast,

lunch, and dinner. I'm writing to you because I think

our school libary needs a new checkout rule.

should

students ~~must~~ be able to check out more

¶ as many books as the number of their

books. ~~Kids can check out only a few books.~~ grade.

finish there books and

That means fast readers have to wait. They

have to wait ~~forever~~ for the next libary day.

~~Everybody likes libary day.~~

Other kids like me want to gobble up all the

Pleese

books they can. Think about a new checkout

or more library days   for reading my letter

rule. ~~I'm begging you~~ Thank you.

Revise
Check your word choice.

Check the words and helping verbs in your letter.

- **Add** verbs that sound polite.

Revising for

Sentence Fluency

Persuasive writing should read smoothly with no short, choppy sentences.

Q. How can I fix short, choppy sentences?

You can fix short, choppy sentences by combining them. Sometimes you can combine sentences by moving a group of words.

Two sentences:
The bus is crowded. It is crowded with older kids.

Combined sentence:
The bus is crowded with older kids.

Practice

Combine the following sentences by moving a group of words.

1. Older kids take up many seats. The seats are in back.
2. The younger kids sit together. They are up front.
3. All the kids are cranky. They are cranky about the crowding.
4. Most kids would agree. They would agree that they need more space.

Revising in Action

Here is how Roku improved the sentence fluency in the first draft of his letter. He added a conjunction and moved a group of words to combine two short sentences.

I love to read. I could eat books for breakfast, lunch, and dinner. I'm writing to you because I think our school libary needs a new checkout rule. ~~should~~ ~~students must~~ be able to check out more ~~as many books as the number of their~~ books. ~~Kids can check out only~~ a few books. ~~grade.~~ ~~finish there books~~ and ~~and~~ That means fast readers have to wait. ~~They~~ have to wait forever for the next libary day.

~~Everybody likes libary day.~~

Other kids like me want to gobble up all the ~~Pleese~~ books they can. Think about a new checkout ~~or more library days~~ ~~for reading my letter~~ rule. I'm begging you. Thank you.

Revise

Check for smooth sentences.

Combine short, choppy sentence by moving groups of words.

- **Move** a word group to make a smoother sentence if possible.

Revising Using a Checklist

 Check your revising.

Number a piece of paper from 1 to 7. If you can answer "yes" to a question, put a check mark after that number. If not, continue working on that part of your essay.

Ideas

____ **1.** Do I have a clear opinion statement?

____ **2.** Do I support my opinion with good reasons that answer the question why?

Organization

____ **3.** Do I state my opinion in the first paragraph?

____ **4.** Does my ending ask the reader to do something?

Voice

____ **5.** Have I used a convincing voice?

Word Choice

____ **6.** Have I used polite words?

Sentence Fluency

____ **7.** Have I combined short, choppy sentences?

 Make a clean copy.

After revising your essay, make a clean copy for editing.

Editing for

Conventions

When you edit for conventions, you check capitalization, punctuation, spelling, and grammar.

Q. How can I check my capitalization?

You can check your capitalization by following the rules listed below.

✔ Capitalize the **first letter of the first word** in each sentence.

✔ Capitalize the **first letter of the names** of people, places, streets, cities, and months.

✔ Capitalize **both letters of a postal state abbreviation**, such as AZ for Arizona.

Practice

Rewrite each of the following lines, using correct capitalization.

1. mr. gaul of Oil city, Pa

2. wadsworth Elementary school

3. we need a light at broad street and main street.

Edit   **Check your letter for conventions.**

Ask yourself the following questions about your paragraph.

1. Add correct punctuation and capitalization.

2. Cut and replace any words that are the wrong word or misspelled.

Edit Read and check your capitalization.

Check each first word, name, and abbreviation.

Editing Checking for Conventions

When editing a letter, check for capitalization, punctuation, spelling, and grammar.

Conventions

Punctuation

_____ **1.** Did I use end punctuation after all my sentences?

_____ **2.** Did I use commas correctly in dates and addresses?

Capitalization

_____ **3.** Did I begin all my sentences with capital letters?

_____ **4.** Did I capitalize names of people, organizations, titles, streets, cities, and states?

Spelling

_____ **5.** Have I carefully checked my spelling?

Grammar

_____ **6.** Do I use correct forms of verbs *(go, went, gone)*?

Practice

Find two errors in each sentence below. Then rewrite the sentences correctly.

1. Their are many reasons to change the rule

2. Kids can be responsibel with more books?

Editing in Action

Here are the editing changes that Roku made in his letter.

Dear Mrs. Lincoln:

I love to read. I could eat books for

breakfast, lunch, and dinner! I'm writing to

Spelling is corrected.
you because I think our school ~~libary~~ *library* needs a

A capital letter is added.
new checkout rule. ~~students~~ should be able to

check out more books.

Kids can check out only as many books

A period is added.
as the number of their grade. Fast readers

A wrong word is replaced.
finish ~~there~~ *their* books and have to wait and

wait for the next ~~libary~~ *library* day.

Other kids like me who want to gobble

Spelling is corrected.
up all the books they can. ~~Pleese~~ *Please* think about

a new checkout rule or more library days.

Thank you for reading my letter.

Sincerely,

Roku Hitsuki

Using a Rubric

The rubric on these pages can help you score your writing.

 Ideas

6 **The opinion and reasons are very convincing.**

5 The opinion is clear, and all the reasons support it.

4 The opinion is clear, but more reasons would be helpful.

Organization

6 **Every part of the writing works perfectly.**

5 The writing is clearly organized.

4 Most parts are organized and work well.

Voice

6 **The voice is polite and convincing.**

5 The voice is convincing.

4 The voice could be more convincing.

 Word Choice

6 **Each word is expertly chosen.**

5 The words make the opinion and reasons clear.

4 Most words work well.

Sentence Fluency

6 **The sentences flow beautifully.**

5 The sentences read smoothly.

4 A few sentences sound choppy.

Conventions

6 **The essay uses conventions well.**

5 Most conventions are correct.

4 Some errors are present.

3 The opinion needs to be clearer with more reasons.

2 The opinion is confusing and needs reasons.

1 The writer needs to state an opinion.

3 Several parts need to be organized better.

2 All parts of the essay run together.

1 The writing needs to be organized to avoid confusion.

3 The writing exaggerates or has a weak voice.

2 The voice comes and goes.

1 The writing needs voice.

3 Some words are unclear.

2 Some words make the writing confusing.

1 Help is needed to find better words.

3 Many sentences are choppy.

2 Some sentences are choppy or incomplete.

1 Many sentences are incomplete.

3 Errors may confuse the reader.

2 Errors make the writing hard to read.

1 Help is needed to make corrections.

Publishing Sending Your Letter

These two pages show you how to put your letter in the correct business letter form.

Heading

1. Write your street address.
2. Write your city, state, and ZIP code.
3. Write the date. (Skip three lines.)

Inside Address

4. Write the name and title of the person you are writing to.
5. Write the school or business name.
6. Write the address: the street, city, state, and zip code. (Skip a line.)

Greeting

7. Write "Dear," the person's name, and a colon. (Skip one line.)

Body

8. Don't indent paragraphs. (Skip a line between paragraphs.)

Closing

9. Write "Sincerely" or "Yours truly" and a comma. (Skip four lines.)

Signature

10. Type your name. Then sign your name above your typed name.

Roku's letter

207 Broad Street
Griffith, IN 46300
February 10, 2009

Mrs. Lincoln, Librarian
Franklin Elementary School
504 Main Street
Griffith, IN 46300

······················· [fold] ·······················

Dear Mrs. Lincoln:

I love to read. I could eat books for breakfast, lunch, and dinner! I'm writing to you because I think our school library needs a new checkout rule. Students should be able to check out more books.

Kids can check out only as many books as the number of their grade. Fast readers finish their books and have to wait and wait for the next library day.

······················· [fold] ·······················

I know other kids like me who want to gobble up all the books they can. Please think about a new checkout rule or more library days. Thank you for reading my letter.

Sincerely,

Roku Hitsuki

Roku Hitsuki

Publishing Addressing an Envelope

The United States Postal Service gives the following directions for addressing an envelope.

Publish

Address your envelope.

1. Write your name and address in the upper left-hand corner.
2. Write the other person's name and address in the middle.
3. Place the proper postage in the upper right-hand corner.

ROKU HITSUKI
207 BROAD STREET
GRIFFITH IN 46300

EarthDay
USA ¢

MRS LINCOLN
FRANKLIN ELEMENTARY SCHOOL
504 MAIN STREET
GRIFFITH IN 46300

Tip Remember: The U.S. Postal Service requests all capital letters and no punctuation on your envelope.

Reflecting on Your Writing

You're done! Now it's time to think about the persuasive letter you wrote and what you learned from it. Here are Roku's thoughts about his letter.

Thinking About Your Writing

Name: _Roku Hitsuki_

Title: _Persuasive Letter_

1. The best part of my essay is . . .

   about how I could eat books for breakfast,

   lunch, and dinner. It gets my reader's attention

   for my ideas about having a new checkout rule.

2. The part that sill needs work is . . .

   the last paragraph. I should have told how

   many books we want to check out.

3. The main thing I learned about narrative writing is . . .

   how to use ideas and reasons to make

   an idea convincing.

Persuasive Writing
Across the Curriculum

Scientists use their skills to create everything from space probes to submarines. Imagine a world without science! Now imagine a world without writers. There would be no books, no Web sites, and no TV shows.

In this section, you'll use your writing skills to create a poster, an e-mail message, and a response to a persuasive prompt. Thanks to students like Miko—and you—we'll never have a world without writers!

Science:
Persuasive Poster

A poster gives information about an event or an idea. Miko's teacher asked students to create a poster to convince people to come to a school event. Miko made a poster for the science fair.

The poster includes information about the event.

Words and pictures help convince the reader to come.

Prewriting Selecting a Topic

One way to think of ideas for a poster is to make a list. Miko wrote this list of upcoming school events.

Ideas List

Make a list.

1. Write "School Events" at the top of a piece of paper.
2. List events that are coming up.
3. Put a star (✳) next to the event you'd like to make a poster about.

School Events

Track and Field Day

Science Fair ✳

student play

spring concert

Gathering Details

A poster should give important information about the event. For example, people need to know *when* and *where* the event will be held.

Answer these questions about your event.

1. What is my event?
2. When does it happen (date and time)?
3. Where is it?
4. Who should attend?
5. Why should people come?

Writing Making Your Poster

Follow these guidelines when you create your poster.

Write **Create a first draft.**

1. Sketch out your poster idea. Include the details about your event. (Refer to the bottom of page 216.)
2. Use a drawing to catch the reader's attention.

Revising Improving Your Poster

A poster must be accurate and easy to read.

Revise **Check your poster for its overall appeal.**

1. Are my details correct? Do they tell what, when, where, and why?
2. Are the words large enough? Are the details spaced so the poster isn't crowded?

Editing Checking for Conventions

Before making your final poster, check your writing for errors.

Edit **Edit your poster.**

1. Have I correctly capitalized any names?
2. Have I used correct punctuation in dates and addresses?
3. Have I checked my spelling?

Health:
An Important Issue

Look Out!

Your eyes are amazing. Because you may not see danger coming, you should follow some safety tips to keep your eyes safe.

Sharp, pointed objects can hurt your eyes. You should carry pencils and scissors with the points down. Always stand behind people throwing darts or shooting arrows. Never put your face near animals with claws.

Machines can harm your eyes. You should stay away from lawnmowers and other machines that can shoot out rocks, bits of metal, or even sparks.

Sports are fun, but they can damage your eyes. Remember to wear a helmet or goggles if your sport needs them. Follow these tips so you can say, "Bye, see you later."

Writing Tips

Before you write . . .

- Think about important health issues you know and care about.
- List as many supporting details for your issue as you can.

During your writing . . .

- Get the reader's attention in the beginning of your persuasive essay.
- Give your reasons in the body paragraph.
- End with a call to action that asks readers to follow your advice.

After you've written a first draft . . .

- Read your essay and see if any important details are missing.
- Give your essay an interesting title.
- Check capitalization, punctuation, spelling, and grammar.

Practical Writing:
E-Mail Message

E-mail allows you to quickly send a friendly note. Maria wrote an e-mail message to her grandpa. Remember to use a greeting and a closing just as you do in a letter.

The **heading** tells where the message is going, and the **subject** tells what it is about.

The **body** gives the message and makes a request.

New Message

To: grampsmacfarland@newarknet.usa

Cc:

Subject: Library Story Hour

Dear Grandpa,

Thank you for the big book about bugs. We are learning about insects at school. Mrs. Owens brought a cage full of caterpillars. She says they will turn into butterflies! I can't wait to see that.

The library is having a story hour about insects. A man from the zoo will bring giant beetles. We can make paper butterflies. I think it would be fun to go. Would you take me? It is Saturday at 1:00 p.m.

Love,
Maria

Writing Tips

Before you write . . .
- Make sure the e-mail address is correct.
- Write a subject line about your message.

During your writing . . .
- Write *Dear*, the person's name, and a comma.
- Tell why you are writing and include all the important details.
- Write sentences that are easy to understand.
- Write a closing (a word like *Sincerely* or *Love),* a comma, and your name.

After you've written an e-mail message . . .
- Read your message carefully.
- Check capitalization, punctuation, spelling, and grammar.
- Make sure your e-mail is complete and correct before hitting "send."

Pretend a special event is coming up. Write an e-mail message to invite someone to the event. Use a computer in your school.

Persuasive Writing

Writing for Assessment

On some writing tests, you will need to write a response to a persuasive prompt. A persuasive prompt asks you to share an opinion about something. It also asks you to give your reasons for the opinion.

Pedro planned his response to the following prompt by making a table diagram like the one below. Then he wrote his essay.

Persuasive Prompt

Some people believe recess should be shorter. What do you think? Write a persuasive essay that tells whether you think school recesses should be shorter or should stay the same. Give reasons for your opinion.

Table Diagram

Recess should not be shorter

kids get exercise   kids learn teamwork   kids do better in reading

Pedro's Response

Save Our Recess

The **beginning** shares the writer's opinion (underlined).

Some people say recess should be shorter. They want kids to work more. I disagree. Kids need a chance to play. <u>I think recess should not be shorter.</u>

The **middle** paragraph gives reasons that support the opinion.

Recess helps kids. Our gym teacher says kids sit around too much, but recess lets us get lots of exercise. For example, my class likes to play games like kickball. Games help us learn teamwork, too. Recess also helps us pay attention. Ms. Dawson says we do better in reading after recess because we "get the wiggles out."

The **ending** asks the reader to do something.

Recess is an important part of the school day. It shouldn't be made shorter because kids would sit too much and not be able to pay attention. Please tell the principal to keep recess the way it is!

After you read . . .

- **Ideas** (1) What is Pedro's opinion?
- **Organization** (2) What sentence in the closing paragraph restates the opinion of the beginning paragraph?
- **Word Choice** (3) Does Pedro sound like he knows what he's talking about? Explain.

Writing Tips

Before you write . . .
- Read the prompt carefully.
- Use a graphic organizer to help you plan your answer.
- Use your time wisely.

During your writing . . .
- Use key words from the prompt as you write your opinion statement.
- In the middle paragraph, give reasons that explain your opinion.
- Restate your opinion in the closing paragraph.

After you've written a first draft . . .
- Check your capitalization, punctuation, and spelling.
- Make neat changes.

Write a persuasive essay in the time your teacher gives you.

Persuasive Prompt

Some people think students should not be allowed to have snacks at school. Do you think students should have snacks or not? Write an essay that gives your opinion and reasons.

Persuasive Writing in Review

When you write a persuasive essay, you try to convince your reader to do something or to agree with you. The guidelines below can help you do that.

Select a topic that you feel strongly about. (See page 188.)

Write an opinion statement about the topic. (See page 189.)

Gather and organize reasons to support your opinion. (See page 189.)

In the beginning part, get your reader's attention and state your opinion. (See pages 190–191.)

In the middle part, give reasons that explain your opinion. (See pages 190–191.)

In the ending part, restate your opinion and ask the reader to do something. (See pages 190–191.)

Check your **ideas, organization,** and **voice** first. Then check your **word choice** and **sentence fluency.** (See pages 192–204.)

Check your writing for conventions. Also have a classmate edit your writing. (See pages 205–209.)

Make a final copy and proofread it for errors before sharing it. (See pages 210–211.)

Responding to Literature

Have you read any good books lately? Good books make you think. When you read **fiction**, you think about make-believe characters and their adventures. When you read **nonfiction**, you think about real people, places, and things.

Sharing your thoughts and feelings about books is called **responding to literature**. In this section, you will respond to both fiction and nonfiction in many different ways.

What's Ahead

- Writing a Response Paragraph
- Writing a Book Review for Fiction
- Writing a Book Review for Nonfiction
- Comparing a Fiction and a Nonfiction Book
- Responding to a Poem
- Writing for Assessment

Writing a

Response Paragraph

Alexis wrote a paragraph about a fiction book she had read. She told how the story made her think of her own life. Writing about it helped Alexis learn more about the book and about herself.

In this unit, you will write a paragraph about a fiction book you have read. You will tell how a part of the story is like something that has happened to you. Remember that a paragraph has three main parts.

1 The **topic sentence** tells what the paragraph is about.

2 The **body sentences** explain the topic sentence.

3 The **closing sentence** leaves the reader with one last idea about the topic.

Alexis' Response Paragraph

Keeping Friends

1   In Amber Brown Is Not a Crayon by Paula Danziger, Amber's best friend moves away. Amber and Justin help each other with their homework, stick up for each other, and plan their school projects together. All of this changes when Justin's family has to move away. I felt like

2   Amber did when my best friend Toni said she was moving. At school, we always laughed and talked during lunch. At first, I didn't even want to talk to my friend

3   Toni about moving. Finally, we found a way that we could still be friends, just like Amber and Justin.

After you read . . .

- ■ **Ideas** (1) How is the writer of this paragraph like Amber, the main character in the book?

- ■ **Organization** (2) What part of this paragraph gives a lot of details about the topic?

- ■ **Word Choice** (3) What words or phrases do you really like? Name two or three.

Prewriting Collecting Ideas

Alexis decided to write about the last book she had read. To collect ideas, she answered four important questions about the book.

 Prewrite **Answer four key questions.**

1. What is the title of the book?
2. Who is the author?
3. What is the main idea of the book?
4. How is the story similar to my life?

Ideas

Alexis's Prewriting

1. What is the title of the book?
   Amber Brown Is Not a Crayon

2. Who is the author?
   Paula Danziger

3. What is the main idea of the book?
   Amber's best friend moves away.

4. How is the story similar to my life?
   My best friend moved away, too.

Writing Creating Your First Draft

As you write your paragraph, remember that it should include three parts: a topic sentence, the body sentences, and a closing sentence.

 Write your response paragraph.

Start with a topic sentence that (1) names the title and author of your book, and (2) tells the book's main idea.

Write body sentences that tell how the story compares to something that has happened to you.

End with a closing sentence that shares a final thought about the topic.

First Draft

In <u>Amber Brown Is Not a Crayon</u> by Paula

Danziger, Amber's best friend moves away.

Amber and Justin help each other . . .

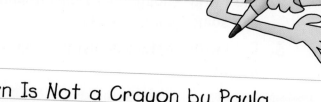

Revising Improving Your Paragraph

When you revise, you make sure that the ideas in the body of your paragraph are clear. Alexis wrote five body sentences to make her idea clear. But what if she had written only three short sentences, like these?

My best friend was moving. I was sad. It helped to talk about it.

These three short sentences would not have been very interesting or fun to read.

Revise — Check your ideas.

Ask yourself the following questions. Then make changes in your paragraph.

1. Did I explain how my life is like part of the story?

2. Did I write enough sentences to show how the story is like something in my life?

3. Did I write sentences that don't fit my topic and need to be cut?

Practice

Which set of sentences below is clearer and more fun to read? Why?

1. Ralph is a mouse. He lives in a hotel. He finds a toy.

2. Ralph is a young mouse who lives in a hotel. One day, his life changes. He finds a motorcycle and learns to ride it. That motorcycle takes Ralph on adventures. It even lets him help a boy with a bad fever.

Editing Checking for

When you edit your paragraph, you look for errors that might confuse your reader. For example, make sure that each sentence has a subject and a verb (predicate).

Ramona Quimby writes a commercial.
   (subject)   (action verb)

Ramona's adventures are funny.
         (subject)   (linking verb)

Check your work.

1. Did I indent the first line of my paragraph?
2. Did I start each sentence with a capital letter?
3. Did I include a subject and a verb in each of my sentences?
4. Have I checked my spelling?

Practice

For each sentence below, write down the subject and the verb.

1. Aunt Dew sings a long song.
2. She is very old.
3. Michael is Aunt Dew's nephew.
4. He counts the pennies in the *Hundred Penny Box*.

Writing a
Book Review
for Fiction

Writing a book review is one way to share a great book with your friends. That's what Ryan did. His book review tells what the book is about without giving away the whole story.

When you write a review, your goal is to make the book sound interesting. Your book review will have three main parts, and each part will answer a different question.

Beginning	What is the book about?
Middle	What is my favorite part?
Ending	What main idea does the author share?

Ryan's Book Review

Freckle Juice

Beginning

    Freckle Juice by Judy Blume is a funny story about a boy named Andrew Marcus. He really wishes he could have freckles. Then a mean girl in class sells him a recipe for freckle juice.

Middle

    My favorite part of the story is reading about the freckle juice recipe. Freckle juice is made from grape juice, vinegar, mustard, mayonnaise, juice from one lemon, pepper, salt, ketchup, olive oil, and a speck of onion. "The faster you drink it, the faster you get freckles," the girl tells him. Then Andrew drinks it.

Ending

    The main idea of *Freckle Juice* is to be yourself. Andrew wants freckles because he likes how they look on a girl in his class. Does Andrew ever get his freckles? You'll have to read the book to find out!

After you read . . .

- **Ideas** (1) What is *Freckle Juice* about?
- **Organization** (2) What question does the ending paragraph ask?
- **Word Choice** (3) Which sentences tell you that Ryan likes this book?

Prewriting Selecting a Book

Kayla thought of two fiction books that she liked. Then she used sentence starters to help her decide which book to write about. Her finished sentences appear below.

 Think of books to review.

1. Write down the titles and authors of two books you have read.

2. Complete these two sentence starters about each book.
   The story is about . . .   I like this story because . . .

3. Put a star (✳) next to the book you want to write about.

Sentence Starters

Book 1: <u>Bunnicula</u> by James Howe
The story is about . . .
    a pet bunny who is really a vampire.
I like this story because . . .
    it is funny. Many of the parts made me laugh.

✳ Book 2: <u>Stone Fox</u> by John Reynolds Gardiner
The story is about . . .
    a boy named Little Willy who enters a
    dogsled race.
I like this story because . . .
    I like adventure stories and dogs.

Gathering Important Details

Next, Kayla used a story map to gather important details about her book. She did not write about the ending because she wanted her classmates to read the book. Her story map appears below.

Prewrite **Make a story map.**

1. Read the story map below.
2. Then fill in your own story map for the book you are writing about.

Story Map

Main Characters:
Little Willy, Searchlight, Grandpa, and Stone Fox
Setting:
Wyoming
Problem:
Willy's grandpa gets sick and may lose his farm.
He owes $500 in taxes.
Most Important Events:
- Willy helps care for Grandpa and the farm.
- Willy and his dog race against Stone Fox to try to win $500.

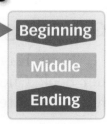

Writing Beginning Your Review

▶ Beginning

Middle

Ending

The first paragraph of your book review should name the book and its author. It should also tell what the book is about.

Write — **Create your beginning paragraph.**

- Answer the following questions in your first paragraph.
  - ● **What is the book's title, and who is the author?**
  - ● **Who are the main characters?**
  - ● **What is the book about?**

Kayla's Beginning Paragraph

Stone Fox is a book by John Reynolds Gardiner. In the story, Little Willy's grandpa gets sick and can't pay the taxes on his farm. Willy and his dog Searchlight enter a dogsled race. The prize money would pay the taxes. They must race Stone Fox. He is a Shoshone Indian who has never lost a race.

Including Details

In a book review, you should give just enough details to make the reader want to read the whole story. Leave out unimportant details.

Don't give away the most surprising parts of the book or the ending. You don't want to spoil the story for your classmates!

Practice

Here is a different beginning paragraph for a book review of *Stone Fox*. Write down the number of each sentence that includes details that are not important.

(1) *Stone Fox* by John Reynolds Gardiner is the story of a boy named Little Willy and his grandfather. (2) Little Willy and Grandpa live on a farm in Wyoming. (3) A farm is a lot of work. (4) Grandpa is too sick to work, so he can't pay his taxes. (5) Usually Grandpa likes to play. (6) Once, he pretended to be a scarecrow. (7) Little Willy and his dog, Searchlight, enter a dogsled race to try to win the tax money. (8) They race against a Shoshone Indian named Stone Fox. (9) He wears a dark-colored headband.

Writing Creating the Middle

Beginning

▶ Middle

Ending

The middle paragraph should tell about your favorite part of the book.

Write **Develop your middle paragraph.**

■ Answer these questions in your middle paragraph.

● **What is your favorite part? Why?**

● **What important events happen in this part?**

Kayla's Middle Paragraph

My favorite part is the big race because it is so exciting. At the starting line, Willy tries to be friends with Stone Fox. "Morning, Mr. Stone Fox," Willy says. Stone Fox just stands there looking big and mean. By the end of the race, everything changes.

Ending Your Book Review

In the last paragraph, you tell about the main idea or theme of the story. One way to find a theme is to think about the big problem the main character faces. You can also ask yourself what the character in the story learns.

Beginning

Middle

▶ Ending

Create your ending paragraph.

■ Answer the following questions as you write the ending for your review.

- What big problem does the main character face?
- What does the main character learn?

Kayla's Ending Paragraph

> <u>Stone Fox</u> shows that no one should ever give up. The race is hard for Willy and Searchlight. Still, they try to beat Stone Fox. When something terrible happens, Little Willy doesn't give up. He learns that some things are worth fighting for.

Revising Improving Your Book Review

Kayla carefully read her first draft. She wanted her book review to answer these three questions:

Beginning	What is the book about?
Middle	Why do I like this book?
Ending	What is the main idea (theme) of the book?

Check your first draft.

■ Answer the following questions. Then make changes in your writing.

- Did I answer the three questions listed above in my book review?
- Did I write about events in correct time order?

Practice

The events below are from the fairy tale "Cinderella," but they are not in the correct time order. Write the numbers of these events in the proper order.

1. Cinderella dances with the prince.
2. The prince announces a big dance.
3. Cinderella's fairy godmother gives her glass slippers.
4. The prince finds the lost glass slipper and searches for its owner.
5. The clock strikes midnight, and Cinderella runs from the dance.

Editing Checking for Conventions

Next, Kayla edited her book review. She checked her writing for capitalization, punctuation, spelling, and grammar.

Conventions

Punctuation

____ **1.** Did I use end punctuation after all my sentences?

____ **2.** Did I underline the book's title?

Capitalization

____ **3.** Did I start all my sentences with capital letters?

____ **4.** Did I capitalize the names of the characters?

Spelling

____ **5.** Did I carefully check my spelling?

Grammar

____ **6.** Did I use subjects and verbs that agree (*He* **races**, not *He* **race**)?

____ **7.** Did I use the right words (*to, two, too; there, their, they're*)?

Practice

Find two errors in each sentence and rewrite the sentences correctly.

1. Little Willy and his dog, searchlight, is brave.

2. They want to help pay the taxs for the farm

3. they know they can count on each other?

Publishing Sharing Your Book Review

Here is Kayla's finished book review.

Kayla's Final Draft

Stone Fox

Beginning
⋯⋯ Stone Fox is a book by John Reynolds Gardiner. In the story, Little Willy's grandpa gets sick and can't pay the taxes on his farm in Wyoming. Willy decides to enter a dogsled race with his dog, Searchlight. If he wins, the prize money will pay the taxes. Stone Fox will race, too. He is a Shoshone Indian who has never lost a race.

Middle
⋯⋯ My favorite part is the big race because it is so exciting. At the starting line, Willy tries to be friends with Stone Fox. "Morning, Mr. Stone Fox," Willy says. Stone Fox doesn't answer him. He just stands there looking big and mean. By the end of the race, everything changes.

Ending
⋯⋯ Stone Fox shows that no one should ever give up. The race is very hard for Willy and Searchlight. Still, they try to beat Stone Fox. Even when something terrible happens, Little Willy doesn't give up. He learns that good things are worth fighting for.

Reflecting on Your Writing

Thinking about your writing can help you grow as a writer. Think about your review by completing the sentences below.

Thinking About Your Writing

Name: Kayla Martins

Title: Stone Fox

1. The best part about my book review is . . .

   the way I ended my report. I didn't give

   away the ending.

2. The main thing I learned about writing a book review is . . .

   that I need to choose just enough details to

   get my reader interested.

3. In my next book review, I would like to . . .

   write about a science-fiction book.

Writing a
Book Review
for Nonfiction

You may be asked to read and review a nonfiction book. A nonfiction book contains information or stories that are true. This sort of review, like other reviews, has a beginning, a middle, and an ending. A 3-2-1 plan, like the one below, works well for a nonfiction book review.

Beginning	**3** What **three** important facts did you learn?
Middle	**2** What **two** surprising details did you discover?
Ending	**1** What **one** thing do you still wonder about?

Nonfiction Review

To Fly

Beginning
········· To Fly, the Story of the Wright Brothers by Wendie Old is a great book. I learned that when Orville Wright was my age, he made wonderful kites and models of flying machines. When he and his brother grew up, they built giant gliders and tried to fly in them. One day, they made an airplane that really worked.

Middle
········· It was so amazing when the airplane stayed in the air for 59 seconds and went 853 feet! Soon, the brothers made airplanes that could swoop, turn, and fly in a figure eight.

Ending
········· The Wright brothers' first airplane is in the Smithsonian Institution in Washington, D.C. I wonder if I will see it someday.

After you read . . .

- **Ideas** (1) What book is this review about? Who is the author?

- **Organization** (2) What three important facts appear in the beginning? What two surprising details appear in the middle? What one thing does the writer wonder about in the ending?

- **Word Choice** (3) What two words are most interesting to you? Why?

Prewriting Choosing a Book

Jared used the following steps to choose a nonfiction book to review. (See his plan below.)

1. List three nonfiction books you have read.
2. Write down the name of each author.
3. Write one sentence about the main idea of each book.
4. Put a star (✳) next to the book you want to review.

Prewrite Choose a book to review.

1. Read through Jared's plan below.
2. Then follow the steps above to make your own plan and choose a book to write about.

Jared's Plan

Book 1: Snakes*
    Author: Seymour Simon
    Main Idea: Snakes are amazing animals.

Book 2: Bridges Are to Cross
    Author: Philemon Sturges
    Main Idea: Bridges are built in different ways.

Book 3: Lou Gehrig: The Luckiest Man
    Author: David A. Adler
    Main Idea: Lou Gehrig was a great
    baseball player and a very brave man.

Gathering Your Details

Jared gathered information for his report by making a 3-2-1 chart. He made the chart below by answering three questions.

 Prewrite Make a 3-2-1 chart.

■ Ask yourself the following questions about your nonfiction book.

3-2-1 Chart

What <u>three</u> important facts did I learn?

1. Snakes are very strong.
2. All snakes eat animals.
3. If there were no snakes, the world would be filled with rats and mice.

What <u>two</u> surprising details did I discover?

1. Snakes smell with their tongues.
2. Some snakes are longer than an elephant.

What <u>one</u> thing do I still wonder about?

If I saw a snake, would I know if it was dangerous?

Writing Creating Your Review

Now it is time to write your first draft. You will create a beginning, a middle, and an ending. Here is what Jared did for each part of his review.

Beginning	In the beginning, Jared named the book and its author. He also explained *three* important facts from the book.
Middle	In the middle part, Jared shared *two* surprising details from the book.
Ending	In the ending, Jared told *one* thing that he still wondered about.

 Develop your first draft.

■ Use your 3-2-1 chart from page 249 as you write your first draft.

Revising Improving Your Writing

Once your first draft is done, you are ready to revise your work. Make sure your ideas are clear and well organized. Then check your writing voice, word choice, and sentence fluency.

Editing Checking for Conventions

Check your review for capitalization, punctuation, spelling, and grammar errors.

Publishing Sharing Your Book Review

Here is Jared's finished review of a nonfiction book.

Jared's Final Draft

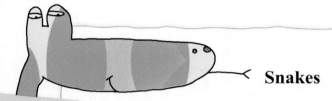

Snakes

Beginning

    Snakes by Seymour Simon is the best book I have ever read about snakes. It is full of interesting facts. Did you know that some big snakes are strong enough to kill a pig or a goat? All snakes eat animals. Without snakes, the world would probably be packed with rats and mice.

Middle

    I learned some surprising facts, too. You probably didn't know that snakes smell with their noses *and* their tongues. Some snakes are longer than an elephant or a giraffe!

Ending

    This book made me think a lot about snakes. Most snakes don't hurt people, but some are very dangerous. I wonder if I would know a snake was dangerous if I saw one.

Comparing a
Fiction and a
Nonfiction Book

A **fiction** book is made-up. For example, you may read a book about a family who lives near Central Park in New York City. The book's facts about New York City may be true, but the story did not really happen.

A **nonfiction** book is true. For example, in a nonfiction book about Central Park, the facts are true and the story is real.

You can write a book review that compares a fiction book to a nonfiction book. This sort of review has three parts, and each part answers different questions.

Beginning — What two books are you comparing? Who are the authors?

Middle — How are the books alike? How are the books different?

Ending — Which book do you like more?

Fiction and Nonfiction Comparison

The Wright Brothers

Beginning

I like airplanes, so I read two books about the Wright brothers. The fiction book is *Wee and the Wright Brothers,* by Timothy R. Gaffney. The nonfiction book is *To Fly, the Story of the Wright Brothers,* by Wendie Old.

These books are alike in some ways. They happen in the same place, and both books contain many facts. For example, the famous flight took place on December 17, a freezing cold day. Orville Wright was lying on the wing of the airplane when he flew.

Middle

The biggest difference is that *Wee and the Wright Brothers* is about a made-up mouse named Wee. He is even a writer! The book says, "On a small printing press above the shop, they published the Mouse News." To get his news story, Wee hides on the airplane and goes along for the famous ride. Of course, none of this is true.

Ending

Both books had many of the same facts, but I liked *Wee and the Wright Brothers* more. The mouse character made it more fun to read. I could imagine being a mouse on the first plane flight!

After you read . . .

- **Ideas** (1) How are the ideas in the two books alike? How are they different?

- **Organization** (2) Which paragraph shows similarities? Which shows differences?

- **Word Choice** (3) What is the main character's name in the fiction book? Find words that describe him.

Prewriting Selecting a Topic

What topics do you love? Jared thinks snakes are amazing. He chose one fiction book and one nonfiction book about snakes.

Prewrite Choose two books.

■ Find a fiction book and a nonfiction book about a topic you enjoy.

Gathering Details

Jared gathered details about each book on a T-chart.

Prewrite Create a T-chart.

1. Read Jared's T-chart below and then make your own chart.
2. Write the names of your books at the top.
3. List interesting details from each book underneath.

T-Chart

Verdi (fiction)	Snakes (nonfiction)
Verdi is a python.	A snake sheds its skin.
He is green.	Big snakes eat pigs and goats.
Verdi likes his color.	Snakes don't see colors well.
He sheds his skin.	The cover shows a python.
He talks and laughs.	
Umbles eats a boar.	

Organizing Your Details

Now that you've gathered your details, you need to organize them. You must decide which details are alike and which are different. A Venn diagram can help you. Jared's Venn diagram appears at the bottom of this page.

 Create a Venn diagram.

1. Draw two overlapping circles.
2. Write the name of each book in the two outside circles.
3. In the center, list similarities (how they are alike).
4. On the two sides, list differences (how they are different).

Venn Diagram

Organization

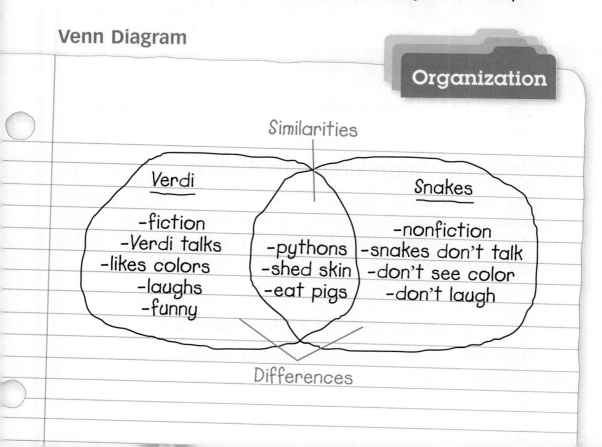

Similarities

Verdi
- fiction
- Verdi talks
- likes colors
- laughs
- funny

- pythons
- shed skin
- eat pigs

Snakes
- nonfiction
- snakes don't talk
- don't see color
- don't laugh

Differences

Writing Creating Your Review

Now you are ready to write your first draft. You will create a beginning, a middle, and an ending. Here is how Jared wrote each part of his review.

Beginning In the beginning paragraph, Jared named the books and their authors.

Middle In the middle paragraphs, Jared explained how the two books were alike and different.

Ending In the ending paragraph, Jared told which book he liked more and why.

 Develop your review.

■ Follow the beginning, middle, and ending plan shown above.

Revising Improving Your Writing

Your first draft is done, and it's time to revise your work. Look over your ideas, the way they are organized, and how your writing voice sounds. You can add, cut, and move details to improve your review.

Editing Checking for Conventions

Check your writing for capitalization, punctuation, spelling, and grammar errors.

Publishing Sharing Your Book Review

Jared compared fiction and nonfiction books.

Jared's Final Draft

Snakes or Verdi?

Beginning

I love snakes, so I read Verdi, by Janell Cannon, and Snakes, by Seymour Simon. Verdi is fiction, and Snakes is nonfiction.

Some things in these books are alike. Verdi looks exactly like the python on the front cover of Snakes. One day, Verdi sheds his skin just like real snakes do. In Snakes, I learned that big snakes can eat big animals, like pigs, sheep, and goats. In Verdi, a big snake named Umbles eats a wild boar.

Middle

These two snake books are different, too. Verdi has made-up animal characters, and Snakes is about real snakes. Verdi talks, laughs, and smiles. For example, he says, "I may be big and very green, but I'm still me!" Verdi likes looking at his green skin, but the Snakes book says that real snakes don't see colors very well.

Ending

My favorite book is Snakes. Verdi is fun, but I learned more interesting facts about snakes by reading Snakes.

Responding to a Poem

The Big, Lazy Dragon
There once was a big, lazy dragon
Who rode everywhere in a wagon.
"I so hate to walk."
That's how he would talk.
"So I ride," he was constantly braggin'.
—Nate Adams

Poetry is a special kind of literature that describes an idea or a feeling. A response to a poem has three basic parts.

Beginning	What is the name of the poem and the poet? What kind of poem is it?
Middle	What are your favorite parts of the poem and why?
Ending	Why do you think the poet wrote the poem?

Alan's Response to a Poem

A Braggin' Dragon

Beginning
· · · · · · · · · · · · · · · ·   "The Big, Lazy Dragon" is a limerick by Nate Adams. Limericks are funny poems. They are five lines long, and they rhyme.

Middle
· · · · · · · · · · · · · · ·   My favorite words in this poem are the rhyming words "dragon," "wagon," and "braggin'." They tell something special about this dragon. I also like the words this dragon says. "I so hate to walk," he says. "So I ride." That's one lazy dragon!

Ending
· · · · · · · · · · · ·   I think the poet wrote this limerick because he likes dragons. This dragon may be lazy, but he's fun. Maybe the poem was written by the dragon himself! It would be just one more thing for him to brag about.

After you read . . .

- **Ideas** (1) What is your favorite idea in this response?

- **Organization** (2) What questions does each part answer?

- **Word Choice** (3) What words from the poem appear in the response?

Prewriting **Selecting a Topic**

First, you need to find a poem. Look through poetry books and children's magazines until you find one you enjoy. You may also choose one of the following poems.

Haiku Poems

Weather Forecast
Icicle melting,
Counting the seconds till spring,
Drip by shining drip.
—Lewis Wright

Bullfrog
A silent bullfrog
Hides in the muddy water
Waiting for dinner.
—Jean Netter

5 W's Poems

The Wolf
Howls
In the woods
At midnight
To call the pack.
—Jana Whiteheart

Grandpa Frank
Tells stories
At the head of the table
During Thanksgiving dinner
Because he remembers so much.
—David Moffet

 Choose a poem to respond to.

■ Make sure to find out what kind of poem you have chosen. (See pages 282–293).

Gathering Details

Next, you need to gather information about your poem. Answering questions can help. Here is the poem that Charise chose. Below, you can read her answers to the questions.

What I Did on Saturday

Watched cartoons. Played with spoons.

Walked the dog. Caught a frog.

Found a hole. Fought a troll.

Turned invisible. Saved our principal.

Came back home. Wrote this poem.

—Craig Eugene

 Prewrite Answer questions about your poem.

1. On your own paper, write the name of your poem and the poet.
2. Then write the underlined questions shown below and answer them.

Detail Questions

"What I Did on Saturday" by Craig Eugene

What kind of poem is it? It is a list poem.

What are my favorite lines or words?

"Found a hole. Fought a troll." Also, I like "Turned invisible. Saved our principal."

Why do I think the poet wrote this poem?

He likes to imagine adventures.

Writing Organizing Your Response

You are now ready to write a response to your poem. Here is how Charise organized her response.

Beginning

In the **beginning paragraph**, Charise named the poem and its author. She also explained what kind of poem she chose.

Middle

In the **middle paragraph**, Charise told about her favorite words or lines in the poem.

Ending

In the **ending paragraph**, Charise told why she thinks the poet wrote the poem.

Write **Develop your response to a poem.**

■ Follow the plan shown above to write your response.

Revising Improving Your Writing

Once your first draft is done, revise your writing. Consider your ideas, the way they are organized, and how your voice sounds. Then work on your word choice and sentence fluency.

Editing Checking for Conventions

Check your response for capitalization, punctuation, spelling, and grammar errors.

Publishing Sharing Your Response Essay

Here is Charise's final draft of her response to a poem.

Charise's Final Draft

A Big Adventure

Beginning .... "What I Did on Saturday" is a list poem by Craig Eugene. This poem rhymes, and it's funny.

Middle .... My favorite part is the middle. The beginning is about usual things, like watching TV and walking a dog. Then the middle is about crazy things, like a hole and fighting a troll. This Saturday gets more and more exciting! I like the next part, too. "Turned invisible. Saved our principal." It makes me feel like I'm a character in a comic book.

Ending .... I think the poet wrote this poem because sometimes he gets bored. Then he imagines wild adventures and has fun writing about them. It's like he said in the ending, "Came back home. Wrote this poem."

Response to Literature

Writing for Assessment

Some writing tests ask you to respond to a short article. You may need to answer questions about the article or write an essay. Here is a prompt you might find on a test.

Response Prompt

Read the article below. In an essay, tell what the article is about. Give a few important facts from the article, and tell one thing you still wonder about.

Mountain Lions on the Move

Mountain lions are on the move. They are showing up in communities all over the United States. Someday, you might see one in your backyard.

For most of the last one hundred years, mountain lions have lived west of the Mississippi River. They usually live in mountain wilderness areas. Lately, these animals have begun moving east into neighborhoods near big cities, like Chicago, Philadelphia, and Boston.

Why are they moving? Scientists say it is because people are building communities in the mountain lion's natural habitat. Buildings, roads, and fences get in the animals' way when they search for food and water. This forces them to look for new places to live where there is plenty to eat and water to drink.

Mountain lions prey on animals like deer, cats, and dogs. If you see a mountain lion, you should stay away from it. Most mountain lions will run from people. However, some have attacked and killed people.

Student Response

Watch Out for Mountain Lions

The **beginning** names the article and tells what it is about.

The article "Mountain Lions on the Move" is about mountain lions in new places. They used to live just out west. Now they are showing up in places like Chicago and Boston.

The **middle** gives facts.

People have caused this problem. They are building homes where mountain lions used to live. Mountain lions are usually afraid of people. Sometimes, though, they have killed people. So don't go near a mountain lion.

The **ending** tells what the writer wonders about.

I liked this article. It made me wonder if a mountain lion will ever show up in my neighborhood. I would like to see one, but not in my yard.

After you read . . .

- **Ideas** (1) Name two important facts the writer shared.

- **Organization** (2) Which part—beginning, middle, ending—named the article and the main idea?

- **Word Choice** (3) What words from the "Response Prompt" appear in this response?

Writing Tips

- Read the prompt and the article carefully.
- Plan your paragraph. Then write your response and check your work.
- Follow all the directions in the prompt.
- Make neat corrections.

Response Prompt

Respond to the following article. Tell what the main idea is, give a few interesting facts, and include one thing you still wonder about.

Still Smiling after Thousands of Years

"She would've had a perfect smile." That is what scientists are saying about Europe's oldest skeleton. The skeleton of a woman is thousands of years old.

One of the most interesting things about this skeleton is her beautiful teeth. They are nearly perfect, straight, and white. In ancient times, people did not take good care of their teeth. A poor diet and poor dental care caused a lot of tooth decay. So, why are this skeleton's teeth so perfect? Scientists think she may have used toothpaste!

The toothpaste was nothing like what we use today. Not long ago, a team of scientists discovered an old Egyptian toothpaste recipe. The ingredients included rock salt, mint, and pepper. These things were pounded into a paste and then put on the teeth. Is some sort of toothpaste what gave the skeleton her beautiful smile? Nobody knows for sure.

Response Writing in Review

When you respond to a book, a poem, or an article, you tell what the writing is about and what it means to you.

Select a book, an article, or a poem that you enjoyed reading. (See pages **236**, **248**, **254**, and **260**.)

Gather and organize details about your reading. (See pages **237**, **249**, **254–255**, and **261**.)

In the beginning paragraph, name the title and author and give the main idea. (See pages **238**, **250**, **256**, and **262**.)

In the middle paragraph, share important details from the reading. (See pages **240**, **250**, **256**, and **262**.)

In the ending paragraph, finish with an interesting thought. (See pages **241**, **250**, **256**, and **262**.)

Look over your **ideas**, **organization**, and **voice** first. Then check your **word choice** and **sentence fluency**. (See pages **242**, **250**, **256**, and **262**.)

Check your writing for conventions. Also have a classmate edit your writing. (See pages **243**, **250**, **256**, and **262**.)

Make a final copy and proofread it for errors before sharing it.

Creative Writing

Senator Robert F. Kennedy once said, "Some people see things as they are and ask why. I dream things that never were and ask why not." Creative writing is one way to dream things that never were and bring them into reality.

In this section, you'll learn how to write imaginative stories and plays and how to create beautiful poems. Set your mind to dreaming, and set your hand to writing!

What's Ahead

- **Writing Imaginative Stories**
- **Creating a Play**
- **Writing Poems**

Writing
Imaginative Stories

"Let me tell you a story!" Ever since prehistoric times, people have been telling stories. Heroes fight monsters, explorers discover new worlds, and adventurers travel through time and space. A story is born in the storyteller's imagination.

In this chapter, you will get a chance to write your own imaginative story. You'll also see how one student, Rosa, wrote her story. Before she began, she thought about how stories are made.

Understanding Stories

All stories have four basic ingredients:

Characters are the people or animals in the story.

Setting is the time when and the place where the story happens. The setting can change throughout the story.

Conflict is a problem or challenge the characters face.

Plot is what happens in the story.
(See page **281** for more information.)

Read the beginning of "Jack and the Beanstalk." Find the characters, the setting, the conflict, and the first thing that happens in the plot.

A long time ago, in a faraway land, there lived a poor widow and her son Jack. They had nothing to live on except their cow's milk. One day, things got so hopeless that the widow sent Jack to the market to sell the cow. . . .

Imaginative Story

Here is the make-believe story that Rosa wrote. It tells about her adventure in a paper boat.

Beginning

The beginning tells about the characters, the setting, and the conflict or problem.

Rising Action

The rising action tells what happens in the first part of the story.

The story shares actions and speaking (dialogue).

Sailing on a Paper Dream

One rainy Saturday, I sat at the kitchen window. What a boring day! I told my mom, "I wish Shelly hadn't moved to Vancouver."

Mom said, "Maybe you can visit her, Rosa."

That gave me an idea. I drew a crayon picture of myself with a life jacket on. Then I made a paper boat and put the picture inside.

"I'm going out for a second," I told my mom. I ran out into the rain! In back of my house, there was a tiny stream of water. I put my boat in the water. It sailed away.

Then something amazing happened. The picture of me jumped on shore. The real me was in the paper boat! I floated down the stream, through a tunnel, and over a huge waterfall!

"Woo!" I shouted and held onto the side.

The boat splashed down in Puget Sound. It floated out across the water. Then the water under the boat turned hard and black. It was the back of a killer whale! "What are you doing on my back?" asked the whale.

High Point
The high point is the most exciting part.
· · · · · · · · · · ·

I said, "I'm going to Vancouver."
The whale turned north and blew hard.
The boat went flying through the air, halfway to Canada.

Suddenly, a seagull flew down, grabbed my boat, and dumped me out. The bird flew off, wearing my boat like a hat. I was left in the water, bobbing around in my life jacket.

Then I felt a hand on my shoulder. Someone pulled me out of the water into another paper boat.

Ending
· · · · · · · · · · ·
The ending tells how everything works out.

"Shelly!" I shouted when I looked up. "What are you doing here?"

My friend smiled. "I was bored, so I made a boat, and I sailed out to find you!"

Answer these questions about my story!

After you read . . .

■ **Ideas** (1) What makes Rosa's story interesting?

■ **Organization** (2) What problem does Rosa have, and how does she fix it?

■ **Word Choice** (3) Find three strong action verbs that make Rosa's story exciting.

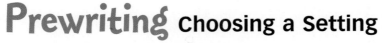

Prewriting Choosing a Setting

You will be the main character in your story. First, you need to choose an interesting setting. Rosa made a list of places and times. Then she drew a line to connect a time and a place to be the setting for her story. (Remember, the setting of a story can change.)

 Prewrite **Make a list of places and times.**

1. List places in one column.
2. List times in another column.
3. Connect a place and a time with a line.

Ideas

Setting List

Places	Times
home	the year 3000
a boat	Valentine's Day
the zoo	my 16th birthday
the moon	a rainy Saturday

Thinking About Your Plot

The plot is what happens in a story. Rosa imagined herself in a boat on a rainy Saturday (her setting). Then she answered the following plot questions.

 Prewrite **Answer these plot questions.**

1. **What big problem do I face?**
2. **What amazing thing do I do?**
3. **What else happens?**
4. **What goes wrong?**

Plot Questions

1. <u>What big problem do I face?</u>
   I feel bored. I miss my friend Shelly.

2. <u>What amazing thing do I do?</u>
   I make a paper boat and sail away to see her.

3. <u>What else happens?</u>
   A whale blows me north!

4. <u>What goes wrong?</u>
   A seagull takes my boat and dumps me out.

Writing Putting Your Story on Paper

Now you have a main character (you!) and a setting. You also know what happens, so you're ready to write.

Write **Write your first draft.**

1. Follow the tips below.
2. When you finish, create a title for your story.

Here are two ways to get started.

Start with action.

> Lightning flashed, and rain pounded on the roof.
>
> OR
>
> "Why did Shelly have to move away?" I asked.

Begin with someone talking.

Here are two ways to keep going.

Introduce a new problem.

> Suddenly, a seagull flew down, grabbed my boat, and . . .
>
> OR
>
> Someone pulled me out of the water . . .

Add a new twist.

Revising Improving Your Writing

When you revise, you make sure your story is clear and exciting, and that it reads smoothly. The questions below can help you.

 Answer these questions.

1. Did I include enough interesting details?
2. Did I tell about a problem?
   Did I solve the problem in the end?
3. Did I use exciting action verbs?

Editing Checking for Conventions

When you edit, you make sure your writing is correct.

 Check your editing.

1. Did I end my sentences with punctuation?
2. Did I begin my sentences with capital letters?
3. Have I used quotation marks for the speaking parts (dialogue)?
4. Have I checked my spelling?

Creating a Play

You can turn your story into a play by acting it out. A play uses dialogue to tell the story. What the characters do is placed in parentheses. Here is the start of Rosa's play.

Sailing on a Paper Dream

List the characters.

Characters: Rosa, Mom, Shelly, Whale, Seagull

Describe the setting.

Setting: Rosa is staring out the kitchen window. Her mom is cooking nearby.

Scene 1

Write dialogue (what each character says).

Rosa: I'm bored. Why did Shelly have to move to Vancouver?

Mom: Maybe you can visit her someday.

Rosa: I know what I'll do! I'll make a boat and sail off to find her! (Rosa grabs some paper.)

Tell what the characters are doing (in parentheses).

Mom: That's nice, honey. (Mom is busy at the stove.)

Rosa: (Rosa draws a picture of herself and makes a paper boat. She jumps up and runs out the door.) Bye, Mom!

Create a
new scene
whenever
the setting
changes.

Scene 2

Setting: Rosa puts the boat in the ditch.
Suddenly she is on board.

Rosa: Excellent! I'm Captain Rosa!
(She floats through a tunnel.)

Oh, no! A waterfall! Woooo!
(Rosa yells as the boat falls.)

That's better. Wait! This water seems
hard! It's black! (The boat begins to
rise on the back of a whale.)

A whale?

Whale: Who said that?

Rosa: It's me, Rosa.

Whale: What are you doing on my back?

Rosa: I'm trying to get to Vancouver.

Whale: Oh, I know where that is. Hold on!
(The whale blows. Rosa and the
boat fly into the air.)

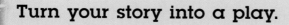

Write Turn your story into a play.

1. List your characters and describe the setting.
2. Use dialogue and lots of action to tell your story.

Learning Elements of Fiction

Writers use the following words and ideas when they write about stories.

The **action** is what happens in a story.

A **character** is a person or an animal in a story.

Conflict is a problem or challenge for the characters.

Dialogue is what characters say to each other.

An **event** is a specific happening.

Fiction is an imaginative or made-up story.

A **moral** is the lesson that a story (fable, tale, or myth) teaches.

The **narrator** is the person or character who is telling the story.

The **plot** is what happens, the series of events. (See the plot line on page **281**.)

The **setting** is the time and place of a story.

The **theme** is the main idea or message.

Understanding a Plot Line

Most stories follow a **plot line** that builds to the most exciting point. The plot line has four parts.

- The **beginning** introduces the characters, the setting, and the conflict.

- The **rising action** tells about problems that come up. It leads to the most exciting part of the story.

- The **high point** is the most exciting part of the story.

- The **ending** tells how things finally turn out.

Right about here, that seagull dumped me in the water!

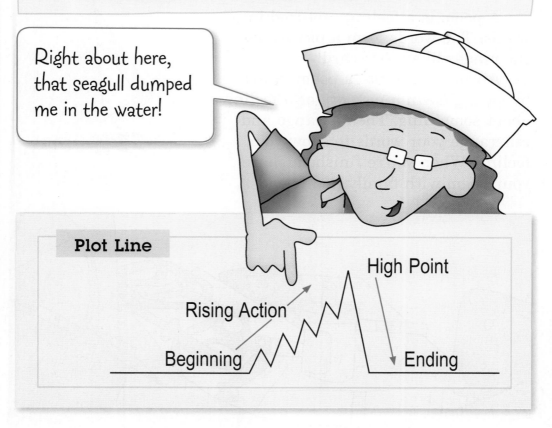

Plot Line

Rising Action

High Point

Beginning

Ending

Creative Writing

Writing Poems

A poem is a feeling captured in words. The words form a picture for the reader like a postcard!

Anyone can write a poem. Start by jotting down a memory or a feeling about something. Then arrange and rearrange your words to show your feeling. When you're finished, share your poem with family and friends.

Rhyming Poem

Some poems use pairs of rhyming words. Rhymes are fun to read and easy to remember. Marta wrote the rhyming poem below to describe how she feels about jumping rope.

Jump to It!

When a *jump* rope starts to spin,
I can't help but get a grin.
I like to hear a *jump* rope whir,
And watch it swinging in a blur.
When a *jump* rope slaps the street,
It gives rhythm to my feet.
I *jump* and *jump* until I pant.
Then I end *my jump* rope chant.

After you read . . .

- **Ideas** (1) What does the poem make you see and hear?
- **Organization** (2) What are the pairs of rhyming words in this poem?
- **Word Choice** (3) How does Marta feel about jumping rope?

Prewriting Selecting a Topic

A poem can be about anything: a pet, a friend, an adventure, a holiday, the mumps. Choose something that gives you a happy or sad feeling. To find a topic, you can list ideas on a T-chart.

 Prewrite Find a topic.

1. Make a T-chart like the one below. List at least three things that make you happy and three that make you sad.

2. Then choose one of these happy or sad things as a topic for your poem.

T-Chart

Organization

Happy Feelings	Sad Feelings
• a new kitten	• cold, rainy days
• jumping rope	• when my goldfish died
• Thanksgiving dinner	• when Sandra moved
• a bubble bath	away
• building a dollhouse	

Gathering Details

A poem builds pictures with words that share sensory details. Once you choose your topic, you can make a sensory chart to gather details.

 Prewrite   **Gather details to create word pictures.**

1. Make a sensory chart like the one below.

2. In each column, list details that will help the reader see and feel your topic.

Sensory Chart

Topic: jumping rope

See	Hear	Smell	Taste	Touch
white rope ends	whirring rope	fresh air	salty sweat on my lips	soft rope
blur	rope slapping the street			rough sidewalk
rope swingers				hair in my face
line of jumpers	everybody chanting			

Prewriting Using Pleasing Sounds

Poets use different ways to make their writing sing!

Rhyme: Rhyme is one way to make pleasing sounds. Poets and songwriters often use rhyming words at the end of lines.

> I bought my pig
> A curly wig.

> Summer is fun.
> Give me the sun!

Sound Words: Poets use words like *buzz* and *snap* that sound like the noise they name. Using these words is called *onomatopoeia* (ŏn ə-măt ə-pē´ ə).

> Buzz, buzz, hummed the bee.

Consonant Sounds: Sometimes poets use words that begin or end with the same consonant sound. This is called *alliteration* (ə-lĭt´ ə-rā shən).

> Wind whispers through the willows.

Rhythm: Rhythm is the pattern of beats in a poem. The beat makes the lines of poetry flow from one idea to the next.

> I bought my pig
> A curly wig.

> Summer is fun.
> Give me the sun!

Prewrite — **Use poetry's pleasing sounds.**

1. Choose some words from your sensory chart.
2. Make a list of words that rhyme with them.
3. Then use this list as you write your poem.

Marta's Prewriting

Marta chose some words from her sensory chart. Then she listed rhyming words under each one. You can use a rhyming dictionary to help you find rhyming words.

Rhyming List

blur	chant	rope	street
fur	ant	hope	feet
purr	can't	mope	heat
sure	pant	soap	meet
whir	slant		

Sometimes poets make up rhyming words or rhyme them in funny ways.
You can't-a-rope
a cantaloupe.

Writing Developing Your First Draft

You've done a lot of thinking about the words you will use in your poem. Now it's time to add your feelings. Have fun writing whatever sounds and feels right! You can make changes later.

Getting Started

If you have trouble getting started, try one of these ideas.

- **Close your eyes** and picture whatever it is you are writing about. Jot down the words that come to mind.

- **Start with your favorite detail**. Then write about your second favorite, and so on.

- **Use a starter phrase**, like "When I see . . ." or "I like to . . . ," and keep going.

 Develop the first draft of your poem.

1. Use all your notes to write your own poem about a happy or sad time. Include the details from your sensory chart.

2. Stop writing when your poem sounds and feels finished to you.

Revising Improving Your Poem

Once you finish your poem, read it aloud to see how it sounds. Next, make changes that will make your poem even better.

- **Add** new lines or details to make your ideas clearer.
- **Cut** parts that don't seem to fit with the rest of your poem.
- **Replace** words to improve your poem's rhythm and rhyme.

Revise Make changes to your poem.

■ Add, cut, and replace words to make your poem better. Work with your poem until every word feels just right.

Editing Fine-Tuning Your Poem

When you edit, you make your writing correct—and easier to read!

Edit Check your poem.

■ Check your poem for punctuation, capitalization, and spelling errors. (Rhyming poems often capitalize the first word of every line.)

Creating a Title

Every poem needs a title. Here are some ideas.
- ■ Use the first or last line: **My Jump Rope Chant**
- ■ Use words from the poem: **Jump Rope Whir**
- ■ Describe the poem: **Jump Rope Song and Dance**

Writing a Limerick

A limerick is a silly rhymed poem with five lines. Lines 1, 2, and 5 rhyme; and lines 3 and 4 rhyme. Limericks also have a special rhythm, as in the example below.

> ## Pete the Fat Cat
>
> There once was a kitten named Pete,
> Who always got too much to eat.
> He soon grew so fat
> That he slipped and fell flat,
> Too heavy to land on his feet.

Rhyming lines may not be next to each other. Notice that **eat** and **feet** are separated in this limerick.

Writing Tips

Select a topic.
- Think of something silly that an animal or a person could do.

Gather details.
- List your ideas. Then circle some funny words and find rhymes for them.

Follow the pattern.
- Write your poem using the limerick pattern.

      There once was . . .
      Who . . .
      She, He, or It . . .
      That . . .

Writing a Clerihew

A clerihew is another funny rhymed poem. It describes a person (or a pet). A clerihew follows this pattern:

- The first line names the person.
- The second line tells a detail about the person and ends with a word that rhymes with the person's name.
- The last two lines tell more details about the person and end with rhyming words.

Ms. Doud

Our gym teacher, Ms. Doud,
must like to be loud!
It makes my hair frizzle
when she blows her whistle.

Some rhyming words match exactly, and some are near rhymes. That's okay!

My Dog Sasha

My dog Sasha
doesn't like when we wash her.
She won't stay in the tub,
but she sure likes a towel rub!

Writing Tips

Select a topic.
- Think of a pet or a person you want to write about.

Gather details.
- List details about the person (or pet).

Follow the pattern.
- Write your clerihew using the pattern above.

Writing a 5 W's Poem

A 5 W's poem is five lines long. Each line answers one of the 5 W's *(who? what? when? where?* and *why?)*. Usually, the lines of a 5 W's poem do not rhyme.

My Bunny Helicopter

Who?	My bunny, Simon,
What?	jumps and spins in midair
When?	when he leaves his cage
Where?	in our backyard
Why?	because he is free!

Writing Tips

Select a topic.
- Make a list of silly and serious "who" ideas. Choose one as the topic for your poem.

Gather details.
- Make a 5 W's chart to list ideas for your poem.

who?	what?	when?	where?	why?

Follow the pattern.
- Write a poem that answers the 5 W's in any order, using details from your chart.
- Add, cut, and replace words until your poem feels just right.

Writing an Alphabet Poem

An alphabet poem is a list poem in alphabetical order. It can start with any letter of the alphabet. The list of single words can be as long as you like. Alphabet poems almost never rhyme.

<u>Parrot Music</u>
Our
Parrot
Quotes
Rap
Songs!

<u>Bear Cubs</u>
Bear
Cubs
Dance
Eat
Fight!

Writing Tips

Select a topic.
- Animals make great topics for alphabet poems. Think of your favorite type of animal.

Gather details.
- Freewrite about the animal you've chosen.

   I love parrots. They're really bright and colorful. They bob their heads up and down and dance from foot to foot. They squawk and talk in a funny voice.

Follow the pattern.
- Name your topic.
- Then list a group of letters from the alphabet in order.
- Be sure each word begins with the letter listed.

Research Writing

Research writing starts with "I wonder" and ends with "Let me tell you." When you look for answers to questions, you're doing research. Afterward, you can share the answers you find by writing about them.

In this section, you'll learn about doing research in the library, writing summaries, and creating a research report. When you're done, you can even make a multimedia presentation.

What's Ahead

- Finding Information
- Writing a Summary Paragraph
- Writing a Research Report
- Creating a Multimedia Presentation

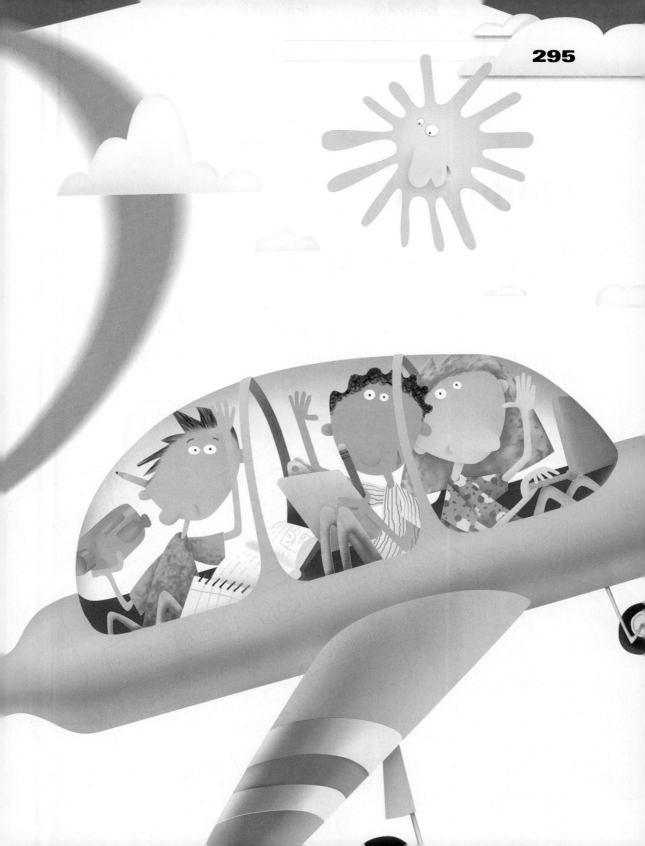

Finding
Information

A library is more than just shelves of books. A library opens the door to a whole world of information. You can find books, magazines, newspapers, encyclopedias, recordings, computers, and even DVD's. Best of all, most libraries have a librarian who can help you find what you are looking for.

Using the Library

A library is organized to help you find information. Usually, different types of books each have their own separate place.

The **books** in a library are divided into three main sections.

1. **Fiction** books include stories and novels. These books are arranged in alphabetical order by the authors' last names.

2. **Nonfiction** (factual) books are arranged on the shelves by call numbers, according to the Dewey decimal system.

> A book numbered **386** comes before a book numbered **714**. One labeled **973A** comes before one labeled **973B.** Some call numbers have decimals, like **973.19** or **973.22**. Your librarian can help you find these books.

3. **Reference** books such as encyclopedias, atlases, and dictionaries are kept in a special section of the library.

In addition to different types of books, your library may include the following:

The **periodicals** area has magazines and newspapers.

The **computer lab** has computers available to use. Some may be connected to the Internet.

The **media section** has DVD's, cassettes, CD's, and videotapes. You may also find computer software in this section.

Using a Card Catalog

In a library full of books, how can you find the one book you need? Simple. Use the card catalog where cards are arranged in alphabetical order. Each book has one *title card* and one *author card*. It may also have a *subject card*. All of these cards tell about the book and where you can find it on the shelves.

1. **Title Card:** If you know the title of a book, look for its title card. If the title begins with *A*, *An*, or *The*, look up the next word in the title.

■ Look under PLANETS to find the book *The Planets*.

2. **Author Card:** You can also find a book by its author's last name. The last name comes first on the author card. All books by that author will be grouped together.

■ Rustad, Martha E. H.

3. **Subject Card:** If you need a book about a particular subject, look for the subject in the catalog. There you will find cards for all sorts of books about that subject.

■ Look under the subject SOLAR SYSTEM to find books about the sun and its planets.

Sample Catalog Cards

Call number

The Planets

J 523.4
RUS

Rustad, Martha E. H.
   The planets/Martha Rustad.—
Mankato, Minn: Pebble Books, 2008.

Author abbreviation

Photographs and simple text introduce
the planets in our solar system.

1. Solar system 2. Space 3. The Sun

Rustad, Martha E. H.

J 523.4
RUS

Rustad, Martha E. H.
   The planets/Martha Rustad.—
Mankato, Minn: Pebble Books, 2008.

Description

Photographs and simple text introduce
the planets in our solar system.

1. Solar system 2. Space 3. The Sun

SOLAR SYSTEM

J 523.4
RUS

Rustad, Martha E. H.
   The planets/Martha Rustad.—
Mankato, Minn: Pebble Books, 2008.

Photographs and simple text introduce
the planets in our solar system.

Related Topics

1. Solar system 2. Space 3. The Sun

Using a Computer Catalog

Many libraries keep their catalog on computer. That makes finding a book even easier. Follow these tips.

- Always read the on-screen directions.
- Search by author or title, if you know the book you want.
- Search by subject to find all books about that subject.
- Use **keywords** in your search. For example, type in *astronomy* to find books about that subject or books with that word in the title.

Author:	Osborne, Will and Mary Pope Osborne.
Title:	*Space*
Series title:	Magic tree house research guide.
Published:	New York: Random House, 2007 137 p.: ill.
Notes:	A nonfiction companion to *Midnight on the Moon*. Jack and Annie present information about the universe, including our solar system, and briefly describe the history of space travel and of the science of astronomy.
Added entry:	Murdocca, Sal, ill.
Subjects:	Astronomy, space flight
Call number:	J 520 OSB
Status:	Checked out
Location:	Children's

Using References

Books are easier to use when you understand their parts.

- The **title page** lists the book's title, author, and publisher. It may also list the book's illustrator.

- The **copyright** page shows important information. It tells the year the book was published. (A new book may be more accurate than an old one.)

- The **table of contents** in the front of the book gives page numbers for chapters and sections of the book.

- Pictures in a book may have **captions** that help to explain them.

- Some books have a **glossary** near the back that defines new words.

- Many books have an **index** in the back. This alphabetical list of topics has page numbers where you can find information on each listed topic.

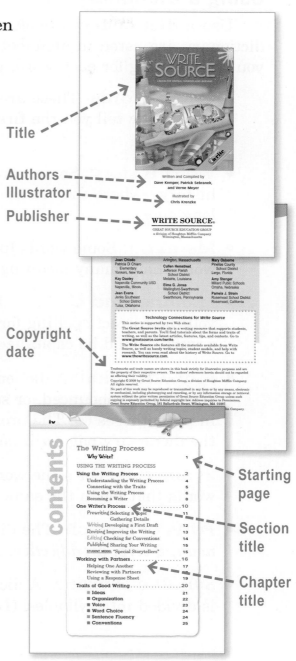

Title

Authors
Illustrator
Publisher

Copyright date

Starting page

Section title

Chapter title

Using a Dictionary

Use a **dictionary** to look up new words. The words in a dictionary are listed in alphabetical order. The dictionary gives you the meaning for each word, plus much more.

- **Guide Words:** These are the words at the top of the page. They tell you the first and last entry words on the page.

- **Word History:** Some words have stories about their history—where they came from and what they meant long ago.

- **Meaning:** Some words have only one meaning. Other words have many meanings.

- **Spelling and Capital Letters:** The dictionary shows you the correct spelling for a word. It also shows whether a word should be capitalized.

- **Pronunciation:** A dictionary shows you how a word should be pronounced, or said. The pronunciation is given in parentheses ( ). The pronunciation key at the bottom of the dictionary page will help you, too.

- **Synonyms:** For some words, the dictionary lists other words that mean the same thing.

- **Parts of Speech:** The dictionary tells you if a word is a *noun,* a *verb,* an *adjective,* or another part of speech.

- **Syllable Division:** A dictionary shows you how a word is divided into syllables. (Look for the heavy black dots.)

Dictionary Page

Guide words ──────▶ **dandelion** ▶ **dangle**

dandelion *noun* A plant with bright yellow flowers and long notched leaves that is a common weed. Its leaves are sometimes eaten in salads. **dan·de·li·on** (dǎn′dl ĭ′ən) ◊ *noun, plural* **dandelions**

Word history ───────▶

Word History

dandelion

Dandelion comes from an old French phrase meaning "tooth of a lion." The leaves of a dandelion have jagged edges that look a little like lions' teeth.

■ **dandelion**

Meaning ───────▶ **dandruff** *noun* Small white flakes of dead skin that are shed from the scalp. **dan·druff** (dǎn′drəf) ◊ *noun*

Spelling and capital letters ───────▶ **Dane** *noun* A person who was born in or lives in Denmark. **Dane** (dān) ◊ *noun, plural* **Danes**

danger *noun* **1.** The chance of harm or destruction; peril: *the danger of a cave-in.* **2.** The condition of being exposed to harm or loss: *in danger of falling.* **3.** Something that may cause harm. **dan·ger** (dān′jər) ◊ *noun, plural* **dangers**

Pronunciation ───────▶

Synonyms

Synonyms ───────▶ **danger, hazard, risk**

The explorer faced many *dangers* in the jungle. ▶ People who live near active volcanoes face certain *hazards*. ▶ It is a *risk* to swim so far, but if you succeed, you will win a prize.

Part of speech ───────▶ **dangerous** *adjective* **1.** Full of danger; risky. **2.** Able or likely to cause harm. **dan·ger·ous** (dān′jər əs) ◊ *adjective*

dangle *verb* To swing or cause to swing loosely: *A key dangled from the chain.* **dan·gle** (dǎng′gəl) ◊ *verb* **dangled, dangling**

Syllable division ───────▶

Pronunciation key

ǎ	pat	ĭ	pit
ā	pay	ī	ride
â	care	î	fierce
ä	father	ŏ	pot
ĕ	pet	ō	go
ē	be	ô	paw, for
oi	oil	th	bath
o͝o	book	th	bathe
o͞o	boot	ə	ago, item
ou	out		pencil
ŭ	cut		atom
û	fur		circus

Using a Thesaurus

A thesaurus is a book that lists words and their synonyms. Synonyms are words with similar meanings. A thesaurus may also list antonyms for some words. Antonyms are words that mean the opposite. You can use a thesaurus to find just the right word and to give your writing variety. For example, the following sample thesaurus entry gives you other choices for the word *small*.

Word	Synonyms	Antonyms
small	little, minor, tiny, trivial, undersized	big, large, major

Using an Atlas

An atlas is a collection of maps. An atlas may include symbols, graphics, and tables. Always check the *key* to learn more about the map you are looking at.

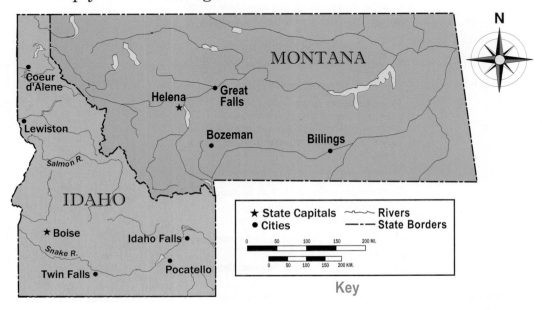

Key

Using an Encyclopedia

An encyclopedia is a set of books that contain articles on many topics. The set is arranged in alphabetical order. Each volume is labeled with letters to show what part of the alphabet it contains. Often, the last volume is an index. It can help you find other articles on topics related to the one you are studying.

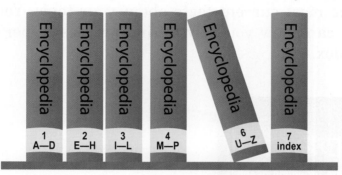

Explore Electronic Encyclopedias

Some encyclopedias are published on a CD or on the Internet. To search for your topic in an electronic encyclopedia, use keywords or words underlined in the article. (See page **300**.)

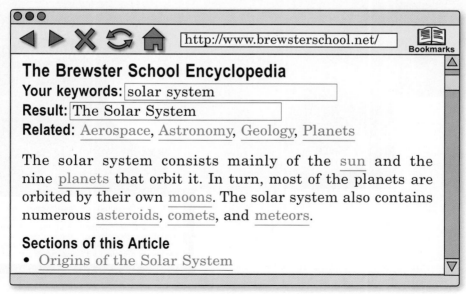

The Brewster School Encyclopedia
Your keywords: solar system
Result: The Solar System
Related: Aerospace, Astronomy, Geology, Planets

The solar system consists mainly of the sun and the nine planets that orbit it. In turn, most of the planets are orbited by their own moons. The solar system also contains numerous asteroids, comets, and meteors.

Sections of this Article
• Origins of the Solar System

Using Periodicals

Periodicals are magazines and newspapers. (*Periodic* means "occurring from time to time.") The periodicals have articles on all sorts of subjects.

Periodicals are published more often than books, so they may have more up-to-date information. Use a recent issue to be sure you have the most current facts about your topic. Your teacher or librarian can show you how to find articles in periodicals by using an index.

Using the Internet

The Internet can be a great place to find information. For example, NASA has its own Web site with lots of photos and information about space exploration. Your teacher may know of other educational sites for you to explore, as well.

Follow the Rules

Be sure to follow your school and library Internet policies. These guidelines and rules are designed to keep you safe.

Know How to Navigate

Arrows move you from page to page.

Bookmarks take you to saved pages.

The **scroll bar** lets you move up and down through the page.

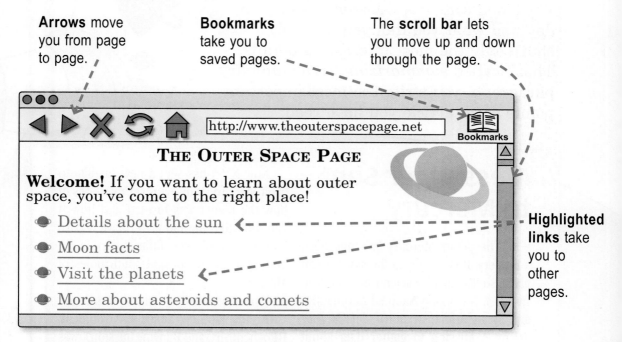

Highlighted links take you to other pages.

Print, Highlight, and Reword

You can print out Internet pages you find and then highlight important parts. Put information in your own words in your writing assignments.

Writing a Summary Paragraph

When someone asks you about your day and what you did, you probably share only the most interesting details. That's called *summarizing*. In a summary paragraph, you write the most important points of an article you have read.

Messenger Sent to Mercury

The planet Mercury has long been a mystery. It is usually in the sun's bright glare, so it's hard for scientists to study it. In 1973, NASA (the **N**ational **A**eronautics and **S**pace **A**dministration) sent *Mariner 10* on a mission to gather data about Venus and Mercury. As the satellite orbited the sun, it flew past Mercury three times between 1974 and 1975. The information it sent back was based on viewing only half the planet's surface.

Now NASA has sent a new satellite to orbit Mercury. It may answer mysteries of how the planet was formed and how it can look like the moon yet have a core like Earth. It will see if there is ice in the craters at the north and south poles of Mercury.

The new satellite, named *Messenger* (**ME**rcury **S**urface, **S**pace **EN**vironment, **GE**ochemistry, and **R**anging mission), was launched on August 14, 2004. *Messenger* will begin orbiting Mercury in March of 2011. It will send back radio signals for a full year. After that it will stop working and crash into Mercury.

Summary Paragraph

After reading the *"Messenger* Sent to Mercury" article, Ugo Garret wrote this summary paragraph.

<u>Messenger Goes to Mercury</u>

The topic sentence states the main idea.

NASA wants to solve some of the mysteries of the planet Mercury. In 1973, NASA sent a satellite named <u>Mariner 10</u> to study Mercury. In 2004, NASA sent a new satellite named <u>Messenger</u> to Mercury to get more information. NASA hopes <u>Messenger</u> will explain how the planet was formed, how it's like Earth, and if there's any ice there. <u>Messenger</u> will start orbiting Mercury in 2011 and send back information about the planet for a year before it crashes.

Important details are put in the writer's own words.

A closing sentence ends the summary.

After you read . . .

- **Ideas** (1) What is the main idea of the summary?
- **Organization** (2) What does the writer do in his closing sentence?
- **Voice** (3) Did the writer use a funny or serious voice? Why?

Prewriting Reading an Article

Your teacher may help you find an article to summarize. As you read, remember to look for the main idea and the most important details.

 Select and read an article.

1. **Find a short article about an interesting subject you are studying.**

2. **Read the article very carefully.**

3. **Write down the main idea and the most important details. (If you have a photocopy of the article, you may underline the details.)**

Ugo's Underlining

Messenger Sent to Mercury

The planet Mercury has long been a mystery. It is usually in the sun's bright glare, so it's hard for scientists to study it. In 1973, NASA (the National Aeronautics and Space Administration) sent *Mariner 10* on a mission to gather data about Venus and Mercury. As the satellite orbited the sun, it flew past Mercury three times between 1974 and 1975. The information it sent back was based on viewing only half the planet's surface.

Now NASA has sent a new satellite to orbit Mercury. It may answer mysteries of how the planet was formed and how it can look like the moon yet have a core like Earth. It will see if there is ice in the craters at the north and south poles of Mercury.

The new satellite, named *Messenger* (**ME**rcury **S**urface, **S**pace **EN**vironment, **GE**ochemistry, and **R**anging mission), was launched on August 14, 2004. *Messenger* will begin orbiting Mercury in March of 2011. It will send back radio signals for a full year. After that it will stop working and crash into Mercury.

Writing Developing the First Draft

Use these guidelines to write your summary paragraph.

 Develop your summary paragraph.

1. Tell the main idea of the article in your first sentence.
2. In your own words, give the most important details in the body of your paragraph.
3. Write the main idea in a new way in the closing sentence.

Revising Reviewing Your Writing

The following questions can help you revise your first draft.

 Improve your work.

1. Did I start with a topic sentence?
2. Did I include the most important details?
3. Did I put my body sentences in a logical order?
4. Did I restate the main idea in a closing sentence?

Editing Checking for Conventions

Check capitalization, punctuation, spelling, and grammar.

 Check your work.

1. Did I include accurate facts from the original article?
2. Have I checked for errors in punctuation, spelling, and grammar?

Writing a Research Report

Writing a research report can be a lot of fun. When you do research, you look for information about a topic that interests you. Then, when you write your report, you tell what you discovered! In this chapter, you will learn how to write a research report.

Research Report

1

Exploring Mercury
by Ugo Garrett

If you lived on Mercury, you would celebrate your birthday every three months! That's because a year on Mercury is only about three Earth months long. Scientists have discovered amazing facts about Mercury.

Mercury is the closest planet to the sun. It is one of the inner planets of our solar system. It travels around the sun in an oval orbit. Its closest distance to the sun is 47 million miles away. Its farthest distance is 70 million miles away. The sun looks three times bigger from Mercury than it does from Earth.

Mercury can be compared to Earth. It is solid like Earth, but it is only half the size of Earth. Unlike Earth, Mercury has no moon. Also, it has no atmosphere to protect it. Meteors and comets are always crashing into its surface. These crashes form many craters. There are no seasons on Mercury because it isn't tilted on its axis. During the day, it can be hotter than the hottest oven. At night, it can be colder than the coldest freezer. Mercury's temperature gets as high as 800 degrees Fahrenheit. At night, it can reach 300 degrees below zero!

Scientists are studying Mercury. In the 1970s, they sent a space probe called *Mariner 10* to orbit Mercury. Cameras on the probe sent back information. In 2004, another probe named *Messenger* was launched. It will send back information on a computer.

Today, scientists want to solve one of Mercury's mysteries. Old radar pictures show something shiny in the craters of the north and south poles. Scientists think the shiny part may be ice on the closest planet to the sun! After 2011, *Messenger* may send back more amazing facts about Mercury.

3

Bibliography

Kipp, Steven L. *Mercury.* Bridgestone Books, Mankato,

MN 2005

McIntyre, Lloyd. Interview. April 12, 2008

"Mercury (planet)." *Microsoft Encarta Online*

Encyclopedia 2008

"*Messenger* Sent to Mercury." *Scholastic News,*

October 4, 2004

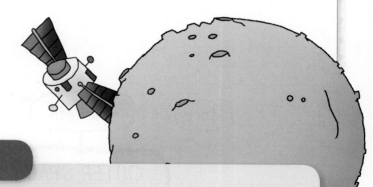

After you read . . .

- **Ideas** (1) How did Ugo get the reader's attention in the first paragraph?

- **Organization** (2) How many paragraphs are in the report?

- **Word Choice** (3) How can you tell that Ugo is excited about his topic?

Prewriting Choosing a Topic

The first step in writing your report is to choose a topic. Ugo's class used a cluster to brainstorm for topic ideas about outer space. When they finished, Ugo chose Mercury as the topic for his report.

Prewrite **Create your cluster.**

1. Write and circle your subject in the middle of a piece of paper.

2. Then write related words around the subject, as shown on the next page.

3. Keep adding words until you find a topic that interests you.

Cluster

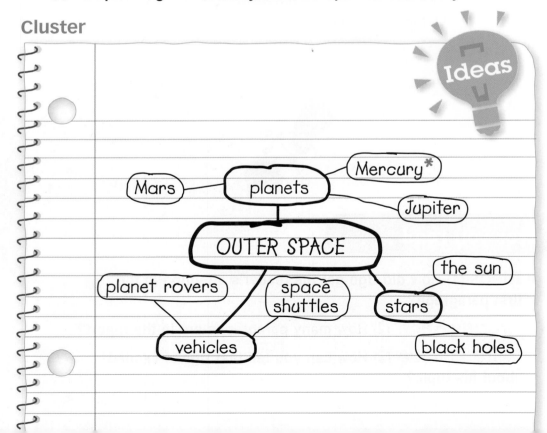

Exploring Your Topic

After choosing your topic, it's time to plan your research. Ugo made the chart on the next page. He thought about what he knew about the topic and about questions he needed to answer.

Prewrite **Plan your research.**

1. Make a chart like Ugo's.
2. In the first column, write the questions you need to answer.
3. In the second column, write facts you already know.
4. In the third column, write the names of sources where you plan to look for answers.

Questions Chart

My Questions	What I Know	Possible Sources
Where is Mercury?	Mercury is the planet closet to the sun.	our online encyclopedia
What is this planet like?		book about the solar system
	It is smaller than Earth.	
How did scientists learn about Mercury?		science magazine
		interview

Prewriting Gathering Information

A research report usually has information from two or more sources. Ugo found information in an encyclopedia, a book, and a magazine. As he found answers to his questions, he wrote them on a gathering grid. Part of Ugo's gathering grid is shown on the next page.

 Prewrite — Make a gathering grid.

1. Get a big piece of paper so you will have space to write your answers.

2. Write your research questions in the first column of your gathering grid.

3. Then list your sources across the top.

4. As you find information, fill in the spaces with answers to your questions.

Ugo's Gathering Grid

Questions

Sources

Answers

Topic Mercury	Encyclopedia: Microsoft Encarta Online	Book: Mercury by Steven L. Kipp	Magazine: "Mission to Mercury" Scholastic News
1. Where is Mercury?	inner planet 47-70 million miles from the sun	oval path around the sun 1/3 of Earth's gravity	closest to the sun sun looks three times bigger from Mercury
2. What is this planet like?	One year there equals three months on Earth. It's less than half the size of Earth.	no rings no moons no seasons no atmosphere solid	800° F days -300° F nights looks like our moon
3. How did scientists learn about Mercury?	Mariner 10 has visited Mercury. Satellites have explored the planet.		MESSENGER will orbit Mercury.

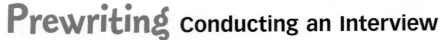

Prewriting Conducting an Interview

You may also want to ask an expert about your topic. That's called *interviewing*. You can interview someone in person, by phone, or even by e-mail.

Before the interview . . .

- Ask your teacher or a parent to help you find an expert and set up the interview.
- Write down a list of questions that need more than a "yes" or "no" answer. Have an adult review your questions.
- Leave space between your questions to write the person's answers.

During the interview . . .

- Tell the person that you will be taking notes.
- Write neatly, so you will be able to read your notes later.
- Repeat the answer to the question out loud. Then the speaker will know you understood what was said.
- Ask the person to explain anything that is confusing.

After the interview . . .

- Thank the person for the interview.
- Read over your notes. If you want, write a few sentences about what you learned during the interview.

Ugo's Interview Notes

Interviewer: Ugo Garrett   Date: April 12, 2008

Expert: Lloyd McIntyre, Astronomer
             Carlyle Planetarium

Question 1: What is Mercury like?

             – small and rocky
             – very hot
             – "It's much like Earth, but smaller
                and closer to the sun."

Question 2: Could people live there?

             – not without a special space suit
             – no atmosphere
             – meteors crash into it
             – no air

Ugo wrote down details about the interview, his questions, notes, and one exact quotation.

Prewriting Organizing Information

An outline is like a road map for writing your paper. You may not follow the map exactly, but it can guide you along the way.

1. **Give your outline a heading.**
   Ugo wrote "The Planet Mercury" as his outline heading.

2. **Write your topic sentences.**
   Each topic sentence should answer one of your research questions from your gathering grid. To write a topic sentence, just answer the question with a statement.

   Where is Mercury?
   Mercury is the closest planet to the sun.

3. **Add in your details.**
   Under each topic sentence, list details from your grid that explain the sentence or tell more about it.

 Create your outline.

1. Read over Ugo's outline on the next page.

2. Then follow the directions above to write your own outline.

3. Use the information from your gathering grid on page 319.

Ugo's Outline

The Planet Mercury

I. Mercury is the closest planet to the sun.

I. Where is Mercury?

- Mercury is one of the inner planets.
- It is 47–70 million miles from the sun.
- It travels in an oval path.
- The sun looks three times bigger from Mercury.

II. Mercury can be compared to Earth.

II. What is this planet like?

- Mercury is solid, like Earth.
- Mercury is less than half the size of Earth.
- It has long days and short years.
- It has no moons or seasons.
- Mercury can be from 800° F to 300° F below zero.
- There is no atmosphere to protect the planet.

III. How did scientists learn about Mercury?

III. Scientists are studying Mercury.

- Mariner 10 has explored the planet.
- Messenger is going to orbit the planet.

Writing **Starting Your Report**

▶ Beginning

Middle

Ending

The Beginning Paragraph

The first paragraph of your report should grab the reader's attention and tell what your report is about. You can use one of the ways listed below to get started.

Ask a question.

> Do you know which planet is closest to the sun?

OR

Make a clever comparison.

> Being first in line isn't always best. Just ask Mercury, the planet closest to the sun!

OR

Connect with the reader.

> If you lived on Mercury, you would celebrate your birthday every three months!

 Write Draft your beginning.

1. Write a beginning paragraph that grabs your reader's attention and tells what your report is about.

2. Try one of the three ways above to get started.

Ugo's Beginning Paragraph

Here is Ugo's beginning paragraph. Notice how he wrote on every other line to leave room for changes.

Beginning
· · · · · · · · · · · · · ·
Ugo makes a personal connection with the reader.

The Planet Mercury

If you lived on Mercury, you would

celebrate your birthday every three months!

That's because a year on Mercury is only

about three Earth months long. This report

will tell you more interesting facts about the

planet Mercury. Scientists have discovered

amazing facts about Mercury.

Writing Developing Your Middle Paragraphs

Beginning
▶ **Middle**
Ending

The Middle Paragraphs

Each middle paragraph covers one main idea. The paragraphs begin with a topic sentence and include sentences that give supporting details.

 Write **Develop your middle paragraphs.**

1. Write your middle paragraphs using your outline from page 323 as a guide.
2. Start each paragraph with one of your topic sentences.
3. Then add sentences that give supporting details.

Ugo's Middle Paragraphs

Middle
Each paragraph begins with a topic sentence (underlined). Supporting details (dotted lines) are added.

Mercury is the closest planet to the sun.

Mercury is one of the inner planets of our

solar system. It travels around the sun in

an oval orbit. Its closest distance to the sun

is 47 million miles away. Its farthest distance

is 70 million miles away. The sun looks three

times bigger from Mercury than it does

from Earth.

Mercury can be compared to Earth. It is solid like Earth, but it is only half the size of Earth. Mercury has no moon. Also, it has no atmosphere too protect it. Meteors and comets are always crashing into its surface. Mercury does not have rings like Saturn.

These crashes form many holes. There are no seasons on Mercury because it isn't tilted on its axis. During the day, it can be hotter than the hottest oven at night it can be colder than the coldest freezer. Mercury's tempeture gets as high as 800 degrees Fahrenheit. At night, it can reach 300 degrees below zero!

Supporting details (dotted lines) are added to each paragraph.

Supporting details are explained.

Writing Ending Your Report

Beginning

Middle

▶ Ending

The Ending Paragraph

The ending of your report should leave the reader with something to think about.

Connect

with the beginning of your report.

Share

a final thought.

Restate

the main idea of the report.

It would be great to have my birthday more often, but I wouldn't like Mercury's hot days and cold nights.

OR

Today, scientists want to solve one of Mercury's mysteries.

OR

There's so much to learn about Mercury. That's why scientists are sending more satellites to the planet.

Write Create your ending paragraph.

1. End your research paper strongly.

2. Use one of the three ideas above to leave the reader with something to think about.

Ugo's Ending Paragraph

Here is Ugo's ending paragraph. He decided to share a final thought with the reader.

Ending
Ugo ends with an interesting detail.

Today, scientists want to solve one of Mercury's mysteries. Old radar pictures show something shiny in the craters of the north and south poles. Scientists think the shiny part may be ice on the closest planet to the sun! After 2011, <u>Messenger</u> may send back more amazing facts about Mercury.

Revising Using a Response Sheet

In a peer conference, you and a classmate discuss each other's reports. The ideas you share can help both you and your partner make your reports better.

Revise **Work with a partner.**

1. Read your report to a partner.
2. Ask your partner to fill out a response sheet.
3. Then listen to your partner's report and fill out a response sheet about the writing.
4. Use your partner's ideas to improve your report.

Response Sheet

Response Sheet

Writer: _Ugo_   Responder: _Caitlyn_

Title: _"Exploring Mercury"_

What I like about your writing:

I liked the part about birthdays coming every

three months!

You include lots of details about Mercury.

I learned a lot from your report.

You sound very interested in your subject.

Questions I have about your writing:

What is a space probe?

Why is Mercury so cold at night?

Revising Improving Your Ideas

Here are several ways to improve your writing. Sometimes you may need to add details to make your ideas clearer. Other times, you may need to cut or change a detail that doesn't fit.

Revise | **Revise the first draft of your paper.**

1. Look for places to add ideas.
2. Also look for places to change or cut ideas to make your report better.

When should I add a detail?

You should **add** a detail to make part of your paper clearer or easier to understand. Use a ∧ (caret) to show where to put the new information.

When should I change a detail?

You should **change** a word if you think it would make an idea clearer. Cross out the word with a neat line and write the new word above it.

When should I cut a detail?

You should **cut** a detail that doesn't belong in your paper. Use a ↜ (delete mark) to show what you are cutting.

Revising in Action

Ugo revised his report by adding a new sentence beginning, cutting an unnecessary detail, and changing a word.

looks three times bigger from Mercury than it

does from Earth.

Add

Mercury can be compared to Earth. It

is solid like Earth, but it is only half the size

Unlike Earth,
of Earth. ∧Mercury has no moon. Also, it has

no atmosphere too protect it. Meteors and

comets are always crashing into its surface.

Cut

~~Mercury does not have rings like Saturn.~~

craters
These crashes form many ~~holes~~. There are no

Change

seasons on Mercury because it isn't tilted on

its axis. During the day, it can be hotter than

the hottest oven at night it can be colder

than the coldest freezer. Mercury's tempeture

gets as high as 800 degrees Fahrenheit. At

night, it can reach 300 degrees below zero!

Editing **Checking for** Conventions

Now that you have finished revising your report, it's time to copy it over. Check the clean copy for errors in punctuation, capitalization, spelling, and grammar.

Conventions

Punctuation
____ **1.** Did I use correct end punctuation for each sentence?
____ **2.** Did I use commas correctly in my sentences?

Capitalization
____ **3.** Did I start all my sentences with capital letters?
____ **4.** Did I capitalize all proper nouns and titles?

Spelling
____ **5.** Have I spelled all my words correctly?

Grammar
____ **6.** Did I use correct verbs (*it **flies***, not *it **fly***)?
____ **7.** Did I use the right words (*there, their, they're; to, two, too*)?

Creating a Title

- Describe the main idea: **Exploring Mercury**
- Be creative: **Mercury, Earth's Cousin**
- Use ideas from the paper: **Mercury, a Mystery Planet**

Editing in Action

Ugo found some mistakes in his revised report.

> looks three times bigger from Mercury than it
>
> does from Earth.
>
>   Mercury can be compared to Earth. It
>
> is solid like Earth, but it is only half the size
>
> of Earth. Unlike Earth, Mercury has no moon.
>
> Also, it has no atmosphere ~~too~~ to protect it.
>
> Meteors and comets are always crashing
>
> into its surface. These crashes form many
>
> craters. There are no seasons on Mercury
>
> because it isn't tilted on its axis. During the
>
> day, it can be hotter than the hottest oven.
>
> at night, it can be colder than the coldest
>
> freezer. Mercury's (tempeture) temperature gets as high as
>
> 800 degrees Fahrenheit. At night, it can reach
>
> 300 degrees below zero!

An incorrect word is replaced.

A run-on sentence is corrected with a period and a capital letter.

A spelling error is corrected.

Publishing Sharing Your Report

Good job! You have worked hard on your report. Now it's time to make a neat final copy and share it.

Make a final copy.

Use the following guidelines to prepare your report.

Put the page number in the upper right corner of each page.

Use one-inch margins on all sides.

Double-space all lines.

Indent every paragraph.

1

Exploring Mercury
by Ugo Garrett

Center your title and name.

If you lived on Mercury, you would celebrate your

birthday every three months! That's because a year on

Mercury is only about three Earth months long.

Scientists have discovered amazing facts about Mercury.

Mercury is the closest planet to the sun. It is

one of the inner planets of our solar system. It travels

around the sun in an oval orbit. Its closest distance to

the sun is 47 million miles away. Its farthest distance is

70 million miles away. The sun looks three times bigger

from Mercury than it does from Earth.

Mercury can be compared to Earth. It is solid like

Earth, but it is only half the size of Earth. Unlike Earth,

Mercury has no moon. Also, it has no atmosphere to

2

into

e are no

is. During

ight, it can

erature gets

reach 300

they sent

Cameras

ier probe

ick

s mysteries.

ers of the

t may be

ssenger

3

Reflecting on Your Writing

After you finish your report, complete each sentence below. Thinking about your work will help you grow as a writer.

Thinking About Your Writing

Name: _Ugo Garrett_

Title: _Exploring Mercury_

1. The best part of my essay is . . .

   the last paragraph. I still wonder if there's

   ice on Mercury.

2. The main thing I learned about writing a report is . . .

   that I have to carefully gather details and then

   I have to organize them before I start writing.

3. In my next report, I would like to research . . .

   sea turtles.

Creating a
Multimedia
Presentation

People can read a written report and listen to a speech. But they can do both with a multimedia presentation. A multimedia presentation is a report or speech that has been turned into a computer slide show. As you read your report aloud, the slide show illustrates each main idea.

Prewriting Selecting a Topic and Details

You can turn almost any report or speech into a multimedia presentation.

 Prewrite Choose a topic and gather details.

1. Choose a report (or speech) that you would like to share with other people.

2. Next, make a list of the main ideas in your report. Each idea will be shown on one slide in your multimedia presentation.

3. Choose pictures, sounds, and animations to go with the words in your report. Make a media grid.

Media Grid

Words from your report	Pictures or videos	Animations	Music or sounds
1. Exploring Mercury	NASA photo of Mercury		exciting music
2. On Mercury, your birthday would happen every three months.		balloons circling the planet	

Writing Making a Storyboard

Use your media grid to create a storyboard like the one below.

 Create a storyboard.

1. In each box, write the words that will appear on the screen.

2. In other colors, make notes about pictures and sounds.

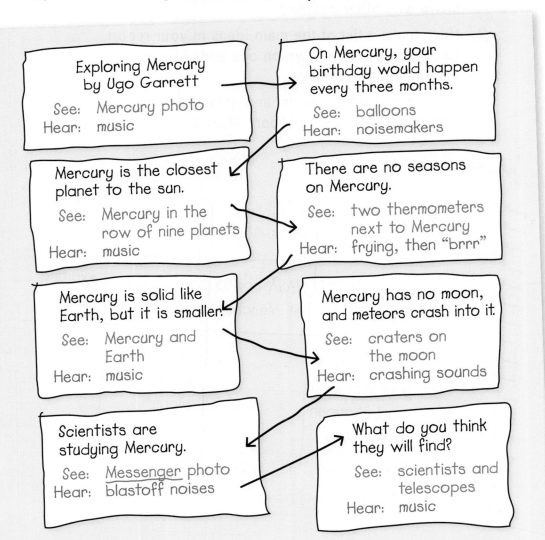

Exploring Mercury
by Ugo Garrett

See: Mercury photo
Hear: music

On Mercury, your
birthday would happen
every three months.

See: balloons
Hear: noisemakers

Mercury is the closest
planet to the sun.

See: Mercury in the
row of nine planets
Hear: music

There are no seasons
on Mercury.

See: two thermometers
next to Mercury
Hear: frying, then "brrr"

Mercury is solid like
Earth, but it is smaller.

See: Mercury and
Earth
Hear: music

Mercury has no moon,
and meteors crash into it.

See: craters on
the moon
Hear: crashing sounds

Scientists are
studying Mercury.

See: Messenger photo
Hear: blastoff noises

What do you think
they will find?

See: scientists and
telescopes
Hear: music

Creating the Slides

Use a computer program to create your slides. You can find pictures and sounds in your software program, on the Internet, or on special CD's.

 Create your slides.

1. Find pictures and sounds for each slide.
2. Design your slides so they are easy to read.

Revising Improving Your Presentation

Practice changing the slides as you speak. You may need to add, cut, or change slides to make your presentation clearer.

 Make changes in your presentation.

1. Practice giving your presentation to family and friends.
2. Listen to their suggestions for making it better.

Editing Checking for Conventions

In a multimedia presentation, even little mistakes on the screen will distract your listeners from your message. So be sure to make everything just right.

 Check your presentation for conventions.

1. Check the text on each slide for errors in punctuation, capitalization, spelling, and grammar.
2. Ask someone else to check your report, too.

The Tools of Learning

You learn in many different ways. You read and write. You speak and watch and listen. Each of these learning skills has certain steps you can follow. For example, you can follow steps to prepare a speech. You can also follow steps to find the important facts in TV programs.

The chapters in this section will help you improve your learning skills. You'll find information about everything from giving speeches to writing in a journal to taking a test.

What's Ahead

- Giving Speeches
- Writing in Journals and Learning Logs
- Viewing and Listening Skills
- Taking Tests

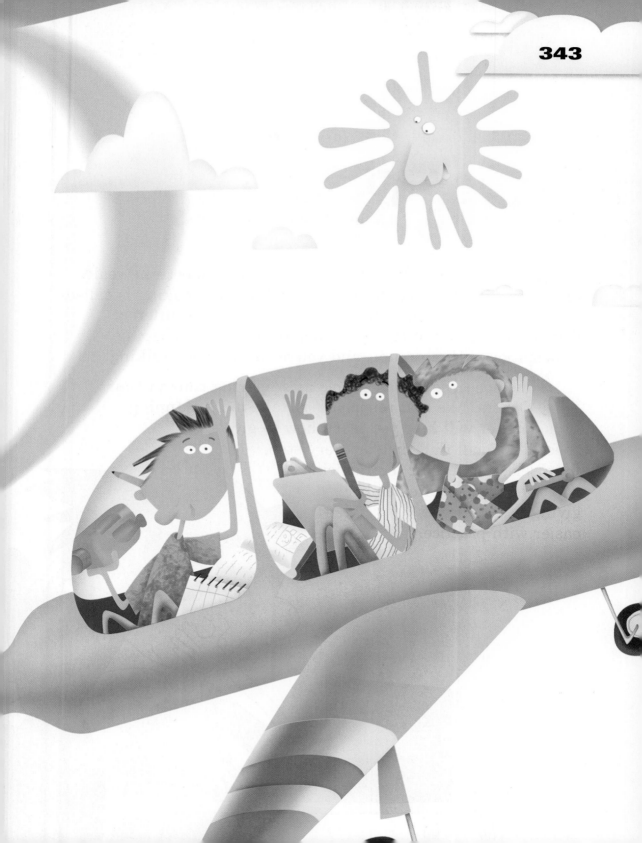

Giving Speeches

Have you ever talked with a friend about something really amazing—like Komodo dragons? This kind of speaking is called a conversation. Giving a speech or a short talk is different from that. Instead of talking to one friend, you're sharing information with a group—and you're the only one talking!

Some speeches are as simple as a sharing time in your class. Others, like oral reports, may take more planning. This chapter will help you learn how to give short speeches. You'll find tips for every step, from selecting a topic to practicing what you will say. Remember, giving speeches gets easier with practice.

Writing Your Speech
5 Put it all together.

To prepare for your speech, write down what you want to say on paper. There are two ways to do this. You can write the main ideas on note cards, or you can write your whole speech on a sheet of paper. (See page **349**.)

Note Cards

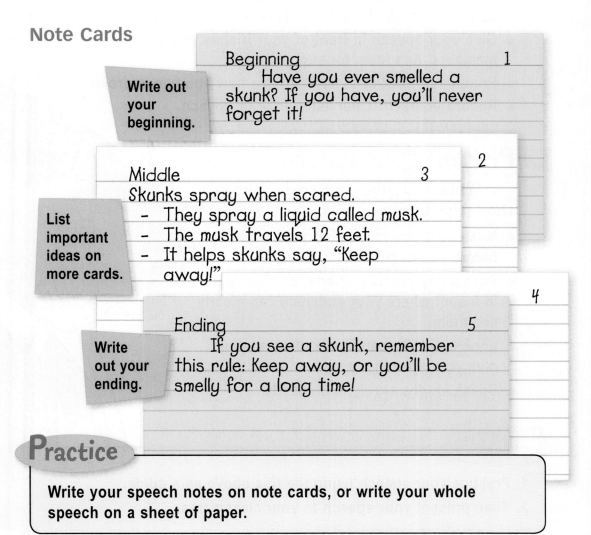

Write out your beginning.

Beginning   1
    Have you ever smelled a skunk? If you have, you'll never forget it!

2

Middle   3
Skunks spray when scared.
    - They spray a liquid called musk.
    - The musk travels 12 feet.
    - It helps skunks say, "Keep away!"

List important ideas on more cards.

4

Write out your ending.

Ending   5
    If you see a skunk, remember this rule: Keep away, or you'll be smelly for a long time!

Practice

Write your speech notes on note cards, or write your whole speech on a sheet of paper.

Giving Your Speech

6 Practice many times.

If you're using note cards, practice saying the ideas listed on each card. Do this over and over until you can repeat all of the ideas easily. If you have written out your speech word for word, practice reading it. Here are some more tips.

- **Start practicing at least two days before your speech.**
- **Give your speech in front of your friends or family members. Ask them for suggestions.**
- **Practice in front of a mirror to see how you can improve.**
- **Record yourself. Then listen to your speech.**

7 Present your speech.

When you give your speech, keep these tips in mind.

- **Make sure you have all of your notes before you begin.**
- **Put up any posters, charts, or objects in a spot where your audience can clearly see them.**
- **Look up at your audience often as you give your speech.**
- **Speak loudly, slowly, and clearly.**

Practice

1. Practice your speech using the tips above as a guide.
2. Then present your speech to your classmates.

Sample Speech

Here's a speech that shares facts about skunks.

Skunks

Name the subject in an interesting way.

Have you ever smelled a skunk? If you have, you'll never forget it!

If you've seen a skunk, it was probably a striped one. They are black with white stripes on their backs, and they're about the same size as a cat. But there are also spotted skunks. They are very small. They weigh only about one pound. When spotted skunks spray, they stand up on their front paws—like doing a handstand!

Share specific facts.

Skunks spray only when they're scared. They spray a liquid called musk. Musk smells awful and can travel about 12 feet. It's the skunk's way of saying, "Keep away!" It works, too!

When you get sprayed by a skunk, you smell really bad. And it's hard to get the smell off. Our dog scared a skunk in our yard. My mom poured tomato juice all over the dog. For some reason, tomato juice helps get rid of the skunk smell.

Repeat the most important idea.

If you see a skunk, remember this rule: Keep away, or you'll be smelly for a long time!

Writing in Journals and Learning Logs

Can you imagine a gymnast who doesn't practice? She would have a hard time doing flips, cartwheels, or spins. A writer won't do very well without practice, either. In fact, to become a good writer, you should try to write something every day!

Writing in a **personal journal** is the best way to practice. All you need is a notebook and a pencil. You can write about anything and everything. The choice is yours. Just make sure to write something every day.

Keeping a Personal Journal

A **personal journal** is your own special place to write. You can . . .

- write about whatever you see and hear around you,
- jot down things you wonder about,
- record what has happened in your life, and
- collect ideas for future writings (stories, poems, plays).

Practice

Start a personal journal notebook. Write your first entry about something you saw, heard, or did today. Be sure to date every entry you write. (See the sample below.)

Sample Journal Entry

Tim's great-grandmother told him about going to school in England. He wrote about what he learned from her in his journal.

March 10, 2009

In Great-Grandma's school, everyone had to learn to swim. They even had to pass a swimming test, and it was hard. She said that because England is an island, the teachers wanted everyone to know how to swim. I was surprised when she told me that the girls and boys had to play on different playgrounds! She had only one dress for school!

Writing in a Reading Journal

A **reading journal** is a place to write about the books and stories you read. Writing about books helps you think about them and enjoy them a second time.

Fiction Books

For a fiction book or story, you can write about . . .
- an exciting or scary part,
- something funny or sad that happens,
- your feelings about one of the characters,
- how your life is like the story, or
- a question that you have.

Practice

Write a reading journal entry for a fiction book or story that you have just read. To get started, use one of the ideas listed above.

Sample Journal Entry for Fiction

Kim read a historical fiction book, and she really liked the main character, Sarah. Kim shares her feelings in her journal.

February 25, 2009
   The Courage of Sarah Noble by Alice Dalgliesh is about being brave. Sarah's mother said, "Keep up your courage." That was before Sarah and her dad went into the wilderness to make a new home for their family. This book made me feel brave. I learned about courage from Sarah.

Nonfiction Books

For nonfiction books, you can write about . . .
- a main idea in the book,
- some surprising or unusual details, or
- your personal thoughts or questions about the topic.

Practice

Write a journal entry for a nonfiction book or article that you have just read. To get started, use one of the ideas above.

Sample Journal Entries for Nonfiction

James read a biography about a famous runner. James' journal entry shows his personal thoughts about this runner.

February 6, 2009
    I read about Jesse Owens for Black History Month. Jesse was a track star. He said, "In America, anybody can become somebody." He won four gold medals in the 1936 Olympics. He was named the World's Fastest Human. Jesse is my hero. I want to be somebody, too!

Eva read a magazine article about volcanoes. Her journal entry tells about some surprising details that she learned.

May 5, 2009
    Yesterday, I read an article about volcanoes. I learned that Earth has about 1,500 volcanoes and that Mount St. Helens might erupt again. Many people are watching Mount St. Helens to see what will happen.

Writing in a Learning Log

A **learning log** is a place to write about the subjects you are studying. Here are some tips to help you get started.

- **Divide** your log into separate parts for each subject.
- **Write** and draw about what you have learned.
- **List** questions that you have about the subject.

Practice

Write about something you have learned in math, social studies, or science. If possible, include a drawing that will help you remember.

Sample Math Entry

In math class, David is learning how to make change. His learning-log entry explains what he knows so far.

May 18, 2010
    Today in math we talked about money and how to make change. One way to make change is to do a subtraction problem to see how much change to give back. If I can make change, I can help my aunt at her garage sale.

Sample Social Studies Entry

Rosie's class visited a Native American burial ground. In her learning log, she tells what she learned and asks a question.

September 20, 2010
    Our class visited a Native American burial ground. These burial grounds were used hundreds of years ago, right in our city. What was it like to live then?

Sample Science Entry

In science, Theo's class conducted an experiment. They made a balloon rocket. In Theo's learning log, he tells about the experiment and draws a picture.

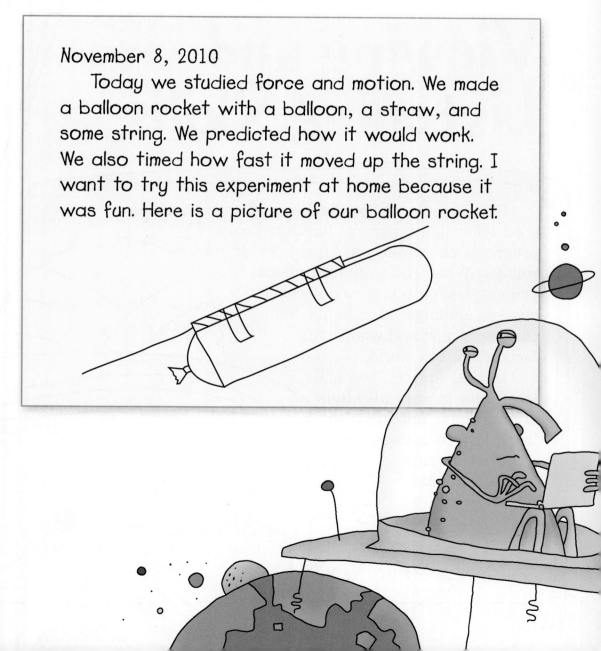

November 8, 2010

Today we studied force and motion. We made a balloon rocket with a balloon, a straw, and some string. We predicted how it would work. We also timed how fast it moved up the string. I want to try this experiment at home because it was fun. Here is a picture of our balloon rocket.

Viewing and Listening Skills

Reading a good book is fun, and so is watching a good television program. Just like books, TV programs can make you laugh, cry, or wonder. When you watch television, you can travel to faraway places or observe endangered animals. You can learn new and wonderful facts about our world.

In this chapter, you will learn how to view all kinds of programs. You will also learn how to understand commercials and how to evaluate a Web site.

Viewing News Programs

Some news programs cover news from your area. Other programs cover news from across the country and around the world. Remember these three things when you watch the news.

1 **News programs show only some of what happens each day.**
Program directors decide which events to cover.

2 **News programs share some of the details from each news story.**
Reporters don't have time to give all the details.

3 **News reporters don't always know all of the facts.**
They can only give the ones they have.

Covering the Basic Facts

A good news story will give you the basic facts. It should answer the 5 W's.

Who? zookeepers

Where? in cold northern states

What? have problems with elephants

When? during winter months

Why? There is not enough room inside to exercise the elephants.

Solution? Maybe elephants should live in warmer southern zoos.

Practice

1. Watch a news report with an adult.
2. Write down the 5 W's for one of the news stories.
3. Did the report answer all of the questions?

Viewing TV Programs

TV programs and educational videos give us information about interesting subjects. These programs can be about animals, people, places, or events. There are even programs about strange creatures like Big Foot. Here are some tips that will help you watch TV programs.

Before Viewing

- Think about what you already know about the subject.
- If your teacher gives you questions to answer, make sure you understand them.

During Viewing

- Listen for new and interesting information.
- Write down key words to help you remember important ideas.
- List any questions you have about the program.

After Viewing

- Talk about the program with someone else who has watched it.
- Answer your teacher's questions.
- Write about the program in your journal.

Practice

1. Watch a TV program and use the viewing guidelines above.
2. Then write about the program in your journal.

Responding to a TV Program

Ellie watched a nature program about zebras. She wrote about the program in her journal.

Ellie's Journal Response

October 17

"Zebras on the Open Plains"

I didn't know that the stripes on zebras protect them. The stripes help zebras hide from their enemies, especially lions. I always thought that zebras looked kind of cuddly, but they are really strong fighters. The program showed two zebra stallions fighting.

Some people in South Africa tame zebras for work. I wish they would just leave them alone. Zebras used to be all over Africa. Now many of them have been killed for food and their hides.

Zebras are part of the horse family. The colts are so cute with their long legs. The narrator of the program said that the young colts sometimes stay together in kindergartens when the mother is away. A male zebra watches the kindergartners. It sounds funny to call a zebra a kindergartner.

Understanding Commercials

Television stations show many commercials! They use different selling methods to make the products seem great. Knowing these methods can make you a smart viewer.

Selling Method	Commercial	Purpose
Bandwagon	Everybody enjoys a certain snack. You should, too!	The ad wants you to feel left out if you don't have the snack.
Famous Faces	A famous runner is shown drinking Superade.	The ad wants you to drink Superade because a famous person drinks it.
Survey Results	Someone may say, "Nine out of ten kids use Stay White Toothpaste."	The ad wants you to feel that you should use the product, too.
Name-Calling	A commercial might say that Healthbars have more protein than Supersnacks.	The ad wants you to believe one product is better than another one.

Practice

1. Watch two commercials.
2. Can you tell which selling method is used in each one?

Evaluating Web Sites

Like television, Web sites can present great information. Many sites include facts that can be checked. Other sites only share people's opinions. How can you be sure the information you find is true? Ask an adult to help you find the best Web site for the information that you need. Then follow the tips below.

Who publishes the Web site?

Find sites that end in **.org**, **.gov**, or **.edu**. These sites are published by organizations, government offices, and educational groups such as schools or universities. These sites usually list true information.

Is the Web site up to date?

Information on the Internet is constantly changing. So look at the date of each site. Be sure the information you find is the latest about your topic.

Do all the facts agree?

Search for information on more than one site. Then compare the facts given on each site. If the facts aren't the same, you may need to check more sites.

Practice

As a class, look up a topic on a few Web sites.
- Who publishes each site?
- Is each site up-to-date?
- Are the facts the same on all the sites?

Learning to Listen

You've learned how to be a smart viewer. Now you'll learn how to become a better listener. You already practice listening every day when you listen to your friends and your teacher.

Remember that you *hear* with your ears, but it takes both your ears and your brain to *listen*. The examples below compare hearing and listening.

Hearing	Listening
A friend's voice	A classmate asking a question
A teacher's voice	A teacher giving directions
Music playing	Paying attention to the words in a song

Are you listening?

Listening is one important way to learn things. The better you listen, the more you'll learn. It isn't easy, though. You have to make sure you don't daydream. You must "stay tuned" to what a speaker is saying.

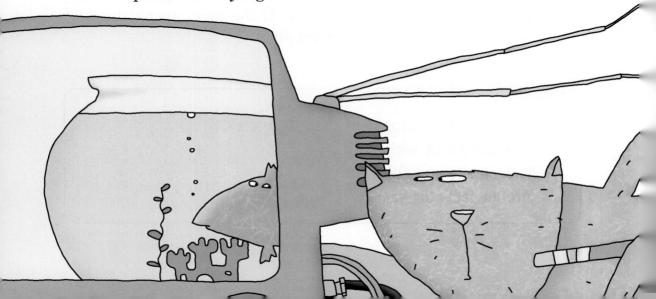

Good-Listener Checklist

✔ **Look at the speaker.**
- Don't look around.
- Keep your mind and your eyes on the speaker.
- Do not talk while the speaker is talking.

✔ **Listen with your eyes as well as your ears.**
- Watch the speaker's expressions.
- Decide how the speaker feels about the subject.

✔ **Listen for key words.**
- The *biggest* planet is Jupiter.
- The planet *closest* to the sun is Mercury.

✔ **Think about what is being said.**
- Do you understand what the speaker is saying?
- What do the speaker's ideas mean to you?

✔ **Take notes.**
- List only the most important words and ideas.
- Write down questions you may want to ask.

✔ **Ask questions.**
- When the speaker is through, ask the questions you wrote down.

Taking Tests

Tests may not be your favorite part of school. You may not like lima beans or going to the dentist, either. Now let's be positive for a moment! Tests are important. They show you what you've learned about a subject and what you still need to work on.

If you keep up with your class work, you can handle the tests. However, it is still important to get ready for each one. In this chapter, you will learn how to study for tests and how to take them.

Studying for a Test

Here are four smart things you can do to get ready for a classroom test. As you develop these good study habits, you will be ready for every test!

1 Listen well.

When your teacher starts talking about your next test, listen carefully to everything he or she says. Write down when the test will be given and what will be on it.

2 Gather all of your materials.

Collect everything you need to study. Find your study guide, your review notes or cards, and your textbook.

3 Plan study time with a partner.

If your test is a week away, ask a friend or an adult to study with you. Do this for a little while each day before the test. Don't wait until the night before the test to start studying.

4 Look over everything.

Start with your textbook. Look over the chapter page by page. Pay special attention to the headings, diagrams, and words in bold print. Answer the review questions at the end of the chapter. Then look over your study guide and review notes or cards.

Understanding Types of Tests

There are different types of tests. The five most common types are **true/false, matching, multiple-choice, fill-in-the-blank,** and **responding to a writing prompt**. You can learn more about these tests on the next five pages.

True/False Test

A **true/false test** is a list of sentences. After reading each sentence, you decide if it is *true* or *false*. Here are some tips.

- If any part of the sentence is false, the answer is false.
- If the whole sentence is true, the answer is true.

Read each sentence below carefully. Then put a "T" before each true statement and an "F" before each false statement.

_____ 1. Citizens pay taxes for goods and services.

_____ 2. Everyone votes to elect local and state officials.

_____ 3. Local government provides fire and police protection.

Answers: 1. T 2. F – "Everyone" is the key word that makes this statement false. 3. T

Tip Words like *always, never, every, all,* or *none* make true/false sentences tricky. Read them carefully.

Matching Test

A **matching test** is two lists of words or phrases. You need to find the words from each list that match, or go together. Here are some tips.

- Before making any matches, read through both lists.
- Put a mark next to each answer you use. Then it will be easier for you to see which answers you have left.

Match the words in the first column with the correct definition in the second column. Write the letter of the definition on the line.

_____ 1. taxes

_____ 2. immigrant

_____ 3. city council

a. a group of people who work with the mayor to run the city government

b. money paid for community services

c. someone who comes to live in a country in which he or she was not born

---

Answers: 1. b, 2. c, 3. a

Tip Go through the whole test and answer those questions that you are sure of first.

Multiple-Choice Test

A **multiple-choice test** is a list of statements or questions with several answer choices. Pick the best choice to complete the statement or answer the question. Here are some tips.

- Read each statement or question very carefully.
- Look for words like *not, never,* or *except.* They can change the meaning of a statement.
- Study all of the choices. Then pick the best one.

Read each statement below carefully. Then write the letter that best completes each sentence.

_____ 1. **Many city governments are led by a**

    (a) mayor   (c) president
    (b) police officer

_____ 2. **Most community workers earn pay for their services except**

    (a) police officers   (c) teachers
    (b) volunteers

_____ 3. **The state government is always located in**

    (a) the largest city   (c) the state capital city
    (b) Washington, D.C.

Answers: 1. a 2. b (The word "except" makes "volunteers" the right answer. They do not get paid for their services.) **3. c** (Although the state capital city may be the largest city, it isn't always.)

TiP If you have time, go back to any questions you may have skipped and work on them.

Fill-in-the-Blank Test

A **fill-in-the-blank test** is a list of sentences with blanks you must fill in. The test may also have a list of possible answers. You select the correct word and write it in the blank. Before you write, however, reread the sentence to check your choice. Here are some tips.

- Be sure you have studied your vocabulary words.
- Ask yourself what kind of information fits in the blank. Does the sentence need a word that answers *who? what? when?* or *where?*

Carefully read each sentence. Choose a word from the list that would make sense and complete the sentence. Write the word on the line.

communities   rural   urban

1. Places where people live, work, and play are called

    _____.

2. A city with many neighborhoods is called an

    _____ area.

Answers: 1. communities 2. urban

TiP Make sure that you have answered every question. If you have time, read over the whole test to be sure your answers sound right.

Responding to Writing Prompts

Some tests ask you to respond to a prompt. (A *prompt* gives you an idea that you have to write about.) See the prompt below.

Sample Writing Prompt

Write a paragraph that compares a one-room school to your school.

Tips for Responding

- **Read the prompt carefully.** Be sure that you know what you are supposed to do.
- **Plan your answer.** Because the sample prompt asks you to compare two things, make two lists—one about a one-room school and one about your school.

One-Room School	My School
kids of different ages	kids close to same age
no janitor	two janitors
lunch from home	lunch in cafeteria

- **Write your answer.**

    A one-room school is not like my school. A one-room school has kids of all ages in the same room. In my classroom, the kids are all close to the same age. Kids in one-room schools help sweep floors and wash blackboards. In my school, janitors do those chores. Kids in one-room schools bring their lunches from home. We have a cafeteria.

Tip Write your answers clearly and neatly.

Remembering for Tests

Idea Maps

An idea map will help you put information in order. It can help you picture and remember what you need to know for a test.

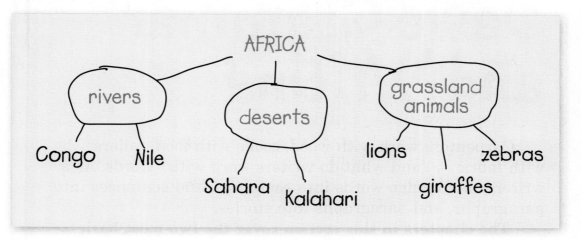

Flash Cards

Write one fact on each card. Carry the cards with you and read one whenever you have a chance. Ask family members or friends to "test" you with the cards.

Memory Tricks

A memory trick can help you remember lists of important names or information. Suppose you want to remember the names of the five Great Lakes.

You could put the names in a special order in which the first letters spell a word. For example, the word HOMES is spelled with the first letters in the names of the lakes: Huron, Ontario, Michigan, Erie, and Superior.

Basic Grammar and Writing

Carpenters work with wood, cooks with food, tailors with fabric . . . and what do writers work with? Words. As a writer, you arrange words into sentences, and sentences into paragraphs, and paragraphs into stories.

The chapters in this section cover the two most basic parts of writing—**words** and **sentences**. As you learn more about these parts, you will begin to build stronger stories, essays, and reports.

What's Ahead

- **Working with Words**
- **Writing Sentences**
- **Building Paragraphs**

Working with
Words

What if all the words in the world disappeared? You wouldn't be able to talk with your friends. You wouldn't be able to read. You wouldn't be able to write stories. Being "wordless" would be totally frustrating!

Luckily, your world is still full of words. This chapter will add to your word knowledge and help you use them more skillfully.

Mini Index

- **Using Nouns** 375
- **Using Pronouns** 379
- **Choosing Verbs** 383
- **Selecting Adjectives** 389
- **Selecting Adverbs** 391
- **Using Prepositions** 393
- **Connecting with Conjunctions** 394

Using Nouns

A **noun** names a person, a place, a thing, or an idea. **Common nouns** name a general person, place, thing, or idea. They are not capitalized. **Proper nouns** name a specific person, place, thing, or idea. They are capitalized.

	Common Nouns	**Proper Nouns**
Person	girl, president	Beth, George Washington
Place	city, theater	Spokane, Lincoln Center
Thing	horse, lake	Seabiscuit, Lake Michigan
Idea	religion	Christianity, Hinduism

Capitalize both words in proper nouns like **L**incoln **C**enter and **L**ake **M**ichigan.

Practice

On your paper, write two proper nouns for each of the following common nouns.

Example: person   Ms. James, Dr. Smith

1. building
2. country
3. river
4. car
5. holiday
6. state

Singular and Plural Nouns

A **singular noun** names one person, place, thing, or idea. A **plural noun** names more than one person, place, thing, or idea.

To form the plural of most nouns, add an -*s* to a singular noun. For nouns that end in *s, sh, ch,* or *x,* add an -*es* to make the plural form. For nouns that end in *y* (with a consonant just before the *y*), change the *y* to *i* and add -*es* to form the plural.

Singular Nouns	Plural Nouns
train, cup, star	trains, cups, stars
bus, wish, box	buses, wishes, boxes
sky, puppy	skies, puppies

Some nouns are irregular, which means they change their spelling when they become plural. For example, **child** becomes **children**.

Practice

Write the plural form for each of the following singular nouns. Use each plural noun in a sentence.

Example: beach
         beaches   The beaches were crowded.

1. cow

2. fox

3. body

4. guess

5. pencil

6. lunch

7. uncle

8. library

Possessive Nouns

A **possessive noun** shows ownership. Singular nouns are usually made possessive by adding an apostrophe and -*s*. In most cases, a plural noun that ends in *s* just needs an apostrophe to make it possessive.

Singular Noun	Singular Possessive	Plural Noun	Plural Possessive
cup	cup's handle	cups	cups' handles
lion	lion's mane	lions	lions' manes

If the plural noun does not end in **s**, make it possessive by adding an apostrophe and an **-s—children's**.

Practice

Rewrite each sentence below. In your new sentence, turn the underlined noun into a possessive noun.

Example: The books belonging to the <u>girls</u> are here.

The girls' books are here.

1. The fur on <u>Henry</u> is shiny.
2. The erasers on the <u>pencils</u> are worn down.
3. The information in that <u>book</u> is helpful.
4. The screen on the <u>computer</u> needs cleaning.
5. The petals on the <u>flowers</u> are very soft.

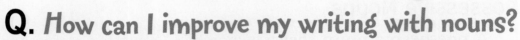

Q. How can I improve my writing with nouns?

A. You can improve your writing by using specific nouns.
A **specific noun** names a particular person, place, thing,
or idea. Using specific nouns will make your writing more
interesting than using general nouns will.

	General Nouns	Specific Nouns
Person	performer	juggler, Jamie Foxx
Place	park	ball park, Wrigley Field
Thing	apple	crab apple, Macintosh
Idea	celebration	birthday, Lincoln's birthday

Practice

Number your paper from 1 to 10. For each of the following general
nouns, write a specific noun.

Example: car   convertible

1. book
2. bread
3. mountain
4. city
5. athlete

6. song
7. street
8. holiday
9. car
10. country

Write **NOW**   On your own paper, write some sentences about your favorite
meal. Use at least four specific nouns in your writing, and
underline them.

Using Pronouns

A **pronoun** is a word that takes the place of a noun. **Personal pronouns** are the most common type of pronoun. Some personal pronouns are used as subjects: *I, you, he, she, it, we, they.* Some are used as objects: *me, you, him, her, it, us, them.*

■ A **subject pronoun** is used as the subject of a sentence.

> She wrapped a ribbon around the big tree.
> They called a reporter.

■ An **object pronoun** is used after an action verb or in a prepositional phrase.

> Suki threw me the ball. (after an action verb)
> My grandma plays with us. (in a prepositional phrase)

Remember that **I** is a subject pronoun and is always capitalized, while **me** is an object pronoun and is not capitalized.

Practice

Number your paper from 1 to 5. For each of the following sentences, write the pronoun and tell whether it is a subject pronoun (SP) or an object pronoun (OP).

Example: I love apples. I, SP

1. We pick apples during the fall.
2. Many people eat them for snacks.
3. Dad takes an apple to work with him.
4. Mom makes us apple pie.
5. She uses Cortland apples.

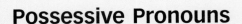

Possessive Pronouns

Possessive pronouns show ownership. They can be either singular or plural. (Possessive pronouns act as adjectives when they come before a noun.)

Billy found my red hat.
The red hat is mine.

Yes, that's our art project.
That art project is ours.

Singular Possessive Pronouns	Plural Possessive Pronouns
my, mine, his, her, hers, its, your, yours	our, ours, your, yours, their, theirs

Always check to make sure you use the correct singular or plural possessive pronoun.

Practice

Number your paper from 1 to 10. Skip one or two lines between each number. Then write a sentence for each possessive pronoun listed below.

Example: their
The Smiths keep their car clean.

1. my
2. her
3. your
4. mine
5. his
6. yours
7. ours
8. theirs
9. our
10. its

Q. *How can I use pronouns correctly?*

A. You can check for pronoun-antecedent agreement. The **antecedent** of a pronoun is the noun that it refers to. If the antecedent is singular, the pronoun must be singular. If the antecedent is plural, the pronoun must be plural.

antecedent   pronoun

The big dog broke its leash.

(The pronoun *its* and the antecedent *dog* are both singular.)

antecedent   pronoun

The students walked to their classrooms.

(The pronoun *their* and the antecedent *students* are both plural.)

Practice

For each of the following sentences, write the correct pronoun from the two in parentheses. Also name the noun it refers to (the antecedent).

Example:
Maria and *(her, their)* friends wanted to go waterskiing.
  her, Maria

1. Before Maria left, *(she, they)* finished her chores.
2. Maria's older brother said *(he, they)* would take Maria.
3. When Maria and her brother got into the car, *(she, they)* talked about waterskiing.
4. Maria's brother and *(his, their)* best friend ski often.
5. The father of one of Maria's friends has *(his, their)* own boat.

Plural Pronouns

Plural pronouns refer to more than one person or thing. Some plural pronouns are used as subject pronouns. Other plural pronouns are used as object pronouns. It is important to know when to use each type of pronoun.

Plural Subject Pronouns	Plural Object Pronouns
we, you, they	us, you, them

- When you use the pronouns *we* and *us*, you are including yourself.
- When you use the pronoun *you*, you are writing about an audience.
- When you use the pronouns *they* and *them*, you are writing about others.

Practice

Rewrite the sentences below. Replace the underlined words with the correct plural pronoun *(we, they, us, them)*.

Example: Grandma took <u>Andy and me</u> to the circus.
Grandma took us to the circus.

1. <u>Andy and I</u> shared a box of popcorn.
2. <u>The boys</u> sat in the front row.
3. A clown threw confetti at <u>Trent and Jake</u>.
4. <u>Grandma, Andy, and I</u> laughed at the clowns.
5. The clown with big shoes shot water at <u>Andy and me</u> from a flower in his hat.

Choosing Verbs

A **verb** is a word that usually tells what is happening. It is the main word in the predicate. There are three types of verbs: **action verbs**, **helping verbs**, and **linking verbs**.

Action Verbs

An **action verb** tells what the subject is doing. If you use specific action verbs, your sentences are more fun to read.

General Action Verbs	Specific Action Verbs
walked	skipped, strolled, pranced
talks	tattles, chatters, whispers
fell	tripped, stumbled, crashed
laugh	chuckle, giggle, hoot

Practice

Rewrite each of the sentences below. Replace the underlined general verb with a more specific one from the list of "Specific Action Verbs" above.

Example: The poodle <u>walked</u> around the show ring.
The poodle pranced around the show ring.

1. The happy child <u>walked</u> down the sidewalk.
2. My parrot <u>talks</u> all the time!
3. Dad <u>fell</u> over the roller skate.
4. Little kids <u>laugh</u> a lot.

Linking Verbs

A **linking verb** links, or connects, a subject to a noun or to an adjective in the predicate.

She is the best math student. (The linking verb *is* links the subject *she* to the noun *student*.)

Linking Verbs
am, is, are, was, were, being, been, appear, become, feel, grow, look, remain, seem, smell, sound, taste

TiP To tell if a word is used as a linking verb or an action verb, change the verb to *is, am,* or *are*. If the sentence still makes sense, the verb is a linking verb.

That soup tastes sour. (*That soup is sour* still makes sense, so *tastes* is a linking verb in this sentence.)

He tastes the soup. (*He is the soup* does not make sense, so *tastes* is an action verb in this sentence.)

Practice

Number your paper from 1 to 4. Then write down the verb from each sentence and write "A" for action verb or "L" for linking verb.

Example: Pablo seemed very excited.
        seemed, L

1. Lightning struck the big tree in our yard.

2. He was happy about the gift.

3. Boats sailed across the quiet lake.

4. Their school was really big.

Helping Verbs

A **helping verb** comes before a main verb. This extra verb helps *to show time* or *to state an action*. Some sentences can have more than one helping verb.

Common Helping Verbs					
has	will	do	may	am	was
have	could	did	can	is	were
had	should	does		are	been
	would				

Ms. Daniels ⟨has⟩ organized a kickball tournament.

(*Has* is the helping verb, and *organized* is the main verb.)

Our team ⟨should have⟩ won the tournament.

(*Should* and *have* are helping verbs, and *won* is the main verb.)

Practice

Copy the following sentences on your own paper. Then circle the helping verbs and underline the main verbs twice. (One of the sentences has more than one helping verb.)

Example: Each class could enter one or two teams.

Each class ⟨could⟩ enter one or two teams.

1. Our team did win our first two games.
2. We had scored seven runs in the second inning.
3. My friend's team should have won their game, too.
4. Pat's team could beat every other team.
5. We will win the next tournament.

Q. How can I show time in my writing?

A. You can show time by using the proper verb tense. The **tense** of a verb tells when the action takes place. The tense of a verb may be either **present**, **past**, or **future**.

- **Present tense verbs** state an action that is happening now or continues happening.

    My bicycle squeaks.

    I swim in the lake every day.

- **Past tense verbs** state an action that happened in the past and is over.

    My bicycle squeaked yesterday.

    Last week, I swam in the pool.

Verbs like *squeak* form the past tense by adding *-ed*. They are called **regular verbs**. Other verbs, like *swim*, change their spelling to form the past tense. These types of verbs are called **irregular verbs**. (See page 542.)

Practice

Number your paper from 1 to 4. For each sentence below, write the verb. Then write "PR" for present tense or "Past" for past tense.

Example: My Aunt Alicia tells me stories about my family.
tells, PR

1. My mother and my aunt played softball.
2. They traveled to many tournaments.
3. My grandmother still keeps the trophies.
4. Now I know something about my mother's life.

■ **Future tense verbs** state an action that will take place at a later time, or in the future.

> My bicycle will squeak until I get it fixed.
> I will swim in the lake next year.

If the present tense verb is singular and ends in **s**, the **s** is dropped from the main verb in the future tense. He **talks**. He **will talk**.

Practice

Number your paper from 1 to 5. Rewrite the following sentences, changing the underlined present tense verbs to future tense. Underline the new verb.

Example: We <u>travel</u> on the train.
We <u>will travel</u> on the train.

1. It <u>zooms</u> through the city.
2. I <u>watch</u> the buildings change.
3. The scenery <u>changes</u> to rolling hills.
4. Juni <u>rides</u> with me.
5. We <u>have</u> a lot of fun on the train.

Write NOW Write three sentences about riding a bicycle.
1. Write one sentence using a present tense verb.
2. Write one sentence using a past tense verb.
3. Write a third sentence using a future tense verb.

Q. How can I use verbs correctly?

A. You can check carefully for subject-verb agreement. All verbs must agree in number with their subjects. If the subject in a sentence is singular, the verb must be singular. If the subject is plural, the verb must be plural.

Freddi hikes with the outdoor club.

(The subject *Freddi* and the verb *hikes* are both singular.)

Many students hike with the outdoor club.

(The subject *students* and the verb *hike* are both plural.)

Freddi and Jeff love hiking. (The compound subject *Freddi* and *Jeff* and the verb *love* are both plural.)

 Tip Singular verbs often end in **s**.
Plural verbs usually do not end in **s**.

Practice

Number your paper from 1 to 5. For each sentence below, write the verb in parentheses that agrees with the subject. Then write "S" if the subject and verb are singular and "P" if they are plural.

Example: Good shoes *(makes, make)* hiking much easier.
    make, P

1. Our first hike *(is, are)* planned for Saturday.
2. We *(needs, need)* our parents' permission to go.
3. The bus *(leaves, leave)* at 8:00 a.m.
4. The handout *(says, say)* that we can wear shorts.
5. Parents and teachers *(has, have)* snacks for us.

Selecting Adjectives

An **adjective** is a word that describes a noun. Adjectives answer four questions about nouns: *what kind? how much? how many?* and *which one?*

What kind?	large dog, American flag, yellow birds
How much?	some salt, more water, less snow
How many?	three steps, fewer questions, one basket
Which one?	that book, this music, those geese

TiP The words **a, an,** and **the** are special adjectives called articles.

Practice

On your own paper, write the adjectives in each sentence below, but do not list the articles *a, an, or the.* (The number in parentheses tells you how many adjectives you should find.)

Example: A desert is a hot, empty region. *(2)*
hot   empty

1. Deserts have a wide variety of prickly plants. *(2)*

2. Most deserts are in warm climates. *(2)*

3. African deserts are home to many herders who wear long robes. *(3)*

4. Sand dunes take many shapes and are formed by high winds. *(3)*

5. The Bedouin people live in desert tribes. *(2)*

Q. How can I use adjectives correctly?

A. You can check the form of each adjective you use. Adjectives have three forms: *positive* (used to describe one thing), *comparative* (used to compare two things), and *superlative* (used to compare three or more things).

Single-Syllable Adjectives

When the adjective is just one syllable, add *-er* to make the comparative form. Add *-est* to make the superlative form.

Positive: Our dog is small.

Comparative: Our dog is smaller than your dog is.

Superlative: Our dog is the smallest one in the neighborhood.

Multi-Syllable Adjectives

When the adjective is two or more syllables, you usually use the word *more* (or *less*) to make the comparative form. Use *most* (or *least*) to make the superlative from.

Positive: Tonight's sunset is beautiful.

Comparative: Tonight's sunset is more beautiful than yesterday's sunset was.

Superlative: That is the most beautiful sunset ever.

Practice

Write the comparative and superlative forms for each adjective below. (Remember to count the syllables in each word first.)

Example: green
greener, greenest

1. clean   **2.** enjoyable   **3.** dull   **4.** old   **5.** afraid

Selecting Adverbs

A word that describes a verb is an **adverb**.

Lori sang softly during the concert.

(The adverb *softly* describes how Lori *sang*.)

Marcus loudly bangs his drums.

(The adverb *loudly* describes how Marcus *bangs* his drums.)

Kinds of Adverbs

■ **Adverbs of time** tell *when* or *how often*.

The kite club met yesterday.

(The adverb *yesterday* tells *when* the club met.)

Mr. Lee always arrives on time.

(The adverb *always* tells *how often* he arrives on time.)

■ **Adverbs of place** tell *where* something happens.

We held our meeting outside.

(The adverb *outside* tells *where* the meeting was held.)

■ **Adverbs of manner** tell *how* something is done.

Andy worked carefully on his kite.

(The adverb *carefully* tells *how* Andy worked.)

Practice

1. Write two sentences using adverbs that tell <u>when</u> or <u>how often</u> an action is done.

2. Write two sentences using adverbs that tell <u>where</u> an action is done.

3. Write two sentences using adverbs that tell <u>how</u> an action is done.

Q. How can I improve my writing with adverbs?

A. You can use adverbs to make your writing more specific. Adverbs will make your sentences clearer and more interesting to read. In the following example, notice how specific adverbs make the sentence clearer and more interesting.

> Maggie trapped the frog under the pail.
> Maggie calmly trapped the frog under the pail.
> Maggie carefully trapped the frog under the pail.

Tip Sometimes the adverb can come after the verb.

She spoke softly to her little prince.

Practice

Rewrite each sentence below, adding one of the following adverbs:

> slowly   easily   politely   poorly   calmly   quickly

Example:
Meg walked up the driveway, bouncing a ball.
Meg walked slowly up the driveway, bouncing a ball.

1. She had played yesterday.

2. Up ahead, her brother stood with his arms crossed.

3. He asked her to play one-on-one.

4. He scored two points.

5. Meg made the next three baskets.

Using Prepositions

A **preposition** is a word that often shows direction or position. It introduces a **prepositional phrase**, which begins with a preposition and ends with the nearest noun or pronoun.

Common Prepositions								
in	at	to	for	with	over	after	before
on	by	up	of	near	from	about	through

The bike in the yard needs a new tire.
(The preposition *in* introduces the prepositional phrase *in the yard*.)

We hid behind the garage.
(The preposition *behind* introduces the prepositional phrase *behind the garage*.)

Practice

On your own paper, identify the prepositional phrase in each of the following sentences. (One sentence has two of them.)

Example:
Mr. Cosford has a huge train set in his basement.
in his basement

1. He always works on the train set.
2. One part of the set includes a little town.
3. Another part includes a big bridge over a river.
4. He is now making a tunnel through a mountain.
5. Mr. Cosford worked for a railroad company, so he knows a lot about trains.

Connecting with Conjunctions

A **conjunction** connects words or groups of words. Coordinating conjunctions like *and, but, so,* and *or* are used to connect words, phrases, and simple sentences.

Coordinating Conjunctions
and   but   or   so   yet

Connecting a Series of Words

At the zoo, we saw <u>elephants</u>, <u>seals</u>, and <u>tigers</u>.

Connecting Two Phrases

The lions eat <u>in the morning</u> or <u>at night</u>.

Connecting Two Simple Sentences

<u>Sally was stung by a bee</u>, but <u>she didn't make a big fuss.</u>

Practice

On your own paper, write each of the following sentences. First, circle the conjunction in each sentence. Then underline the words, phrases, or simple sentences that the conjunction connects.

Example:
Are grizzly bears or black bears found in our state?
Are <u>grizzly bears</u> (or) <u>black bears</u> found in our state?

1. Seals and otters are fun to watch.
2. A buffalo has a huge head, but the rest of its body seems small.
3. The hippos rest in the river or on the grassy bank.
4. Hyenas look very odd, and they do not really laugh.

Q. How can I use conjunctions in my writing?

A. You can use conjunctions to combine your ideas. For example, you can use conjunctions like *and, but,* and *or* to combine two simple sentences into a compound sentence. A **compound sentence** is two simple sentences joined by a comma and a conjunction.

Two Simple Sentences

> Jack went to the store. Sam stayed home.

One Compound Sentence

> Jack went to the store, but Sam stayed home.

Practice

On your own paper, combine each set of short sentences into a compound sentence. (Use the conjunction in parentheses.)

Example:
Mr. Snyder blew his whistle. He started practice. *(and)*
Mr. Snyder blew his whistle, and he started practice.

1. Most of us took batting practice. Two players practiced pitching. *(but)*

2. Next, the infielders caught ground balls. The outfielders caught fly balls. *(and)*

3. Then Mr. Snyder blew his whistle again. We had to line up for base running. *(and)*

4. At the end of practice, we could play a game. We could have a hitting contest. *(or)*

Writing
Sentences

Does "I spinach" make sense? No, something is missing. Does "I like spinach" sound better? It should (even if you don't like spinach). The second example states a complete thought.

A group of words that states a complete thought is called a **sentence**. You use sentences when you talk to other people. You also use them in your writing and read them in your favorite stories and books. In other words, you use sentences all the time.

This section will show you what you need to know about sentences.

Mini Index

- **Writing Complete Sentences** 397
- **Fixing Sentence Problems** 403
- **Improving Sentence Style** 407
- **Preparing for Tests** 414

Writing Complete Sentences

Q. How can I write clear sentences?

A. You can write clear sentences by making sure each sentence expresses a complete thought. A sentence begins with a capital letter and ends with a period, a question mark, or an exclamation point.

travel	trucks	the	on	freeway

The group of words above does not make sense. But these same words can be arranged into a sentence that does express a complete thought.

Trucks	travel	on	the	freeway.

Practice

On your own paper, rearrange each group of words below so that it is a clear sentence. Remember to capitalize and punctuate your sentences.

Example: food   our   from   places   many   comes
Our food comes from many places.

1. Florida   our   from   come   oranges
2. potatoes   come   some   Idaho   from
3. lakes   and   oceans   fish   caught   are   in
4. are   many   farms   on   raised   vegetables   huge
5. countries   sugar   and   tea   other   produce

Write NOW Write at least five sentences about your favorite meal. Remember: A sentence starts with a capital letter and ends with a period, a question mark, or an exclamation point.

Complete Subjects

All sentences have a subject and a predicate (verb). The **subject** tells who or what the sentence is about. The **complete subject** may be just one word or more than one word.

Ronnie scored a touchdown.
(*Ronnie* is the complete subject.)

Many fans cheered loudly.
(**Many fans** is the complete subject.)

The team's new kicker made the extra point.
(*The team's new kicker* is the complete subject.)

The subject usually comes at the beginning of a sentence.

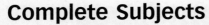**Practice**

Write the sentences below on your own paper. Then underline the complete subject in each one.

Example:
The crowd watched the football game in the rain.
The crowd watched the football game in the rain.

1. A marching band performed at halftime.
2. Our team's uniforms are red and white.
3. My favorite player is the quarterback.
4. The linemen block for the quarterback.
5. Long passes are fun to watch.

Complete Predicates

The **predicate** includes the verb and tells something about the subject or what it does. The predicate can also tell what is being done to the subject. The **complete predicate** may be just one word, or it may be several words.

Maria celebrated.

(*Celebrated* is the verb and the complete predicate.)

We ate cold slices of watermelon.

(*Ate cold slices of watermelon* is the complete predicate.)

Her party was so much fun.

(*Was so much fun* is the complete predicate.)

The complete predicate contains the verb and all the words that describe it or complete it.

Practice

Write the sentences below on your own paper. Then underline the complete predicate in each sentence.

Example:
Maria was excited about her party.
Maria <u>was excited about her party.</u>

1. Her friends arrived at noon.

2. They played shadow tag.

3. Maria's older sister organized many other games.

4. Her dad made hamburgers.

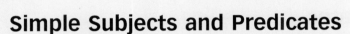

Simple Subjects and Predicates

The **simple subject** is the subject without the words that describe it. The **simple predicate** is the verb without the words that modify it.

Our art <u>teacher</u> draws funny cartoons.
(*Our art teacher* is the complete subject, and *teacher* is the simple subject.)

Our chorus teacher <u>sings</u> very well.
(*Sings very well* is the complete predicate, and *sings* is the simple predicate, or verb.)

Practice

Copy sentences 1 to 5 on your own paper. Then underline the simple subjects with one line and the simple predicates with two lines.

Example:
Our teacher announced the date of our art show.
Our <u>teacher</u> <u>announced</u> the date of our art show.

1. The parents received invitations.
2. My mom marked the date on the calendar.
3. We painted pictures for weeks.
4. Every student was ready on the big day.
5. My best friend wished me good luck.

Write NOW Write three sentences about a special program at your school. Then underline the simple subjects with one line and the simple predicates with two lines.

Compound Subjects and Predicates

A **compound subject** has two or more simple subjects. A **compound predicate** has two or more simple verbs.

Lions and tigers do not look alike.
(*Lions* and *tigers* make up the compound subject.)

Tigers move with speed and attack with power.
(*Move* and *attack* make up the compound predicate.)

> Compound subjects and predicates are usually joined by **and, but,** or **or.**

Practice

Copy sentences 1 to 5 on your own paper. Then underline the simple subjects with one line and the simple predicates with two lines. (Watch for compound subjects and compound predicates.)

Example:
Lions and tigers are huge.
Lions and tigers are huge.

1. Some tigers grow 10 feet long and weigh 500 pounds.
2. Tigers eat deer, wild boars, and even cattle.
3. Tigers hunt alone at night.
4. Lions and tigers in the wild live about 15 years.
5. Wild lions live only in Africa and India.

Write NOW   Write three sentences about an animal you find interesting. Try to use a compound subject or a compound predicate in at least one of your sentences.

Capitalization and Punctuation

Every sentence should begin with a capital letter. A sentence that tells something is called a **statement**. It should end with a period. A sentence that asks something is called a **question**. It should end with a question mark.

Statements

Popcorn is a popular snack.
It has an interesting history.

Questions

Do you like popcorn?
How do you make it?

Practice

Write sentences 1 to 5 on your own paper. Begin each sentence with a capital letter and end it with a period or a question mark.

Example:
native americans made popcorn a long time ago
Native Americans made popcorn a long time ago.

1. they ate popcorn and used it for necklaces
2. where is popcorn grown
3. popcorn is grown in many Midwestern states
4. why does popcorn pop
5. heat causes the kernels to pop

Write **NOW** Write three sentences about your favorite snack. At least one of your sentences should ask a question. Remember to use correct capitalization and punctuation.

Fixing Sentence Problems

Q. *How can I write correct sentences?*

A. You can learn to avoid fragments and other sentence errors. A **sentence fragment** is a group of words that looks like a sentence but isn't. It is missing a subject, a verb, or both.

Fragment	Sentence
My yo-yo smoothly. (The verb is missing.)	My yo-yo spins smoothly. (A verb is added.)
Were first made in China. (The subject is missing.)	Yo-yos were first made in China. (A subject is added.)
From the Philippines. (The subject and the verb are missing.)	Modern yo-yos come from the Philippines. (A subject and a verb are added.)

Practice

Number your paper from 1 to 5. Write "S" for each complete sentence and "F" for each fragment below. Rewrite each fragment to make it a complete sentence.

Example:
One of the oldest toys.
F, The yo-yo is one of the oldest toys.

1. Dolls are as old as yo-yos.
2. Made of clay.
3. Yo-yos in India looked like little boxes.
4. Went only up and down.

Write NOW Write five sentences about your favorite toy. Make sure that each sentence has a subject and a predicate.

Run-On Sentences

A **run-on sentence** is two sentences that run together. To correct this problem, add end punctuation and a capital letter between the two sentences.

Run-On Sentence

> Sarah and I rode our bikes to school we left my house at 7:30. (Two sentences run together.)

Corrected

> Sarah and I rode our bikes to school. We left my house at 7:30. (A period ends the first sentence. The capital **W** begins the second sentence.)

Practice

On your own paper, rewrite the following run-on sentences. Add end punctuation and a capital letter between the two sentences.

Example:

Most of our trip was easy we had only one big hill to go over.

Most of our trip was easy. We had only one big hill to go over.

1. Sarah's bike is red my bike is yellow.
2. We took a shortcut through the park I liked going that way.
3. Sarah always rides her bike to school I was doing it for the first time.
4. We talked all along the way the trip went really fast.
5. We parked our bikes in the bike rack I made sure to use my lock.

Rambling Sentences

A **rambling sentence** is one that goes on and on. A writer may use the word *and* too many times in a rambling sentence. To correct this problem, the writer can drop the *and* whenever possible. Then add capital letters, commas (if needed), and end punctuation to make new sentences.

Rambling Sentence

> Josie and I went to our Girl Scout meeting and we learned about making bead necklaces and each of us made one and we also planned our summer camping trip. (The word *and* is used too often.)

Corrected

> Josie and I went to our Girl Scout meeting. We learned about making bead necklaces, and each of us made one. We also planned our summer camping trip. (The word *and* is dropped in two places. Then capital letters, periods, and a comma are added to make three sentences.)

Practice

On your own paper, turn the rambling sentence below into shorter sentences. (You will need to drop the word "and" two or three times. Also, use capital letters, periods, and commas correctly.)

On rainy days, we don't have outside recess and everyone has to do things in the room and we play board games and we also build things with construction sets.

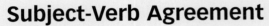

Subject-Verb Agreement

The subject and the verb must agree in a sentence. If the subject is singular, the verb must be singular, too. If the subject is plural, the verb must be plural, too.

Sentences with Singular Subjects and Verbs

Ms. Peterson writes funny stories.

She reads them to us.

Sentences with Plural Subjects and Verbs

My older sisters write a lot of notes.

They talk on the phone, too.

> Remember that singular means **one**, and plural means **more than one**.

Practice

Number your paper from 1 to 5. For each sentence below, select the verb in parentheses that agrees with the subject. Write that verb on your paper.

Example: Mr. Hayes (*play, plays*) softball with us.

plays

1. Mr. Hayes (*pitch, pitches*) to us.
2. Travis usually (*hit, hits*) the ball on the ground.
3. Sam and Mike (*hit, hits*) long fly balls.
4. My best friends (*like, likes*) running the bases.
5. Our games (*is, are*) four innings long.

Write **NOW** Write three sentences about one of your favorite games. Be sure that the subject and the verb agree in each of your sentences.

Improving Sentence Style

Q. How can I write better sentences?

A. There are four ways to improve the sentences that you use in your paragraphs, essays, and stories.

1 Combine short sentences.

2 Use compound sentences.

3 Use different kinds of sentences.

4 Model sentences written by other writers.

Basic Sentences

My friends and I went bowling. We went on Saturday. I was throwing gutter balls. In the first five frames my score was 26. I got better. I had only one more gutter ball. I got one spare. My score was 70.

Improved Sentences

On Saturday morning, my friends and I went bowling. In the first five frames, I threw some gutter balls. My score was only 26. Then I started to do better. I had only one more gutter ball, and I even got one spare. One of my friends asked me, "How did you do that?" By the end of the game, my score was 70!

 Write NOW Write four or five sentences about something that you really like to do. Be sure that your sentences are fun to read.

Combine Sentences with Key Words or Words in a Series

You can combine short sentences using a **key word** or a **series of words**.

Short Sentences

The butterfly landed on me. It was a monarch butterfly.

Combined with a Key Word

The monarch butterfly landed on me.

Short Sentences

Monarchs have beautiful black wings. They also have white and orange on their wings.

Combined with Words in a Series

Monarchs have beautiful black, white, and orange wings.

Practice

On your own paper, combine each set of short sentences below. Use the examples above as a guide.

Example:

Butterfly wings have scales. The scales are powdery.
Butterfly wings have powdery scales.

1. Butterflies live in rain forests. They also live in woodlands and fields.

2. Most butterflies have thin bodies. The bodies are hairless.

3. A butterfly's body has a head. It also has a thorax and an abdomen.

4. Butterflies have two antennae. The antennae are slender.

Combine Sentences with Compound Subjects and Predicates

You can combine two sentences by making a **compound subject** or a **compound predicate**.

Short Sentences

Stuart speaks Spanish. Olivia speaks Spanish.

Combined with a Compound Subject

Stuart and Olivia speak Spanish.

 Tip You may need to change a singular verb to a plural verb for a compound subject.

Short Sentences

Anna plays the clarinet. She sings in the chorus.

Combined with a Compound Predicate

Anna plays the clarinet and sings in the chorus.

Practice

Combine each of the sentence pairs below. Use a compound subject or a compound predicate to make your new sentence.

Example:

Julia is in gymnastics. Missy is in gymnastics, too.
Julia and Missy are in gymnastics.

1. Kyle swims on Mondays. He plays soccer on Tuesdays.
2. Ruby loves to read. Sheri also loves to read.
3. Luke reads comic books. He draws superheroes.
4. Erin joined the computer club. Her brother also joined.

Use Compound Sentences

A **compound sentence** is two or more simple sentences joined by a comma and a conjunction *(and, but, or)*.

Two Sentences

Most spiders spin webs. They use their webs to catch food.

One Compound Sentence

Most spiders spin webs, and they use their webs to catch food.

Practice

Combine each of the sentence pairs below by making a compound sentence. (Use the conjunction in parentheses.)

Example:
Some spiders live in buildings. Many other spiders live outside. *(but)*

Some spiders live in buildings, but many other spiders live outside.

1. Many people call spiders insects. Scientists call them arachnids. *(but)*

2. A spider's eyes are on top of its head. The eyes vary in number and size. *(and)*

3. Spiders cannot chew food. They eat only liquids. *(and)*

4. A spider can drop from its web. It can hang from a dragline in the air. *(or)*

5. Jumping spiders have short legs. They can jump very far. *(but)*

Use Different Kinds of Sentences

You can add variety to your writing by using different **kinds of sentences**.

- **Declarative** sentences make a statement.

    Mercury is the closet planet to the sun.

- **Interrogative** sentences ask a direct question.

    What other planets can you name?

- **Imperative** sentences give a command.

    Name the largest planet.

- **Exclamatory** sentences show strong emotion or surprise.

    Jupiter has more than 60 moons!

Practice

On your paper, label each sentence as "D" for declarative, "Int" for interrogative, "Imp" for imperative, or "Ex" for exclamatory. Add the correct end punctuation mark for each sentence.

Example:
Did you know that Venus is the planet closest to Earth
Int, ?

1. The solar system is amazing
2. Scientists are still studying the planets
3. Will they find new information
4. People use telescopes to view the planets
5. Please name the planets

Write
NOW
Write at least five sentences about the solar system. Include the four kinds of sentences.

Try Sentence Modeling

You can improve your writing by following the patterns of sentences written by professional authors. This type of practice is called **sentence modeling**.

Guidelines for Modeling

1. Find a sentence that you really like.
2. Decide what you will write about in your own sentence.
3. Following the author's pattern, build your sentence one part at a time.

One Student's Modeling

Anthony really likes *Shiloh Season* by Phyllis Reynolds Naylor. Anthony decided to model two of the author's sentences.

See how Phyllis Naylor's sentences line up with Anthony's sentences.

1. Shiloh just sits on the grass in the shade, smiling at us.

   Sam just lies on the bed in his room, talking to me.

2. The bus comes around the bend, and Shiloh barks and backs away.

   The milk spills on the floor, and Jenna cries and runs outside.

Practice

Write your own sentence modeled after one of Phyllis Naylor's sentences above.

Study Model Sentences

Here are some sentences that you can use as models.

■ "It was Sunday, and I was riding my bike back from Robbie's."

    —from *The Journal of Ben Uchida* by Barry Denenberg

■ "She looks at me closely, and I see a change in her face."

    —from *Train to Somewhere* by Eve Bunting

■ "My grandmother is lining up the rolled and folded tamales ready for cooking."

    —from *Family Pictures* by Carmen Lomas Garza

■ "Down the well she went, step over step."

    —from *Addie Across the Prairie* by Laurie Lawlor

Practice

Choose three of the sentences above to model. Write your own sentences, using the "Guidelines for Modeling" on page 412 to help you.

Write NOW   Save a spot in your notebook to list special sentences from books that you really like. Use these sentences as models to write your own sentences.

Preparing for Tests

Check Sentence Sense

1 Choose the group of words that is a complete sentence.

    Ⓐ Last time others in the sun.

    Ⓑ Warm weather near the favorite.

    Ⓒ Rain helps the crops grow.

    Ⓓ Thunder and lightning in the sky.

2 Choose the group of words that is **not** a complete sentence.

    Ⓐ Two teams with their coaches.

    Ⓑ Our team played hard during the whole game.

    Ⓒ The home team scored the first points.

    Ⓓ Fans shouted and cheered for the players.

3 Find the sentence that is **not** correct.

    Ⓐ The girls play outside all day.

    Ⓑ They build a snow fort.

    Ⓒ The sun were shining all afternoon.

    Ⓓ Slowly the fort melted away.

4 Which sentence best combines the following short sentences?

I like pizza. I like pizza with pepperoni. I like mushrooms on pizza, too.

    Ⓐ Mushrooms on pepperoni pizza taste great.

    Ⓑ I like pizza with pepperoni and mushrooms.

    Ⓒ The best pizza for me has pepperoni.

Answer Questions with Sentences

1 **Which sentence answers the following question?**
Question: What is the largest planet in our solar system?

  Ⓐ Earth and Venus are close to the same size.

  Ⓑ The largest planet in our solar system is Jupiter.

  Ⓒ Mercury is the smallest planet in the solar system.

2 **Which question would have this answer?**
Answer: The best speller wins a trophy.

  Ⓐ Who will be the best speller in our class?

  Ⓑ Will Jen or Aaron win the spelling trophy?

  Ⓒ What will the best speller in the spelldown win?

  Ⓓ Who will give the winner a trophy?

3 **Which question would be best for this answer?**
Answer: The temperature usually rises during the day
and falls in the evening.

  Ⓐ What is the length of a day?

  Ⓑ How hot does it get during July?

  Ⓒ How does the temperature change from day
  to night?

4 **Which sentence answers the following question?**
Question: What book would you use to find the meaning of
a word?

  Ⓐ You would use the dictionary to find word meanings.

  Ⓑ The encyclopedia would help you find information.

  Ⓒ You would use the thesaurus to find different words.

Building
Paragraphs

You could tell someone why living with your little brother is hard. You could also write a paragraph about it. A **paragraph** is made up of several sentences, all about the same subject.

A paragraph has three main parts. The first part is the **topic sentence**. The second part includes the **body sentences,** or middle, of the paragraph. The last part is the **closing sentence**.

Paragraph Parts

1 The **topic sentence** tells what the paragraph is about.

2 The **body sentences** support the topic.

3 The **closing sentence** wraps up the paragraph.

Parts of a Paragraph

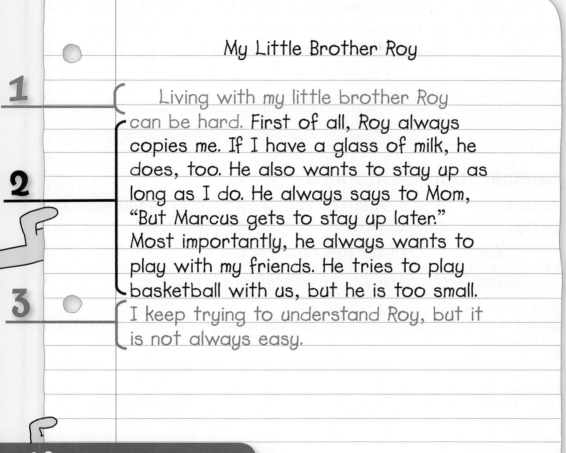

My Little Brother Roy

1   Living with my little brother Roy can be hard. **2** First of all, Roy always copies me. If I have a glass of milk, he does, too. He also wants to stay up as long as I do. He always says to Mom, "But Marcus gets to stay up later." Most importantly, he always wants to play with my friends. He tries to play basketball with us, but he is too small. **3** I keep trying to understand Roy, but it is not always easy.

After you read . . .

- **Ideas** (1) What is the topic of this paragraph? What three reasons does Marcus give to explain the topic?
- **Organization** (2) What words are used to put the reasons in order?
- **Voice** (3) How does Marcus show he's interested in the topic?

Writing Strong Topic Sentences

A strong topic sentence does two things: (1) It names the topic, and (2) it states the main idea (or focus) of the topic.

Topic	Main Idea (or Focus)

Living with *my little brother Roy* can be hard.

Our neighborhood needs better sidewalks.

My baseball team won the championship game.

Special Topic Sentences

Numbers ▪ A topic sentence can use a number to tell what the paragraph will be about.

Topic	Main Idea (or Focus)

My cat Henry hides in three different places.

Lists ▪ A topic sentence can list the things that the paragraph will cover.

Topic	Main Idea (or Focus)

The fitness test includes running, jumping, and throwing.

Practice

Choose the best main idea (or focus) for the topic below.

Topic	Main Idea (or Focus)
Our school	1. has hundreds of students.
	2. is brick.
	3. needs new playground equipment.

Writing Closing Sentences

The closing sentence in a paragraph should be just like a special treat—something the reader will like and remember. Here are three ways to write closing sentences.

1 Remind the reader of your main idea.

Topic sentence:
> Living with my little brother Roy can be hard.

Closing sentence:
> I'm trying to understand Roy, but it is not always easy.

2 Give a final thought about the topic.

Topic sentence:
> The fitness test includes running, jumping, and throwing.

Closing sentence:
> The fitness test is fun, and I don't even have to study for it.

3 Convince the reader of your opinion.

Topic sentence:
> Our neighborhood needs new sidewalks.

Closing sentence:
> Better sidewalks will make our neighborhood safer for everyone.

A good closing sentence wraps up the paragraph.

Using Details

The sentences in the **body**, or middle part, of a paragraph include details. **Details** are the specific words and ideas that tell about the topic. Details can include reasons and facts.

Reason: A reason *answers the question* why?

Topic sentence ———— Living with my little brother Roy can be hard. First of all, Roy

Reason ———— always copies me.

Fact: A fact *adds information*.

Topic sentence ———— Last summer, my baseball team won the championship game.

Fact ———— We beat the Cardinals 2 to 1.

Practice

Choose two facts that tell more about the topic sentence below.

Topic sentence: My cat Henry hides in different places.

Facts: Henry has black fur and long whiskers.
His main hiding place is under my bed.
Cats are nosy animals.
Henry also curls up in my sister's closet.

Other Details

Most paragraphs also include examples and explanations. They give the reader even more information about the topic.

Example: An example *shows something.*

Topic sentence — Living with my little brother

Roy can be hard. First of all,

Reason — Roy always copies me. If I have

Example — a glass of milk, he does, too.

Explanation: An explanation *makes an idea clearer.*

Topic sentence — Last Summer, my baseball

team won the championship game.

Fact — We beat the Cardinals 2 to 1.

Explanation — We scored both of our runs in the

last inning.

Organizing Paragraphs

The sentences in a paragraph must be organized so the reader can follow your ideas. Here are three ways to organize your paragraphs.

Time Order . . .

When you use time order, you give the details in the order in which they happened. You can use words like *first, next,* and *then* to help organize your ideas.

Order of Location . . .

With order of location, you describe a topic from one point to another, like top to bottom. Use words and phrases like *on top, down the sides,* and *at the bottom* to help you organize your ideas in this way.

Order of Importance . . .

With order of importance, you give the most important detail first or last. You can use words or phrases like *first of all, also,* and *most importantly* to help you organize your ideas in this way.

Practice

Which type of organization would you use to write about each of these topics? (There may be more than one answer.)

- describing a pet
- baking cookies
- making a snowman
- telling why recess should be longer

My grandpa takes very good care of his garden. First, he walks up and down the rows pulling weeds. Next, he gathers any vegetables that are ready to eat. He always seems to find something that needs to be picked. Then he plants new seeds in the open spaces. Finally, he waters everything.

McKinley Hill towers over our neighborhood. There are oak trees on top of the hill. My friends and I sometimes climb the trees. Steep paths run down the sides of the hill. We ride down these paths on old pieces of cardboard. At the bottom of the hill, we have a homemade baseball diamond where we play baseball all summer.

Living with my little brother Roy can be hard. First of all, Roy always copies me. If I have a glass of milk, he does, too. He also wants to stay up as long as I do. He always says to Mom, "But Marcus gets to stay up later." Most importantly, he always wants to play with my friends. He tries to play basketball with us, but he is too small. I keep trying to understand Roy, but it is not always easy.

Writing Guidelines

The guidelines on these two pages will help you write strong paragraphs.

 **Prewriting**

Selecting a Topic

- **Choose a topic that interests you.**
- **Make sure that the topic is the right size.**
    Too big: *Our team's whole baseball season*
    Too little: *One time at bat*
    Just right: *Our championship game*

Collecting Details

- **Gather plenty of details.**

    For **narrative** or story paragraphs, answer the questions *who? what? where?* and *when?*

    For **descriptive** paragraphs, collect *sights, sounds, smells,* and *tastes.*

    For **expository** (factual) paragraphs, gather important *facts* and *examples.*

    For **persuasive** paragraphs, list *reasons* that explain your opinion.

- **Use graphic organizers.**
    Choose a cluster, time line, sensory chart, 5 W's chart, or story map to help you organize your details. (See pages **438–444** for sample organizers.)

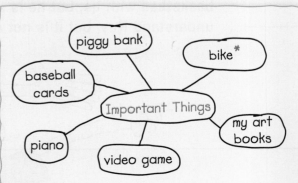

 **Writing**

Creating Your First Draft

- Write a topic sentence that tells the main idea (or focus) of your paragraph.
- Explain the topic in the body or middle sentences.
- End with a sentence that wraps up the paragraph.

 **Revising**

Improving Your Paragraph

- Have I included a topic sentence, the body, and a closing sentence in my paragraph?
- Did I include enough details about my topic?
- Did I put my sentences in the best order?
- Have I used the best words to explain my topic?

 **Editing**

Checking for Conventions

- Did I start each sentence with a capital letter?
- Did I end each sentence with a punctuation mark?
- Did I indent the first line of my paragraph?
- Did I spell words correctly?

Practice

1. Write a paragraph about your favorite hobby.

2. Include two reasons that explain why this is your hobby.

Marking Paragraphs

If you're really excited about a story idea, you may keep writing and writing to get all your thoughts on paper. In the end, you may have a long piece of writing that must be divided into paragraphs. If that happens, try the following idea.

Mark-Ask-Read-Find

You can find the paragraphs in your stories and essays by following these steps.

1 **Mark** the first sentence with a paragraph sign. ¶

2 **Ask** yourself what the main idea of the writing is.

3 **Read** until you **find** a new main idea.

1 **Mark** that sentence with a paragraph sign. ¶

2 **Ask** yourself what the main idea of this part is.

3 **Read** until you **find** another new main idea.

Response to a Book (No Paragraphs)

Grow It Again

Grow It Again by Elizabeth Macleod tells how to grow plants from fruits and vegetables. This book tells how to grow plants from beans, potatoes, and peanuts. I guess I never thought about all the plants that produce the foods I eat. I didn't know potatoes and peanuts grow underground. This book also tells how fruits and vegetables are good for you, and beautiful, too. There are lots of food surprises in Grow It Again.

Following the Steps

Notice how the model book response can be divided into paragraphs using the **Mark-Ask-Read-Find** steps.

1 **Mark** the first sentence with a paragraph sign.

¶ Grow It Again by Elizabeth Macleod tells how to grow plants from fruits and vegetables.

2 **Ask** yourself what the main idea of the writing is.

The main idea is what the book is about.

3 **Read** until you find a new idea.

1 **Mark** that sentence with a paragraph sign.

¶ I guess I never thought about all the plants that produce the foods I eat. I didn't know potatoes and peanuts grow underground.

2 **Ask** yourself what the main idea of this part is.

The main idea is what the writer thinks.

3 **Read** until you find a new idea.

1 **Mark** with a paragraph sign.

¶ This book also tells how fruits and vegetables are good for you, and beautiful, too. There are lots of food surprises in Grow It Again.

2 **Ask** what the main idea is.

It tells what else the book is about.

Grow It Again

Grow It Again by Elizabeth Macleod tells how to grow plants from fruits and vegetables. This book tells how to grow plants from beans, potatoes, and peanuts.

I guess I never thought about all the plants that produce the foods I eat. I didn't know potatoes and peanuts grow underground.

This book also tells how fruits and vegetables are good for you, and beautiful, too. There are lots of food surprises in Grow It Again.

Preparing for Tests

On a test, you may be asked to write a paragraph that summarizes a reading selection. A **summary** includes only the most important ideas found in the reading.

Writing Tips

Before you write . . .
- Read the selection at least twice.
- Use a graphic organizer to plan your paragraph and make notes.

During your writing . . .
- Start with a topic sentence that names the main idea of the reading.
- Write about the information in your own words.

After you've written . . .
- Make sure that your ideas are clear.

Reading Selection

Little Horses Take the Lead

Miniature horses make fine guide animals for the blind. They are the size of large guide dogs. These horses are usually only 20 to 34 inches at the tallest part of their back.

Miniature horses can be trained to stay calm. They are hard workers that are not bothered by noises.

Horses have their eyes on the sides of their heads. This allows them to see in almost all directions. Horses can also see very well at night.

Horses are good guides because they seem to know when danger is near. They naturally look for a safe way to get somewhere else.

Table Diagram

Main Idea

Miniature horses as guide animals

Facts

| good size | can be trained | good sight | know danger |

Sample Summary

Mini Horses to the Rescue

Topic Sentence (underlined)

Miniature horses are great guide animals for blind people. They are the right size

Facts

because they are only 20-34 inches tall. They learn to stay calm. Because horses see well, they also know when danger is near.

Practice

1. Write a summary paragraph of the essay "Chocolate in His Pocket" on page 113 in your book.

2. Use the tips and sample on these two pages as a guide.

A Writer's Resource

Writing is fun, but sometimes it's hard to get started. Finding a topic to write about is the first step. The best topics are often things that you already know about.

This chapter will help you get started. You will also find ways to put your ideas in order and get them on paper. Remember that good writing is like walking—you take one step at a time.

What's Ahead

- Selecting Ideas 432
- Improving Organization 438
- Discovering Your
  Writing Voice 446
- Building Word Choice 449
- Improving
  Sentence Fluency 458
- Polishing Your
  Presentation 460

How can I find a good topic to write about?

Keep a writer's notebook.

Keep a list of writing ideas in a notebook. Then use them for your writing assignments. Here are some ways to collect ideas.

> **TIP** When you see or hear a good idea for a topic, write it down!

1 **Keep your eyes open.**

Sometimes a topic will find you! You might see a cat sitting on a fence. What is it looking for? Does it belong to someone? What is its name? Write ideas in your notebook about things that you see.

2 **Make a list of your bests, worsts, and favorites.**

Here are a few ideas to get you started. Look over your list when you need a writing idea.

Bests	Worsts	Favorites
My best day	My worst subject	My favorite book
My best subject	My dumbest moment	My favorite animal
What I'm best at	My worst accident	My favorite place
My best sport	My worst mistake	My favorite person
My best friend	My least favorite chore	My favorite food
		My favorite music

3 Read a lot.

Read books and magazines. Read about things you've never read about before—space travel, raising rabbits, the Civil War. Write ideas in your notebook as you read.

4 Try different things.

Try new games. Join new clubs. Help people in your neighborhood. The more you do, the more you'll have to write about.

5 Write often.

In a journal, or in your writer's notebook, write about things you see, hear, and do.

6 Finish sentence starters.

Finish some of these sentence starters in as many ways as you can.

I wonder how . . .   I hope our school . . .

I just learned . . .   One place I like . . .

Everyone should . . .   I remember . . .

Here's how to . . .   When I grow up . . .

I'm afraid of . . .   I wish I . . .

Where can I find more writing ideas?

Look at a list of topics.

You can look at a basics-of-life list to think about topic ideas.

animals	art	books	community
environment	exercise	family	food
friends	health	hobbies	jobs
music	school	sports	weather

Here's how to use the "Basics-of-Life" list:

1. Choose one of the topics.
2. Connect it to your writing assignment.
3. Make a list of possible subjects.

My topic is hobbies.

My assignment:
    Write an expository essay explaining one
    of your hobbies.

I could write about . . .
    - collecting old postcards.
    - making my poetry notebook.
    - learning how to ride a unicycle.

Consider topics for each form of writing.

Descriptive Writing

People: someone in your family, a friend, your bus driver, your family doctor/veterinarian, a teacher, a babysitter, a coach

Places: the dentist's office, a campground, a noisy place, a forest, a neighborhood store, your classroom

Things: a leaf falling from a tree, rain on the roof, a very old object, a special gift

Narrative Writing

Tell about . . . your first ride on a roller coaster, being surprised, learning to do something, playing with a friend, helping someone

Expository Writing

Explain how to . . . care for a pet, make a snow fort, pitch a tent, play a favorite board game, make pancakes

Explain different kinds of . . . trucks, horses, airplanes, rocks, storms, dances, skateboards, trees

Explain the meaning of . . . family, teamwork, bravery, love, fear, friendship

Explain why . . . you like or don't like where you live, you like a certain school subject, you need to be organized

Persuasive Writing

Convince your reader about the importance of . . . getting enough sleep, playing an instrument, having recess, having a classroom pet, having quiet times

How can I start learning about a topic?

Start thinking.

To begin with, you should start thinking about your topic. Here are ways to do this.

Listing Write your topic on the top of a piece of paper. Then start listing ideas about it.

The Big Blizzard
-two feet of snow
-howling wind
-huge drifts
-buried cars
-closed roads

Cluster (Web) Write your topic in the middle of a piece of paper and circle it. Then write related ideas around it. Write as many ideas as you can!

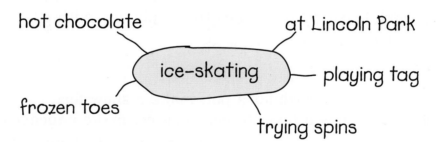

hot chocolate

at Lincoln Park

ice-skating

playing tag

frozen toes

trying spins

Describing Wheel Write your topic in the middle. Write words that describe the topic on the wheel's spokes.

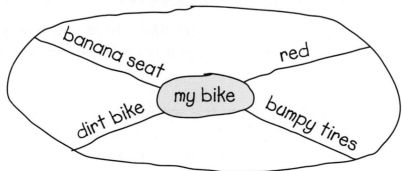

banana seat

red

my bike

dirt bike

bumpy tires

How can I write good topic sentences?

Check your purpose first.

Your topic sentence should fit the purpose of the paragraph: *to share a story, to describe, to explain,* or *to persuade.*

Remember: A topic sentence does two things: (1) it names the topic and (2) it tells what you plan to say about the topic (the *focus*).

To Describe

Descriptive paragraphs describe a topic. Here is a topic sentence for a descriptive paragraph.

Our dog **(topic)** looks like an old dust mop **(focus)**.

To Share a Story

Narrative paragraphs share a story. Here is a topic sentence for a narrative paragraph.

I swam in deep water **(topic)**
for the first time **(focus)**!

To Explain

Expository paragraphs explain or tell about a topic. Here is a topic sentence for an expository paragraph.

You can make a snowman **(topic)** in four steps **(focus)**.

To Persuade

Persuasive paragraphs give an opinion. Here is a topic sentence for a persuasive paragraph.

Afternoon recess **(topic)** should be longer **(focus)**.

Which graphic organizers should I use?

Try a Venn diagram to compare subjects.

Use a **Venn diagram** to show how two subjects are alike and how they are different. Begin by drawing two interlocking circles like the example below.

In area 1, list details about one of your subjects.

In area 2, list details about the other subject.

In area 3, list details that are true for both subjects.

Sample Venn Diagram

Area 1   Area 3   Area 2

Alligator
- wide snout
- very dark
- nests in plants
- found in SE United States

- large reptile
- meat eater
- nocturnal

Crocodile
- narrow snout
- olive brown
- lays eggs in mud
- found in Southern Florida

Make a time line to put events in order.

Use a **time line** to put events or actions in the order they happened for a story. You can also use a time line to list the steps in a process.

Sample Time Line

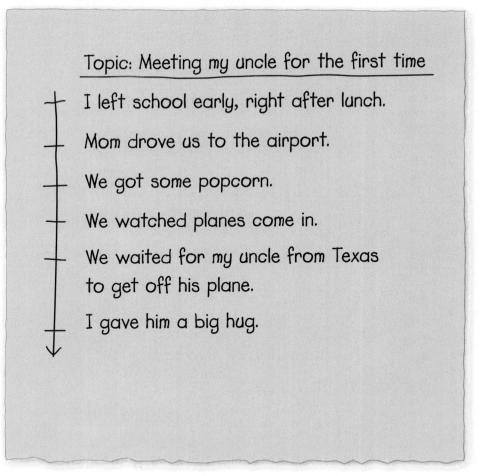

Topic: Meeting my uncle for the first time

I left school early, right after lunch.

Mom drove us to the airport.

We got some popcorn.

We watched planes come in.

We waited for my uncle from Texas to get off his plane.

I gave him a big hug.

Use a story map to make a plan.

Use a **story map** to plan your next story. Just fill in the main ideas and events. (You do not have to tell everything.)

Sample Story Map

Title:	A Very Far Hit
Main character:	Billie, a baseball player
Other characters:	Billie's coach his grandmother
Setting:	A baseball diamond
Conflict (Problem):	Billie was afraid he would strike out.
Plot (What happens?):	1. His team comes up to bat, and Billie is getting nervous.
	2. He remembers his coach's advice.
	3. Billie smashes a hit.
Ending:	Billie tells his grandmother about his hit.

Draw a life map to remember events.

You can use a life map to help you remember and choose an experience you want to write about. Start with the day you were born and map out events up to the present time.

Sample Life Map

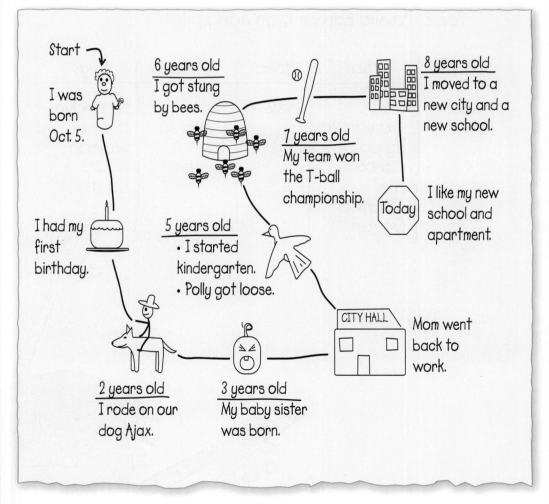

Start
I was born Oct. 5.

6 years old
I got stung by bees.

7 years old
My team won the T-ball championship.

8 years old
I moved to a new city and a new school.

Today
I like my new school and apartment.

I had my first birthday.

5 years old
• I started kindergarten.
• Polly got loose.

Mom went back to work.

CITY HALL

2 years old
I rode on our dog Ajax.

3 years old
My baby sister was born.

Make a 5 W's chart to list ideas.

Use a **5 W's chart** to list the important information that you need for an essay or a report. Try to answer each of the 5 W's.

Sample 5 W's Chart

Topic: Amelia Earhart, an early pilot

Who?	What?	When?	Where?	Why?
Amelia Earhart	first woman to fly solo across the Atlantic Ocean	1932	from Canada to Ireland	to prove that a woman could do it

Make a sensory chart to find details.

Use a **sensory chart** to organize details for a description. List details for each of the five senses.

Sample Sensory Chart

Topic: My picnic party

Sight	Sound	Smell	Taste	Touch
big slices of water-melon	people talking	popcorn	salty peanuts	new soft shirt
picnic tables piled with food	party noisemakers	hot dogs	crunchy pretzels	sticky table-tops
red and yellow balloons	kids laughing and shouting	smoke from the grill	sour pickles	warm hot-dog buns

Make an outline to organize details.

One way to organize the information for a report or a short talk is to make a topic outline.

Sample Topic Outline

Write your topic at the top.

Use Roman numerals for main ideas.

Use capital letters for supporting details.

My Saturday

I. Morning (main idea)
   A. Cartoons
   B. Breakfast   (details)
   C. Bowling
II. Afternoon (main idea)
   A. Lunch
   B. Cleaning my room   (details)
   C. Going to Natalie's
III. Evening (main idea)
   A. Supper
   B. Dishes   (details)
   C. Board-game time

How do I organize a friendly letter?

Use the five parts of a friendly letter.

Friendly letters have five parts: the *heading*, the *salutation*, the *body*, the *closing*, and the *signature*.

1 The **heading** includes your address and the date.

1 978 Cedar Trail
Lodi, Wisconsin 53590
August 17, 2009

2 The **salutation**, or greeting, is capitalized and followed by a comma.

2 Dear Miranda,

Wow, it's been two weeks already since your visit! It was so much fun seeing you and your family.

3 The **body** is the main part of the letter.

I bet you were glad to be here in Wisconsin when it was so hot in Nevada. Our summer probably feels cool to you!   **3**

Thanks again for the great poncho. The colors remind me of the desert pictures you showed me. I'm going to wear my poncho on the first day of school.

4 The first word of the **closing** is capitalized. The closing is followed by a comma.

Write back and tell me all about your school.

4 Adios my friend,

5 Your **signature** is written below the closing.

5 Andres

How can I find the right writing voice?

Make your voice fit your purpose.

Your writing voice will be right if you think about why you are writing and who will be reading it.

Descriptive Voice

One way to improve your descriptive voice is to show your reader what's happening.

■ **Telling:** The writer simply tells about a character.

> Muriel always chewed gum.

■ **Showing:** Author Katherine Paterson clearly describes a character's action in *The Great Gilly Hopkins*.

> Galadriel Hopkins shifted her bubble gum to the front of her mouth and began to blow gently.

Narrative Voice

Your narrative voice will sound natural and real if you write as though you were telling your story to a friend.

In *Amber Brown Is Not a Crayon* by Paula Danziger, the main character, Amber, thinks about her friend Justin. Notice how natural her words sound when she describes him.

> *Who else is going to make faces when some goofy grown-up says, "So your name is Justin, like in the song 'Justin-Time' "?*

Expository Voice

Your expository voice will work well when you use specific details to explain the topic, as in the following example. Notice how easy it is to picture this process.

■ In *Shiloh Season,* Phyllis Reynolds Naylor tells how to eat biscuits.

> *I show David how to mix a spoonful of honey with a spoonful of margarine—stir it up till it turns creamy, and then spread that on a hot biscuit.*

Persuasive Voice

Your persuasive voice will work if you use good reasons to convince the reader to agree with you.

■ **Unconvincing:**

Uncle Mark is a good baseball player. It is fun to watch him play.

■ **Convincing:**

Every time Uncle Mark gets up to bat, the crowd goes crazy. In his last game, he hit a home run. He also tagged two guys out at second base. His teammates call him a power player.

What forms of writing can I try?

Try these forms of writing.

You can learn a lot by writing in different forms. Here are some that you should try.

Personal Journal A personal journal is your own special place to write about anything and everything.

Lists Making lists can help you remember things, think in different ways, or just have fun. For example, you could make a list of winter words.

Family Stories These stories show how families can be brave, funny, or kind.

Alphabet Books An alphabet book puts funny or interesting information in alphabetical order.

Newspaper Stories A news story reports on an important event.

Photo Essays A photo essay tells a story using words and photographs.

Tall Tale A tall tale is a funny story about a character who can do impossible things.

Time-Travel Fantasy In this type of story, you write about any time and place that interests you.

Free-Verse Poems A free-verse poem can be short or long. It can rhyme, but it doesn't have to. You can choose!

How can I learn new words?

Keep a new-word notebook.

Make a special notebook for new words. Write the meaning and a sentence for each new word.

My Vocabulary Notebook

Word	Meaning	Sentence
ibis	long-legged wading bird	The ibis is a wading bird with a long, curved bill.
microscope	an instrument used to see very small objects	Carla's mom uses a microscope to study water pollution.

TIP **Read, read, read!**
The best way to learn new words is to read a lot.

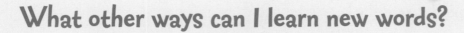

What other ways can I learn new words?

Use the dictionary.

The dictionary can teach you many facts about words. (See pages **302–303**.) Each entry shows . . .

- how to divide the word into syllables,
- how to say the word,
- how the word can be used, and
- the different meanings of the word.

> **gen·e·ra·tion** *(jen´ə rā´shən) noun* **1.** A group of people born and living at about the same time. **2.** A stage or step in the line of descent from an ancestor.

Use the context of a word.

When you are reading and you come to an unfamiliar word, look at the context (the words around it) to help you figure out what the word means. (See the next page for more ways to use context.)

Use a thesaurus.

A thesaurus can help you find just the right words to use in your writing. You can learn synonyms for the word you are trying to replace. (See page **452** for more.)

Think about word parts.

You can figure out the meanings of new words by learning about prefixes, suffixes, and roots. (See pages **453–457**.)

Root words: The main part of the word or base word
Prefix: A word part that comes before the root word
Suffix: A word part that comes after the root or base word

Use the context of a word.

"Context" means the words around a word. Looking at the context can help you figure out its meaning. Try the hints below to help you. The key words and phrases are underlined.

- Read the sentence that includes the word. Also read the sentence before and after it for clues to its meaning.

  > From the edge of the prairie, we watched the **kestrel** dive from the air into the grass and swoop up with a mouse.

  (A *kestrel* is a small falcon or hawk.)

- Search for synonyms (words with the same meaning).

  > The **aroma** of the odd-looking plant reminded me of the unmistakable scent of a skunk.

  (*Aroma* means the same thing as *scent*.)

- Search for antonyms (words with the opposite meaning).

  > The weatherman said the sky would be **overcast**, but it was completely clear.

  (*Overcast* means "cloudy." The word *but* is a clue that "clear" means the opposite of *overcast*.)

- Look for a definition of the word.

  > I dug through the pile of rocks looking for a **geode**, a rock with crystals in its center.

  (A *geode* is a hollow rock that has crystals inside.)

Use a thesaurus.

Use a **thesaurus** to find the right word for your sentence. A thesaurus is a book of synonyms, or words that mean almost the same thing. For example, if you look up *walk* in a thesaurus, you may find *stroll, hike,* and *step.*

Look for the Right Word

Let's say you use a thesaurus to find just the right word for *hop* in the following sentence.

Cassie and her friends _____ over the pile of snow.

Look up the word *hop* in the thesaurus.

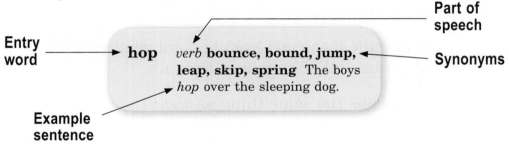

Part of speech

Entry word → **hop**   *verb* **bounce, bound, jump, leap, skip, spring** The boys *hop* over the sleeping dog.

Synonyms

Example sentence

Choose the Right Word

Review the list of synonyms. Choose the word that works best for your sentence. In the example, the best word seems to be *leap.*

Cassie and her friends <u>leap</u> over the pile of snow.

How can I figure out what a new word means?

Divide the word into parts.

You can figure out the meaning of new words by learning about the three basic word parts: prefixes, roots, and suffixes.

unicyclist
1. **Prefix:** **uni**   means *one*
2. **Root:**   **cycl** means *wheel*
3. **Suffix:** **ist**   means *someone who does something*

A *unicyclist* is someone who rides a one-wheeled cycle.

Learn prefixes.

Prefixes are word parts that come at the beginning of a word, *before* the root. They often change the meaning of the root. Here are some common prefixes.

anti- *[against]*
   antibody (part of the blood that works against germs)

bi- *[two]*
   bicycle (two-wheeled cycle)

dis- *[apart]*
   disagree (apart from agreeing)

ex- *[out]*
   external (outside)

mis- *[wrong]*
   misbehave (behave wrongly)

non- *[no, not]*

nonfiction (not fiction; factual)

pre- *[before]*

preview (view before)

re- *[again]*

retry (try again)

sub- *[under]*

submarine (underwater ship)

un- *[not]*

unhealthy (not healthy)

Study suffixes.

Suffixes are word parts that come at the end of a word, *after* the root. They often change the meaning of the root. Here are some common suffixes.

-able *[can do]*

changeable (can change)

-ed *[past tense]*

learned (to learn something in the past)

-er, -or *[a person who]*

baker (a person who bakes)

-est *[most]*

funniest (most funny)

-ful *[full]*

   helpful (full of help)

-ing *[doing something]*

   talking (doing what it is to talk)

-ist *[a person who]*

   pianist (a person who plays the piano)

-less *[without]*

   careless (without care)

-ly *[in some manner]*

   completely (in a complete manner)

-logy *[study of]*

   biology (study of living things)

-ment *[act of]*

   movement (the act of moving)

-ness *[state of]*

   carelessness (state of being careless)

-s, -es *[plural, more than one]*

   trees (more than one tree)

-sion, -tion *[state of]*

   expansion (state of expanding)

   addition (state of adding)

-y *[having]*

   rosy (having a rose color)

Remember root words.

The **root** is the main part of a word. It helps you understand the word's meaning. Here are some common roots.

aud *[hear]*
auditorium (a place to hear something)

bio *[life]*
biography (writing about a person's life)

chron *[time]*
chronological (the time order in which things happened)

cycl, cyclo *[wheel, circular]*
bicycle (a vehicle with two wheels)
cyclone (a circular wind)

dent, dont *[tooth]*
dentist (a person who treats teeth)
orthodontist (a person who straightens teeth)

derm *[skin]*
dermatology (the study of skin)

flex *[bend]*
flexible (able to bend)

geo *[earth]*
geology (the science that describes the earth)

hab, habit *[live]*
inhabit (to live in)

meter *[measure]*

thermometer (an instrument that measures heat)

phon *[sound]*

telephone (far sound)

photo *[light]*

photograph (a picture formed by light)

port *[carry]*

portable (able to be carried)

scope *[see]*

otoscope (an instrument used for seeing inside the ear)

tele *[far]*

telescope (an instrument for seeing things that are far away)

vid, vis *[see]*

video (part of an electronic program that can be seen)

supervise (to oversee or look over)

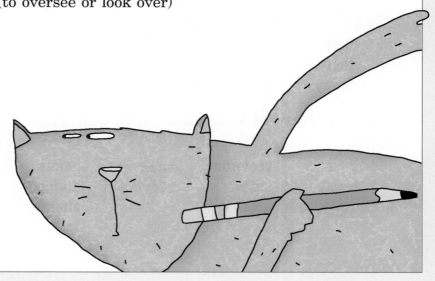

How can I make my sentences easy to follow?

Use transitions.

Transitions are words that help the reader to follow your ideas. Each transition is a signal that a new, important idea is coming. In the following paragraph, four transitions are used.

> A butterfly leads an incredible life. *First,* it starts out as an egg. The eggs are very tiny and round. *Second,* a larva hatches from the egg. Butterfly larvae are usually called caterpillars. *Third,* when a caterpillar finishes growing, it becomes a pupa. The pupa often forms inside a cocoon. *Finally,* when the pupa finishes changing, an adult butterfly comes out.

Some transitions help you show time.

Use these transitions to explain the steps in a process. (See the paragraph above.)

first	second	third	next	last
then	now	soon	later	finally
today	yesterday	tomorrow	before	after

These **groups** of transitions work well when showing time.

first	yesterday	now	before	first
second	today	soon	during	next
third	tomorrow	later	after	finally

Some transitions help you show location.

Use these transitions to describe a person, place, or thing.

above	behind	below	beneath	beside
between	down	in back of	in front of	inside
outside	near	off	on top of	over
under	to the right	to the left	nearby	
in the distance				

These **groups** of transitions work well in descriptions.

in front of	on top of	above	over
beside	next to	below	under
in the distance	in back of	beneath	nearby

Some transitions help you show more information.

Use these transitions to write about a topic in an essay or a report.

again	another	in addition	also	next
as well	besides	along with	other	finally
for example				

These **groups** of transitions work well when adding information.

for example	next	another	in addition
along with	finally	also	as well

How can I make my writing look better?

Add graphs to your writing.

Are you ever confused when you read about numbers? Graphs can show how numbers are related to each other. Put graphs in your writing to help your reader understand the information. A sample bar graph is shown below.

Bar Graph

A **bar graph** uses bars to compare two or more things. The bar graph below compares the number of different-colored jackets in one classroom.

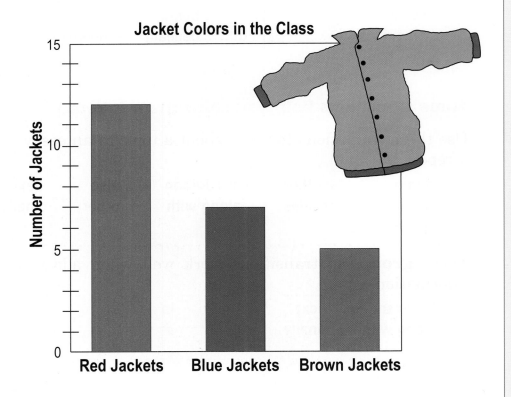

Jacket Colors in the Class

Make tables to share information.

A **table** is a graph that has two basic parts: *rows* go across, and *columns* go down. Here are two examples.

Schedule for Special Classes

	10 a.m.	11 a.m.	1 p.m.	2 p.m.
Monday	Art			
Tuesday		Gym	Music	
Wednesday	Library			
Thursday		Gym		Music
Friday		Art		

Teachers Who Play Instruments

Kind of instrument	Women	Men	Total Players
Guitar	2	5	7
Piano	5	3	8
Flute	3	0	3
Trumpet	3	3	6
Violin	3	2	5

Proofreader's Guide

What's Ahead

- Marking Punctuation **463**
- Editing for Mechanics **486**
- Improving Spelling **502**
- Using the Right Word **510**
- Understanding Sentences **526**
- Using the Parts of Speech **532**

Marking Punctuation

Periods

A **period** is used at the end of a sentence. A period has other important uses, too.

You've been using periods for years.

At the End of a Sentence	Use a period at the end of a sentence that makes a statement. *Claudia rides her bike to school.* (statement) Also use a period at the end of a command. *Make sure you lock your bike.* (command)
After an Initial	Use a period after an initial in a person's name. *A. A. Milne Mary E. Lyons*
After an Abbreviation	Use a period after an abbreviation that shortens a word. (See page **496**.) *Ms. Mrs. Mr. Dr. W. First St.*
To Separate Dollars and Cents	Use a period to separate dollars and cents. *It costs $2.50 to get into the fair.* *I have $6.31 in my piggy bank.*

Question Marks

A **question mark** is used at the end of a direct question.

At the End of a Question	Who put the hot sauce on my taco? Will I ever be able to taste again? Where's the mild sauce?

Exclamation Points

An **exclamation point** is used to express strong feeling. It may be placed after a word, a phrase, or a sentence.

To Express Strong Feeling	Awesome! (word) Happy birthday! (phrase) There's an alligator! (sentence)

 Don't use too many exclamation points in your writing. They lose their value when they are used again and again.

End Punctuation

▶ **Write a period, a question mark, or an exclamation point to end each sentence.**

Example: Do you like fruit ?

1. Fruit is a healthful food choice

2. Strawberries contain vitamin C

3. Do nectarines or peaches have a fuzzy skin

4. Brazil grows the most oranges in the world

5. Over 200 different kinds of raspberries are grown

6. Wow, settlers once used watermelons as canteens

7. Most cranberries are eaten during the Thanksgiving and Christmas holidays

8. Did you know there were so many interesting facts about fruit

Next Step: Write a question about a fruit. Then answer the question.

Commas

Commas tell a reader where to rest or pause in a sentence. They make your writing easier to read.

Reed likes to read books, and his dog Chase likes to chase squirrels.

Between Items in a Series	Use a comma between words or phrases in a series. (A series is a list of three or more things.) I like pizza, pickles, and pretzels. (words) Shawn drinks orange juice every morning, milk after school, and water with dinner. (phrases)
In Letter Writing	Use a comma after the greeting in a friendly letter. Dear Auntie Liz, (greeting) Use a comma after the closing in all letters. Yours truly, (closing) Sally
To Keep Numbers Clear	Use a comma in numbers of four or more digits. Our school collected 22,000 soda cans! My brother's used car cost $1,500.

Commas 1

■ Commas in a Series

▶ **Rewrite each sentence below, placing commas where they belong.**

Example: I learn about food health
and fitness at school.
I learn about food, health,
and fitness at school.

1. Eating lots of candy French fries and pie isn't good for you.

2. Avoid eating too many sweets fats and oils.

3. At least three servings of low-fat milk yogurt and cheese should be eaten each day.

4. Meat eggs and nuts contain iron and many other nutrients.

5. Eat lots of vegetables and fruits (such as grapes apples and bananas).

6. About half of the bread cereal and pasta you eat should be made with whole grains.

Next Step: Write a sentence that lists a series of vegetables.

Commas . . .

Between a City and a State	Use a comma between a city and a state in a sentence or in an address at the top of a letter. He moved to Sleepy Hollow, New York. (sentence)
In Addresses	110 Hill Street Hannibal, MO 63401 (address) Do not use a comma between a state and a ZIP code.
In Dates	Use a comma between the day and the year in a sentence or in the heading of a letter. I saw Uncle Sam on July 4, 2009. (sentence) July 4, 2009 (heading of a letter) Do not use a comma between a month and a year. July 2009
In Compound Sentences	Use a comma before the connecting word in a compound sentence. A compound sentence is made up of two simple sentences that are connected by *or, and, but, so, yet,* and *for.* I usually feed Linus, but I don't clean his litter box!

Commas 2

■ In Compound Sentences

▶ **Rewrite each sentence below, inserting a comma where needed.**

Example: I had seen the car before but I had to look again.
I had seen the car before, but I had to look again.

1. Its headlights looked like eyes and the grille looked like a mouth.

2. This car was laughing at me or maybe it was just smiling.

3. I couldn't believe my eyes so I rubbed them to make sure they were okay.

4. I looked at the car again and it still had that goofy grin!

5. I must have been dreaming that day for I never saw the car "smiling" after that.

Next Step: Write a compound sentence about a time your eyes played tricks on you. Don't forget the comma!

Commas . . .

To Set Off a Speaker's Words	Use a comma to set off the exact words of a speaker from the rest of the sentence.

> Maddie said, "If I have four eggs and you have six eggs, what do we get when we put them together?"
>
> "We get scrambled eggs," said her mother.

After an Introductory Word or Group of Words

A Word That Shows Surprise
Use a comma to set off an interjection. An interjection is a word that shows surprise.

> Wow, you hit that ball a mile!

The Name of a Person Spoken To
Use a comma to set off the name of someone you are speaking to.

> Mom, why didn't you come to the game?

A Group of Words
Use a comma to set off a group of words that comes before the main part of a sentence.

> Because she had to work late, Mom missed the game.

Between Describing Words

Use a comma between two words that describe the same noun.

> His pet is a hairy, black spider!

Commas 3

■ **After Introductory Words**

▶ **For each sentence below, write the word or group of words that should be followed by a comma. Also write the comma.**

Example: Gee that frog looks big!
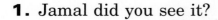
Gee,

1. Jamal did you see it?

2. Before we let it go let's weigh it.

3. Cristi see if you can grab it.

4. If I stand over here the frog can't escape.

5. Uh-oh it's getting away!

6. Hopping into the pond the frog made a big splash.

7. Aw maybe we will catch it another time.

Next Step: Write a sentence about an experience with a wild animal. Include an introductory group of words and use commas correctly.

Apostrophes

An **apostrophe** is used to make contractions or to show ownership. An apostrophe looks like a comma, but it is placed between letters like this:

It**'**s lunchtime!

In Contractions	Use an apostrophe to form a contraction. The apostrophe takes the place of one or more letters.

"Not" Contractions

aren**'**t (are not)   hasn**'**t (has not)
can**'**t (can not)   haven**'**t (have not)
couldn**'**t (could not)   isn**'**t (is not)
didn**'**t (did not)   wasn**'**t (was not)
doesn**'**t (does not)   weren**'**t (were not)
don**'**t (do not)   won**'**t (will not)
hadn**'**t (had not)   wouldn**'**t (would not)

Other Common Contractions

I**'**m (I am)   I**'**ll (I will)
you**'**re (you are)   you**'**ll (you will)
they**'**re (they are)   I**'**ve (I have)
we**'**re (we are)   they**'**ve (they have)
should**'**ve (should have) I**'**d (I would)
it**'**s (it is **or** it has)   you**'**d (you would)
that**'**s (that is)   she**'**s (she is)

Apostrophes 2

■ **Possessives**

▶ **Use an apostrophe to show possession of the items listed below.**

Example: soup that Aunt Ida makes
Aunt Ida's soup

1. a pencil that belongs to Mark

2. the funny ears on those dogs

3. the flowers that Ms. Gardner grows

4. the fruit salad that our neighbors brought

5. the ring tone on my phone

6. the glasses that Dr. Wiler wears

7. the new movie that Hillary Duff is in

8. homework that Tracy dropped

9. the color of the sky

Next Step: Write a sentence about something that belongs to a friend. Use an apostrophe to show ownership.

Quotation Marks

Quotation marks are used to punctuate titles and to set off a speaker's exact words. Remember that quotation marks always come in pairs. One set comes before the quoted words, and one set comes after them, like this:

Porky Pig says, **"**That's all, folks!**"**

To Set Off Spoken Words	Use quotation marks before and after the exact words of the speaker in a sentence. **"**What's that?**"** I asked. Dad said, **"**It's just a pile of rags.**"** **"**Dad,**"** I asked, **"**do rags have a pink nose?**"** Dad looked carefully into the chicken coop. **"**It's a possum!**"** he said, surprised. In almost all cases, punctuation (periods, commas, question marks) is placed inside quotation marks.
To Punctuate Titles	Use quotation marks to punctuate titles of songs, poems, and short stories. **"**This Land Is Your Land**"** is a great song. Ms. Barr read a poem called **"**Whispers.**"** Lu read a story called **"**Swamp Monster.**"** Use underlining or italics for titles of books, magazines, and movies. (See page **478**.)

Quotation Marks

■ In Dialogue

► Write the following sentences on your own paper. Add quotation marks where they are needed.

Example: Mom said, Here's a surprise.

Mom said, "Here's a surprise."

1. What is it? I asked.

2. She said, We are going to get a dog!

3. Wow! I exclaimed.

4. Mom explained, We will choose a dog from the animal shelter.

5. You will need to help take care of it, she added.

6. I said, I'm so glad we are getting a dog. I will be happy to take care of it.

7. Great! Let's go, Mom said.

Next Step: Write a few lines of dialogue without quotation marks (like those above). Then exchange papers with a classmate and add quotation marks to each other's sentences.

Underlining and Italics

Underlining is used to mark titles of books, plays, movies, television programs, and magazines. If you use a computer, you can put titles in *italics* instead of underlining them.

For Titles

Underlining: The Ghostmobile ←

or

Italics: *The Ghostmobile* (a book) ↖

Fantasia or *Fantasia* (a movie)

Nature or *Nature* (a television program)

Cricket or *Cricket* (a magazine)

 Use quotation marks (" ") for titles of poems, songs, and short stories. (See page **476**.)

For Names of Aircraft and Ships

Use underlining (or italics) to mark the names of aircraft and ships.

Pinta, Santa Maria, Niña or *Pinta, Santa Maria, Niña* (Columbus' ships)

Discovery or *Discovery* (spacecraft)

Underlining and Italics

■ In Titles

For each sentence below, write the word or words that should be in italics. Underline them.

Example: In the movie Babe, all the animals could talk.

<u>Babe</u>

1. Grandma gave me The Boxcar Children, a book about orphans.

2. I get the magazine Highlights once a month.

3. Tay saw a TV show he liked called Reading Rainbow.

4. Tiff is reading the book Henry Huggins.

5. My dad likes to watch Nova, a TV science show.

6. The Iron Giant is a cartoon movie about a robot.

7. I like to read the jokes in old Reader's Digest magazines.

Next Step: Write a sentence about a book you have read recently. Underline its title.

Colons

A **colon** is used in three special cases: to show time, to introduce a list, and after the greeting in a business letter. To make a colon, put one dot on top of another one (**:**).

Between Numbers in Time	Use a colon between the parts of a number showing time. My school starts at 7**:**45 a.m. I'll meet you on the playground at 3**:**30.
To Introduce a List	Use a colon to introduce a list. I don't like to do these things**:** go shopping, do chores, or go to bed early. Here are my favorite foods**:** pizza, spaghetti, and pancakes. **T¡P** When introducing a list, the colon is used after words like *the following* or *these things*. Do not use a colon after a verb or preposition.
In a Business Letter	Use a colon after the greeting in a business letter. Dear Ms. Yolen**:** Dear Editor**:** Dear Mr. Wilson**:** Dear Office Manager**:**

Colons

■ To Introduce a List

▶ **Answer each question below with a complete sentence that lists three or more items. Use colons to introduce your lists.**

Example: What things do you use every morning?

I use these things every morning: a hairbrush, a toothbrush, and lip balm.

1. What are some funny names for dogs?

2. What three things do you like about yourself?

3. How do you spend your free time?

4. Which colors might you see in a rainbow?

5. Which chores might you be asked to do?

6. Which three foods do you like best?

7. What are the names of some of your friends?

Next Step: Write a question that could be answered with a list. Exchange papers with a classmate. Then answer each other's question in a complete sentence with a colon.

Hyphens

A **hyphen** is used to divide words. Hyphens can come in handy when you run out of room at the end of a line.

> **To Divide a Word**
>
> Hawks really like to eat mice, grass-
> hoppers, and even snakes. A hawk can
> see a mouse from a mile in the sky.
>
> Divide words only between syllables.
> (The word *grass-hop-per* can be divided
> in two places.) If you are not sure
> where the word gets divided, check
> your dictionary.

Parentheses

Parentheses are used to add information. Parentheses always come in pairs.

> **To Add Information**
>
> The map (see figure 2) will help you
> understand the trail.
>
> When you find important information, write
> down only the main ideas. (This is called note
> taking.)

Hyphens

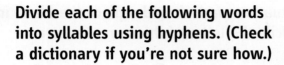

> Divide each of the following words into syllables using hyphens. (Check a dictionary if you're not sure how.)

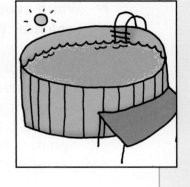

Example: swimming

swim-ming

1. almost

2. question

3. something

4. people

5. before

6. pencil

7. circus

8. happen

9. subtract

10. prepare

11. breakfast

12. winter

13. insect

14. monster

Next Step: Write two sentences about the last time you went swimming. Use a hyphen to divide a word at the end of the line if you need to.

Practice Test

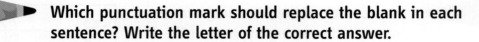

Which punctuation mark should replace the blank in each sentence? Write the letter of the correct answer.

1 Maggie, Darren__ and I love to read.
ⓐ question mark (**?**)
ⓑ comma (**,**)
ⓒ apostrophe (**'**)
ⓓ period (**.**)

2 Do you have a library card__
ⓐ period (**.**)
ⓑ comma (**,**)
ⓒ apostrophe (**'**)
ⓓ question mark (**?**)

3 Robert__s mom works in the school library.
ⓐ apostrophe (**'**)
ⓑ comma (**,**)
ⓒ period (**.**)
ⓓ question mark (**?**)

4 I couldn__t find the book I wanted.
ⓐ period (**.**)
ⓑ comma (**,**)
ⓒ apostrophe (**'**)
ⓓ question mark (**?**)

5 Mrs. Ramer helped me find it__
ⓐ period (**.**)
ⓑ question mark (**?**)
ⓒ apostrophe (**'**)
ⓓ comma (**,**)

6 I read a whole chapter last night__ and I can read some more today.
ⓐ period (**.**)
ⓑ comma (**,**)
ⓒ apostrophe (**'**)
ⓓ question mark (**?**)

7 Wow, you read fast__
- Ⓐ period (.)
- Ⓑ exclamation point (!)
- Ⓒ question mark (?)
- Ⓓ apostrophe (')

8 When I am done with the book__ I will return it to the library.
- Ⓐ period (.)
- Ⓑ apostrophe (')
- Ⓒ question mark (?)
- Ⓓ comma (,)

9 Then I__ll get a new book!
- Ⓐ period (.)
- Ⓑ apostrophe (')
- Ⓒ question mark (?)
- Ⓓ comma (,)

10 How many books can I check out__
- Ⓐ period (.)
- Ⓑ apostrophe (')
- Ⓒ question mark (?)
- Ⓓ comma (,)

11 We are allowed to get six books at a time__
- Ⓐ period (.)
- Ⓑ apostrophe (')
- Ⓒ question mark (?)
- Ⓓ comma (,)

12 Once I had to put two of my books in Anna__s backpack.
- Ⓐ period (.)
- Ⓑ apostrophe (')
- Ⓒ question mark (?)
- Ⓓ comma (,)

Editing for Mechanics
Capitalization

Proper Nouns and Proper Adjectives	Capitalize all proper nouns and proper adjectives. A proper noun names a specific person, place, or thing. Proper adjectives are formed from proper nouns.

Do you know who Rosa Parks is?
She worked for civil rights in Alabama.
(proper nouns)

Where's my Spanish book?
You left it on the Great Lakes ferry.
(proper adjectives)

Words Used as Names	Capitalize words such as *mother, father, mom, dad, aunt,* and *uncle* when these words are used as names.

If Dad goes, Uncle Terry will go, too.

 No capital letter is needed if you use *our* mother, *my* dad, and so on.

My dad asked me to set the table.

Titles Used with Names	Capitalize titles used with names.

President Abraham Lincoln
Mayor Barbara Long

 Do not capitalize titles when they are used alone: the president, a mayor.

Capitalization 1
■ **Proper Nouns and Adjectives**

▶ **For each sentence, write the word or words that should be capitalized.**

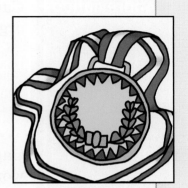

Example: A russian speed skater
won the gold medal.

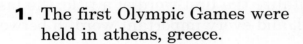

Russian

1. The first Olympic Games were
held in athens, greece.

2. Devon understands the french language.

3. He has been to paris.

4. Rodrigo will live in kansas with aunt tanya
this summer.

5. Do you know anything about the jewish holiday
of Hanukkah?

6. A black iron fence surrounds the white house
in Washington, D.C.

7. The name of Grandpa's favorite cereal is
toasted oats.

Next Step: Write a sentence about a famous person.
Remember to capitalize correctly.

Capitalization . . .

Abbreviations	Capitalize abbreviations of titles and organizations.
	
	    Mr. (Mister) Dr. (Doctor)
	
	    ABC (American Broadcasting Company)
	
	    NFL (National Football League)

Titles	Capitalize the first word of a title, the last word, and every important word in between.
	
	    "There's a Hole in the Bucket" (song)
	
	    Beauty and the Beast (movie)
	
	    Tracks in the Snow (book)

First Words	Capitalize the first word of every sentence.
	
	    The first day at school is exciting.
	
	Capitalize the first word of a direct quotation.
	
	    Mr. Hon said, "Welcome to my class."

Days, Months, and Holidays	Capitalize the names of days of the week, months of the year, and special holidays.
	
	    Friday April Memorial Day
	    Thanksgiving Arbor Day

 Do not capitalize the seasons: *winter, spring, summer, fall.*

Capitalization 2

- **First Words**
- **Days, Months, and Holidays**

▶ **Number your paper from 1 to 10 (for each line in the following paragraph). Write the word or words from each line that should be capitalized. There are 12 mistakes in all.**

Our

1   our family's birthdays are

2   at different times of the year. my

3   sister Margy's birthday was last tuesday, october

4   12. I have to wait until november 26, the day after

5   thanksgiving this year, for my birthday. Dad's

6   birthday, june 5, was on a saturday this year. he

7   liked that! Mom's day was february 16, which

8   was presidents' day. Margy gave her a quarter

9   with Washington's picture. a penny with Lincoln's

10   picture was my gift!

Next Step: Write a sentence that tells the day and date of your birthday this year.

Capitalize Names of Places

Planets and heavenly bodies	Earth, Mars, Milky Way
Continents	Europe, Asia, Africa, North America, South America, Australia, Antarctica
Countries	Canada, Mexico, United States of America
States	Utah, Ohio, Washington, Maine, Indiana
Provinces	Nova Scotia, Quebec, Newfoundland
Cities and counties	Buffalo, New York City, Mexico City, Los Angeles County
Bodies of water	Red Sea, Lake Michigan, Mississippi River, Atlantic Ocean
Landforms	Rocky Mountains, Mount Everest, Hawaiian Islands
Public areas	Liberty Island, Yellowstone National Park
Streets, roads, and highways	Santa Monica Freeway, Main Street, Rock Road, Skyline Drive, Park Avenue, Interstate 95
Buildings	Sears Tower, Petronas Towers

Capitalize	Do Not Capitalize
January, October	spring, summer, winter, fall
Mother (as a name)	my **mother** (describing her)
President Washington	our first **president**
Mayor Hefty	Ms. Hefty, our **mayor**
Lake Erie	the **lake** area
the **South** (section of the country)	**south** (a direction)
planet **Earth**	the **earth** under our feet

Capitalization 3

■ **Names of Places**

▶ **For each sentence, write the word or words that should be capitalized.**

Example: Some people in parts of asia live in tents called *yurts.*
Asia

1. The planet most like earth is venus.

2. We saw the gateway arch in st. louis, missouri.

3. The nile river goes through egypt.

4. Most of the world's highest mountains are in the himalayas.

5. The deepest lake on the planet is lake baikal in russia.

6. Cleveland's tallest building is the key tower.

7. Mom enjoys driving on lake shore drive in chicago.

Next Step: Write a sentence containing a surprising fact about a place.

Plurals

Most Nouns	Plurals of most nouns are made by adding an -*s*. balloon ➜ balloons shoe ➜ shoes
Nouns Ending in *sh*, *ch*, *x*, *s*, and *z*	The plurals of nouns ending in *sh*, *ch*, *x*, *s*, and *z* are made by adding -*es* to the singular. wish ➜ wishes lunch ➜ lunches box ➜ boxes buzz ➜ buzzes dress ➜ dresses
Nouns Ending in *y*	Nouns that end in *y* with a consonant letter just before the *y* form their plurals by changing the *y* to *i* and adding -*es*. sky ➜ skies story ➜ stories puppy ➜ puppies city ➜ cities Nouns that end in *y* with a vowel before the *y* form their plurals by adding -*s*. monkey ➜ monkeys day ➜ days toy ➜ toys key ➜ keys
Irregular Nouns	Some nouns form a plural by taking on a different spelling. child ➜ children mouse ➜ mice goose ➜ geese

Plurals

■ Nouns Ending in *sh*, *ch*, *x*, *s*, and *z*

 ▶ **Number your paper from 1 to 15. Write the plural of each noun below.**

Example: inch
        inches

1. tax

2. pass

3. dash

4. catch

5. six

6. bush

7. watch

8. fox

9. batch

10. kiss

11. lash

12. itch

13. guess

14. waltz

15. bus

Next Step: Write two sentences. Include the plural form of *match* in one and *dish* in the other.

Numbers

Writing Numbers

Numbers from one to nine are usually written as words; all numbers 10 and above are usually written as numerals.

one four 23 45 365 5,280

Except: Numbers being compared should be kept in the same style.

Students in the choir are between 6 and 10 years old.

Very Large Numbers

You may use a combination of numbers and words for very large numbers.

18 million   1.5 billion

Sentence Beginnings

Use words, not numerals, to begin a sentence.

Eleven students in the class had brown hair.

Numerals Only

Use numerals for any numbers in the following forms:

money $1.50
decimals 98.6
percentages . . . . 50 percent
pages . . . . pages 12–21
chapters . . . . chapter 5
addresses . . . . 701 Hill St.
dates . . . . June 6
times . . . . 3:30 p.m.
statistics . . . . a score of 5 to 2

Numbers

▶ **If the number in a sentence is written correctly, write "OK." If it is not, write it correctly.**

Example: There are about twenty peppers in the basket.
20

1. 14 third and fourth graders were absent yesterday.

2. Why are there only fifteen crayons in this box?

3. My grandpa is 59 years old.

4. Kendrick drew ten pictures of his dog.

5. The Hensens drove two hundred and twenty miles to visit family.

6. Ivan can put 9 cherries in his mouth at once!

7. I read forty pages of my book last night.

8. Mexico has 31 states.

9. Seven cars are parked in the Wells' driveway.

Next Step: Draw a picture to illustrate one of the sentences above.

Abbreviations

Common Abbreviations

An **abbreviation** is the shortened form of a word or phrase. Many abbreviations begin with a capital letter and end with a period.

Mrs.   Mr.   Dr.   Sr.   Ave.   a.m.   p.m.

Days of the Week

Sun.	(Sunday)	Thurs.	(Thursday)
Mon.	(Monday)	Fri.	(Friday)
Tues.	(Tuesday)	Sat.	(Saturday)
Wed.	(Wednesday)		

Months of the Year

Jan.	(January)	July	(July)
Feb.	(February)	Aug.	(August)
Mar.	(March)	Sept.	(September)
Apr.	(April)	Oct.	(October)
May	(May)	Nov.	(November)
June	(June)	Dec.	(December)

Acronyms

An acronym is a word formed from the first letter or letters of words in a phrase.

radar (**ra**dio **d**etecting **a**nd **r**anging)
DEAR (Drop Everything And Read)

Initialisms

An initialism is like an acronym, but the initials (letters) are said separately.

CD (compact disc)   TV (television)
PTA (Parent-Teacher Association)

Abbreviations 1

■ **Common Abbreviations**

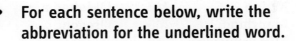 For each sentence below, write the abbreviation for the underlined word.

Example: Today is <u>Tuesday</u>, July 1.

Tues.

1. I have an appointment with my dentist, <u>Doctor</u> Miller.

2. My last appointment with her was in <u>February</u>.

3. Her office is located on Dry <u>Avenue</u>.

4. My neighbor <u>Mister</u> Link works in the same building.

5. He won't be at work this <u>Friday</u>.

6. He must take a trip to <u>Saint</u> Louis.

7. He wants to visit his father, William P. Link, <u>Senior</u>.

Next Step: Ask a classmate in what month his or her birthday is. Tell each other the abbreviations for your birthday months.

State Abbreviations

Alabama	AL	Kentucky	KY	North Dakota	ND
Alaska	AK	Louisiana	LA	Ohio	OH
Arizona	AZ	Maine	ME	Oklahoma	OK
Arkansas	AR	Maryland	MD	Oregon	OR
California	CA	Massachusetts	MA	Pennsylvania	PA
Colorado	CO	Michigan	MI	Rhode Island	RI
Connecticut	CT	Minnesota	MN	South Carolina	SC
Delaware	DE	Mississippi	MS	South Dakota	SD
District of		Missouri	MO	Tennessee	TN
Columbia	DC	Montana	MT	Texas	TX
Florida	FL	Nebraska	NE	Utah	UT
Georgia	GA	Nevada	NV	Vermont	VT
Hawaii	HI	New Hampshire	NH	Virginia	VA
Idaho	ID	New Jersey	NJ	Washington	WA
Illinois	IL	New Mexico	NM	West Virginia	WV
Indiana	IN	New York	NY	Wisconsin	WI
Iowa	IA	North Carolina	NC	Wyoming	WY
Kansas	KS				

Address Abbreviations

Avenue	AVE	Heights	HTS	South	S
Boulevard	BLVD	Highway	HWY	Square	SQ
Court	CT	Lane	LN	Station	STA
Drive	DR	North	N	Street	ST
East	E	Road	RD	West	W

 Use these postal abbreviations when addressing envelopes. (See page 212.)

Abbreviations 2

■ **State Abbreviations**

▶ **For each state abbreviation below, write out the complete state name. A clue is given for each.**

Example: ME (lighthouses)
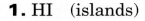
Maine

1. HI (islands)

2. RI (smallest state)

3. MS (long river)

4. CA (Hollywood)

5. FL (hurricanes)

6. TX (cowboys)

7. NM (not old)

8. AK (biggest state)

9. SD (Mt. Rushmore)

10. NY (skyscrapers)

11. CO (Pike's Peak)

12. KY (horse farms)

13. ID (potatoes)

14. MI (great lake)

Next Step: Write a short paragraph about a state you have visited or would like to visit.

Practice Test

▶ **For each sentence, look for mistakes in capitalization, abbreviations, or use of numbers. (Write the letter of the line that has a mistake.) If there are no mistakes, write "D."**

1. Peter and I asked   mr. Lerm for a
     Ⓐ   Ⓑ
   glass of water.   No mistakes
       Ⓒ   Ⓓ

2. 17 kids at school   got a letter from
      Ⓐ   Ⓑ
   Mayor Hillen.   No mistakes
      Ⓒ   Ⓓ

3. Aunt Marta would   like a visit from us
      Ⓐ   Ⓑ
   next wednesday.   No mistakes
      Ⓒ   Ⓓ

4. Every winter, this   area gets two feet
      Ⓐ   Ⓑ
   or more of snow.   No mistakes
      Ⓒ   Ⓓ

5. <u>Our class welcomed</u>   <u>a new student from</u>
         Ⓐ   Ⓑ
   <u>korea in November.</u>   No mistakes
            Ⓒ   Ⓓ

6. <u>when Dean went</u>   <u>to Hawaii, he surfed</u>
         Ⓐ   Ⓑ
   <u>some giant waves.</u>   No mistakes
            Ⓒ   Ⓓ

7. <u>Sitka is one of the</u>   <u>largest alaskan cities,</u>
          Ⓐ   Ⓑ
   <u>with about 8,800 people.</u>   No mistakes
                Ⓒ   Ⓓ

8. <u>At my checkup on Friday,</u>   <u>my dentist, Dcr. Wall,</u>
                 Ⓐ   Ⓑ
   <u>told me I am healthy.</u>   No mistakes
               Ⓒ   Ⓓ

9. <u>Mom makes sure that I</u>   <u>replace my toothbrush</u>
               Ⓐ   Ⓑ
   <u>every 3 months.</u>   No mistakes
            Ⓒ   Ⓓ

Improving Spelling

Learning some basic spelling rules can help you spell many words. But remember that there are **exceptions** to the rules. (An exception is a word that doesn't fit the rule.)

Silent *e*	If a word ends with a silent *e*, drop the *e* before adding an ending that begins with a vowel, like *-ed* or *-ing*. share ➜ shared, sharing care ➜ cared, caring
Words Ending in *y*	When you write the plurals of words that end in *y*, change the *y* to *i* and add *es*. If the word ends in *ey*, just add *s*. (Also see page **492**.) puppy ➜ puppies pony ➜ ponies turkey ➜ turkeys donkey ➜ donkeys

Consonant Ending	When a one-syllable word with a short vowel needs an ending like *-ed* or *-ing*, the final consonant is usually doubled. *Exception*: Do not double the consonant for words ending in *x*, as in *boxed* or *boxing*.
	
	stop ➜ stopped quit ➜ quitter
	         stopping quitting
	swim ➜ swimming star ➜ starred
	         swimmer starring

i before e

Use *i* before *e* except after *c* or when these letters "say" *a* as in *neighbor* or *weigh*.

i before *e* words:
> friend, piece, relief, believe, audience, chief, fierce

exceptions to *i* before *e* rule:
> either, neither, their, height, weird

Spelling Words

The spelling words are listed in alphabetical (ABC) order by their first letter, and then by each following letter. For example, in the "A" column, the words *almost, alone,* and *always* begin with *al*. For these three words, you must look at the third letter to see their alphabetical order.

A
about
afraid
after
again
almost
alone
a lot
always
angry
animal
another
answer
anybody
anyone

April
aren't
around
asked
asleep
August
aunt
author

B
beautiful
because
before
behind
believe

better
bicycle
body
both
bought
break
breakfast
bright
brought
built
bunch

C
cannot
care
catch
caught
cause
change
children
climb
clothes
coming
could
country
cousin

D

dance
daughter
dear
December
decided
didn't
different
dirty
doesn't
done
don't
down
dressed
drive
dropped
during

E

early
earth
either
engine
enough
everyone
everything

F

family
famous
favorite
February
few
field
fight
finally

finished
first
flew
floor
flying
follow
forest
fought
found
Friday
friend
from
front

G

ghost
girl
goes
ground
group
guess
gym

H

half
happen
happiness
have
heard
heart
high
hospital
how
huge
hungry
hurry
hurt

I

idea
I'll
I'm
important
inches
inside
instead
interest
island
isn't
it's

J

January
join
July
June

K

kept
kitchen
knew
knife
knocked
know

L

laugh
learn
leave
library

listen
live
loose
loud
lunch

M

mail
many
March
May
maybe
metal
middle
might
minute
mirror
Monday
monster
morning
mouse
mouth
music
myself

N

near
neighbor
ninety
nobody
noise
north
nothing
November
now

Spelling 1

▶ **Write the correct spelling of the missing word in each sentence below. Look at the letters given and the number of blanks for clues.**

Example: I enjoy rap, rock, and classical m _ _ _ _.
music.

1. My mother, father, brothers, and sisters are my f _ _ _ _ _.

2. We play basketball in the _ _ m at school.

3. The man who lives next door is my n _ _ _ _ b _ _.

4. Hawaii is an _ s _ _ _ d in the Pacific Ocean.

5. When I hear a joke, I _ _ _ _ h.

6. You might lose a button if it is l _ _ _ _.

7. We borrow books from the _ _ b _ _ _ y.

Next Step: Write a sentence about a song you like. Use a word from page **504** in your sentence.

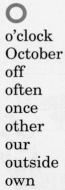

O

o'clock
October
off
often
once
other
our
outside
own

P

paint
paper
parents
past
people
person
phone
picture
piece
pleased
police
poor
president
pretty
probably

Q

question
quick
quiet
quite

R

reached
ready
really
reason
receive
remember
rhyme
right
river
rough
round

S

said
Saturday
scared
school
science
secret
September
sight
since
someone
something
special
stairs
started
straight
strange
strong
Sunday
sure
surprise

T

taught
than
their
then
there
they're
thought
threw
through
Thursday
together
tomorrow
tonight
trouble
truth
Tuesday

U

uncle
understand
until
upon
usual

V

very
visit
voice

W

want
was
watch
wear
weather
Wednesday
went
where
which
while
whole
without
woman
women
won't
world
would
write
wrong

X

X-ray
xylophone

Y

young
your
you're

Z

zero

Spelling 2

▶ **For each set of words below, write the correct spelling of the misspelled word.**

Example: **a)** person, **b)** quick, **c)** saprize
            c) surprise

1. **a)** speshul, **b)** world, **c)** very

2. **a)** through, **b)** rough, **c)** straigth

3. **a)** police, **b)** reddy, **c)** where

4. **a)** shure, **b)** without, **c)** picture

5. **a)** Wendseday, **b)** round, **c)** wrong

6. **a)** strange, **b)** recieve, **c)** usual

7. **a)** thought, **b)** surprise, **c)** ryme

8. **a)** parents, **b)** scool, **c)** remember

9. **a)** zero, **b)** which, **c)** sience

10. **a)** peice, **b)** sure, **c)** women

Next Step: Write five words from page **506** that you might have trouble spelling correctly.

Practice Test

▶ Write the letter of the misspelled word in each group.

1
- Ⓐ animal
- Ⓑ girl
- Ⓒ write
- Ⓓ neer

2
- Ⓐ beleive
- Ⓑ Tuesday
- Ⓒ remember
- Ⓓ might

3
- Ⓐ round
- Ⓑ comeing
- Ⓒ while
- Ⓓ than

4
- Ⓐ scool
- Ⓑ December
- Ⓒ maybe
- Ⓓ sure

5
- Ⓐ friend
- Ⓑ question
- Ⓒ whare
- Ⓓ please

6
- Ⓐ myself
- Ⓑ dear
- Ⓒ untill
- Ⓓ decided

7
- Ⓐ because
- Ⓑ people
- Ⓒ which
- Ⓓ leeve

8
- Ⓐ coud
- Ⓑ own
- Ⓒ knife
- Ⓓ interest

9
- Ⓐ their
- Ⓑ finally
- Ⓒ children
- Ⓓ woud

10
- Ⓐ Wendsday
- Ⓑ catch
- Ⓒ monster
- Ⓓ pretty

11
Ⓐ mous
Ⓑ wrong
Ⓒ high
Ⓓ afraid

12
Ⓐ quick
Ⓑ first
Ⓒ beter
Ⓓ another

13
Ⓐ Febuary
Ⓑ together
Ⓒ both
Ⓓ again

14
Ⓐ minite
Ⓑ behind
Ⓒ guess
Ⓓ October

15
Ⓐ group
Ⓑ feild
Ⓒ women
Ⓓ ready

16
Ⓐ idea
Ⓑ dressd
Ⓒ important
Ⓓ November

17
Ⓐ lern
Ⓑ early
Ⓒ zero
Ⓓ parents

18
Ⓐ voice
Ⓑ whole
Ⓒ world
Ⓓ allmost

19
Ⓐ upon
Ⓑ recieve
Ⓒ lunch
Ⓓ half

20
Ⓐ kept
Ⓑ past
Ⓒ realy
Ⓓ science

Using the Right Word

In your writing, you use words that can be easily confused, such as *blue* and *blew*. This section covers two kinds of problem words that are often confused—*homophones* and *homonyms*.

Homophones are words that sound alike but have different spellings and meanings.

> The doghouse was made of wood.

> Would Mugsy like it?

Homonyms sound alike *and* are spelled the same, but they have different meanings.

> Be careful; don't break that vase!

> We should take a break.

ant, aunt	An **ant** is an insect that works hard. My **aunt** is my mom's sister.
ate, eight	We **ate** all the popcorn. (The past tense of *eat* is "ate.") The number **eight** comes between seven and nine.
bare, bear	If you have **bare** feet, you have no shoes or socks on. A **bear** is a big, furry animal.
blew, blue	The wind **blew** hard. (The past tense of *blow* is "blew.") A clear sky is the color **blue**.

Using the Right Word 1

■ ant, aunt; ate, eight; bare, bear; blew, blue

▶ **For each sentence below, write the word (in parentheses) that is correct.**

Example: Does every *(bare, bear)* sleep through the winter?
bear

1. If I slept in a cave all winter, I would turn *(blew, blue)*!

2. Maybe I would be warm enough if *(ate, eight)* big, furry animals slept with me.

3. Serena and her *(ant, aunt)* bought some tomato plants for the garden.

4. One plant was almost *(bare, bear)*.

5. Serena *(ate, eight)* some great tomatoes from that plant a few months later.

6. She noticed an *(ant, aunt)* crawling on one tomato.

7. Serena just *(blew, blue)* it off the tomato.

Next Step: Using two words from the list above, write a sentence about a food you have eaten.

brake, break	A car's **brake** makes it stop. If you **break** a glass, it shatters into pieces. Taking a **break** means resting for a bit.
buy, by	When you pay for an item, you **buy** it. The word *by* means "near."
cent, scent, sent	One **cent** is the same as one penny. A pine tree's **scent** is the way it smells. We **sent** Aunt Carole a valentine. (The past tense of *send* is "sent.")
close, clothes	**Close** the window so no bugs can get in. People wear **clothes**, such as shirts and pants.
creak, creek	A squeaky kind of sound is called a **creak**. A **creek** is a stream or a tiny river.
dear, deer	Juan is fond of his **dear** grandmother. **Deer** are animals that live in the woods.
dew, do, due	The moisture on the morning grass is **dew**. When you're given a job, always **do** your best. Homework is usually **due** on a certain day.

Using the Right Word 2

■ buy, by; cent, scent, sent; close, clothes; dear, deer

▶ **Write a word from the list above to complete each sentence.**

Example: Some of these flowers have a very strong _____ .

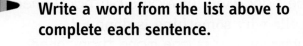
scent

1. I would like to _____ some for my grandma.

2. I need one more _____ to have enough money.

3. My grandma is very _____ to me.

4. The _____ she wears are old, but they always look nice.

5. Once she _____ me a long letter.

6. She described playing in the woods _____ her house when she was young.

7. She remembers leaving corn out for the _____ .

8. Grandma often tells me, "Never _____ your mind to new ideas."

Next Step: Write two sentences that show your understanding of the words *by* and *buy*.

eye, I	A mammal's **eye** allows it to see. **I** love the zoo. (The pronoun *I* refers to the person who is speaking.)
for, four	I made pancakes **for** Mom's birthday breakfast. (*For* tells why something is done.) The number **four** is one more than three.
hare, hair	A **hare** looks like a large rabbit. **Hair** covers a person's head.
heal, heel	Her cut should **heal** within a week. The **heel** is the back part of the foot.
hear, here	We use our ears to **hear** sound. Someone who is **here** is in this place.
heard, herd	We **heard** sirens all night. (The past tense of *hear* is "heard.") A **herd** is a group of animals.
hole, whole	An area that's been hollowed out is a **hole**. Something that is **whole** has nothing missing.
hour, our	One **hour** lasts 60 minutes. **Our** dog barks at strangers. (*Our* shows ownership.)

Using the Right Word 3

■ for, four; hear, here; heard, herd; hour, our

▶ **For the sentences below, write the right word from each pair (in parentheses).**

Example: My watch tells the date, the *(hour, our)*, the minute, and the second.
   hour

1. I got it *(for, four)* my birthday.

2. At night I keep it right *(hear, here)* on my bedside table.

3. Once I *(heard, herd)* its alarm go off at *(for, four)* o'clock in the morning!

4. The alarm also woke up *(hour, our)* three dogs.

5. Of course, they *(hear, here)* every little sound.

6. When they come running, it sounds like a *(heard, herd)* of buffalo!

Next Step: Write a sentence about a time you were frightened. Use one of the words from the list above correctly.

its, it's	The cat licked **its** paw. (*Its* shows ownership.) **It's** hot today! (*It's*—with an apostrophe—is the contraction for "it is.")
knew, new	Dauna **knew** how to read at age four. (The past tense of *know* is "knew.") Something that is **new** is not old.
knight, night	Long ago, a **knight** was a soldier in armor. At **night** it's dark outside.
know, no	To **know** something is to understand it. The opposite of "yes" is "**no**."
made, maid	Grandma **made** waffles for us. (The past tense of *make* is "made.") A **maid** is someone hired to do housework.
main, mane	The **main** idea is the most important one. The long hair on a horse's neck is its **mane**.
meat, meet	Some people eat the **meat** of animals. We come together to **meet** with others.
one, won	**One** is the number before two. We **won** the game! (The past tense of *win* is "won.")

Using the Right Word 4

■ it's, its; knew, new; know, no; one, won

▶ **For each sentence below, write the word (in parentheses) that is correct.**

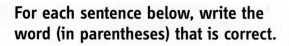

Example: Let's shoot some hoops with my *(knew, new)* ball.

new

1. *(It's, Its)* one of the prizes for a hoops contest I entered.

2. I *(one, won)* third place.

3. I *(knew, new)* I couldn't beat Calvin.

4. I *(know, no)* of only *(one, won)* other player who might have beaten him.

5. While doing a layup, Reggie almost broke the hoop off *(it's, its)* backboard.

6. Calvin wanted *(know, no)* prize other than first.

7. *(It's, Its)* not surprising that he got it!

8. Now he has a *(knew, new)* bike!

Next Step: Write a sentence about entering a contest. Use one of the words from the list above.

pair, pare, pear	A **pair** of items is two things. When you trim off the outside of a **pear** or an apple, you **pare** it.
peace, piece	The opposite of war is **peace**. A **piece** of bread is part of a loaf.
plain, plane	Bonita's bedroom is **plain**, not fancy. A **plain** is a large, flat area of land without trees. The shortened word for "airplane" is "**plane**."
read, red	I've **read** that book twice. (The past tense of *read* is "read.") We picked some ripe, **red** tomatoes. (*Red* is a color.)
right, write	**Right** is the opposite of left. Something that is correct is **right**. You put words on paper when you **write**.
road, rode, rowed	A **road** is a path for cars and trucks. Sammy **rode** his tricycle down the driveway. (The past tense of *ride* is "rode.") The friends **rowed** the boat across the lake. (The past tense of *row* is "rowed.")
scene, seen	A **scene** is a place and its surroundings. The dog had **seen** the rabbit before it took off running. (*Seen* is a way to state "see" in the past tense.)

Using the Right Word 5

■ peace, piece; right, write; road, rode, rowed

▶ **For each sentence below, write the word (in parentheses) that is correct.**

Example: The sign beside the
(road, rode) wasn't helpful.
road

1. The arrow pointing (right, write)
only had triangles on it!

2. Maybe a (peace, piece) of the sign had broken off.

3. We (rode, rowed) on in the car, not knowing
where we were.

4. Mom said she'd (right, write) someone a letter
about it.

5. We wanted to get to the (peace, piece) and quiet
of the lake.

6. Finally, we put the boat in the water and
(rode, rowed) away on the gentle waves.

Next Step: Write a sentence about getting lost. Use a
word from the list above.

sea, see	A **sea** is a large body of water. People use their eyes to **see**.
sew, so, sow	A needle and thread are needed to **sew**. We were **so** tired. (*So* means "very." *So* can also mean "as a result," so it can connect word groups.) When *you* plant seeds, *you* **sow** them.
soar, sore	A high-flying bird is said to **soar**. Muscles that ache are **sore**.
some, sum	Get **some** sleep. (*Some* refers to an amount.) A **sum** is the total of numbers added together.
son, sun	A male child is his parents' **son**. The **sun** is the closest star to the earth.
tail, tale	A happy dog wags its **tail**. Colin's story was an exciting **tale** about elves.
their, there, they're	The boys finished **their** homework. (*Their* shows ownership.) If you are here, you cannot be **there**. **They're** outside playing. (*They're*—with an apostrophe—is the contraction for "they are.")
threw, through	Matt **threw** a baseball over the fence. (The past tense of *throw* is "threw.") To go **through** a tunnel, you go in one side and out the other.

Using the Right Word 6

■ son, sun; their, there, they're; threw, through

For each sentence below, decide which word (in parentheses) is correct. Write it on your paper.

Example: In the morning, the *(son, sun)* rises in the east.

sun

1. It peeks *(threw, through)* my bedroom curtains.

2. I have a shade *(their, there, they're)*, but I forget to close it.

3. Dad is Grandma and Grandpa's *(son, sun)*.

4. *(Their, There, They're)* his parents.

5. Once Dad *(threw, through)* a baseball into Grandma's kitchen window.

6. Grandma and Grandpa fixed *(their, there, they're)* window right away.

Next Step: Write a sentence or two about people in your family. Use the word *they're*.

to, two, too	*To* suggests moving toward something. The number **two** is one less than three. *Too* can mean "very" or "also."
waist, waste	Your **waist** is between your chest and hips. You **waste** a thing if you don't use it wisely.
wait, weight	I will stay here and **wait** until you get back. A man's **weight** tells how heavy he is.
way, weigh	Knowing the **way** helps you get somewhere. To find out how heavy you are, **weigh** yourself.
weak, week	The opposite of strong is "**weak**." A **week** is seven days.
wear, where	Stefan and his brother **wear** jeans every day. **Where** is Scott? (*Where* means "in what place.")
witch, **which**	A **witch** is a woman who is thought to have magical powers. **Which** magazine do you want? (*Which* identifies one thing out of a group.)
wood, **would**	**Wood** comes from trees. I **would** vote for you. (*Would* suggests a choice.)
your, you're	**Your** drawing is neat! (*Your* shows ownership.) **You're** an artist. (*You're*—with an apostrophe—is the contraction for "you are.")

Using the Right Word 7

■ weak, week; wood, would; your, you're

▶ **Write the correct word from the list above to complete each sentence below.**

Example: It will be a ___week___ before school starts again.

1. Did you remember to cover all _____ new books?

2. I think _____ going to do fine in school this year.

3. Raj _____ like summer to last a little longer.

4. He is building a birdhouse out of _____.

5. He might not finish it in just a _____.

6. If he stays up too late working on it, he may feel _____ the next day.

7. You can offer him _____ help if you'd like to.

Next Step: Write two sentences about school. Use the words *your* and *you're* correctly.

Practice Test

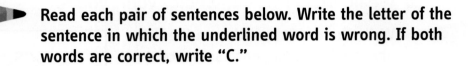

Read each pair of sentences below. Write the letter of the sentence in which the underlined word is wrong. If both words are correct, write "C."

1
  (A) <u>Would</u> you please get ready?
  (B) <u>Its</u> time to go now.
  (C) Correct as is

2
  (A) I'd like a <u>peace</u> of that pie.
  (B) It has a wonderful <u>scent</u>.
  (C) Correct as is

3
  (A) This <u>road</u> is very bumpy.
  (B) <u>No</u> one rides a bike on it.
  (C) Correct as is

4
  (A) Jan <u>herd</u> a noise.
  (B) The cat got a <u>new</u> collar bell.
  (C) Correct as is

5
  (A) He wants a pair of <u>blue</u> jeans.
  (B) Will Dad <u>buy</u> them?
  (C) Correct as is

6
  (A) Luther <u>sent</u> me a postcard.
  (B) He is spending <u>for</u> months in Florida.
  (C) Correct as is

7
  (A) I <u>ate</u> a taco for lunch.
  (B) I had some last <u>weak</u>, too.
  (C) Correct as is

8
  (A) An <u>ant</u> is on my sandwich.
  (B) It is not the only <u>one</u>!
  (C) Correct as is

9
  (A) Uncle Dave has a <u>bare</u> in his yard.
  (B) Don't worry; it is made of <u>wood</u>.
  (C) Correct as is

10
(A) It has been cloudy for <u>six</u> days.
(B) When will we see the <u>son</u> again?
(C) Correct as is

11
(A) Jill <u>rode</u> the bus to the zoo.
(B) The ride took an <u>our</u>.
(C) Correct as is

12
(A) Is this <u>you're</u> book?
(B) Yes—I can tell by <u>its</u> torn cover.
(C) Correct as is

13
(A) Mr. Lee's <u>son</u> isn't feeling well.
(B) He is <u>weak</u> and has a fever.
(C) Correct as is

14
(A) Mark saw <u>eight</u> jays in a tree.
(B) He could <u>here</u> them, too.
(C) Correct as is

15
(A) Kenna walked <u>by</u> the river.
(B) All the trees were <u>bare</u>.
(C) Correct as is

16
(A) I didn't <u>clothes</u> my dresser drawer.
(B) I <u>threw</u> a pair of socks toward it.
(C) Correct as is

Understanding Sentences
Parts of a Sentence

Simple Subject	The subject names someone or something. The subject is often doing something. The **simple subject** is the main word—without any other words—in the complete subject. My big sister threw the balloon. (*Sister* is the simple subject.) My best friend caught the balloon. (*Friend* is the simple subject.)
Complete Subject	The **complete subject** is the main word along with any other words that describe it. My big sister threw the balloon. (*My big sister* is the complete subject.) The huge balloon is full of water. (*The huge balloon* is the complete subject.)
Compound Subject	A **compound subject** is made up of two or more simple subjects joined by *and* or *or*. My big sister and my best friend played catch with the balloon. (*Sister* and *friend* make up the compound subject.)

Parts of a Sentence 1

■ Complete and Simple Subjects

▶ **For each sentence below, write the complete subject.**

Example: One famous author of children's books was Theodor Seuss Geisel.

One famous author of children's books

1. Most people know him simply as Dr. Seuss.

2. Odd creatures in fantastic places fill his books.

3. The main character in *Green Eggs and Ham* is Sam-I-Am.

4. A bored brother and sister are entertained by *The Cat in the Hat*.

5. Dr. Seuss's book of wonderful noises is *Mr. Brown Can Moo! Can You?*

6. Dr. Seuss may have taught your parents to read!

Next Step: For each answer you wrote, circle the simple subject. (One is a compound subject, so you will circle two words.)

Parts of a Sentence . . .

Simple Predicate (Verb)	The predicate tells what the subject is or does. The **simple predicate** is the main word—the verb—in the complete predicate.
	Rocky is the fastest dog on the block. (*Is* is the simple predicate.)
	Rocky runs faster than the other dogs. (*Runs* is the simple predicate.)
Complete Predicate (Verb)	The **complete predicate** is the verb along with the other words that describe and complete it.
	Rocky is the fastest dog on the block. (*Is the fastest dog on the block* is the complete predicate.)
	Rocky runs faster than the other dogs. (*Runs faster than the other dogs* is the complete predicate.)
Compound Predicate (Verb)	A compound predicate is made up of two or more simple predicates (verbs) joined by *and* or *or*.
	Rocky runs fast and barks loud. (*Runs* and *barks* make up the compound predicate.)

Parts of a Sentence 2

■ Complete and Simple Predicates

▶ **For each sentence below, write the complete predicate.**

Example: Rabbits are mammals
with long ears and
short tails.

*are mammals with long ears
and short tails*

1. These animals are blind and hairless at birth.

2. Rabbits hop and run fast with their powerful hind legs.

3. They can escape foxes, badgers, and birds of prey.

4. Rabbits are very active at night.

5. Rabbits eat lots of different plants.

6. Many gardeners think of them as pests.

Next Step: For each answer you wrote, circle the simple predicate. (One is a compound predicate, so you will circle two words.)

Practice Test

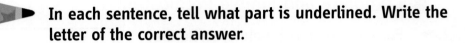

In each sentence, tell what part is underlined. Write the letter of the correct answer.

1 Giraffes <u>are the tallest animals.</u>
- Ⓐ simple subject
- Ⓑ complete subject
- Ⓒ simple predicate
- Ⓓ complete predicate

2 A baby giraffe <u>is</u> about six feet tall at birth.
- Ⓐ simple subject
- Ⓑ complete subject
- Ⓒ simple predicate
- Ⓓ complete predicate

3 They <u>can grow</u> to be 18 feet tall!
- Ⓐ simple subject
- Ⓑ complete subject
- Ⓒ simple predicate
- Ⓓ complete predicate

4 <u>High treetops</u> provide food for giraffes.
- Ⓐ simple subject
- Ⓑ complete subject
- Ⓒ simple predicate
- Ⓓ complete predicate

5 They <u>use their long tongues and stretchy lips to get leaves.</u>
- Ⓐ simple subject
- Ⓑ complete subject
- Ⓒ simple predicate
- Ⓓ complete predicate

6 Like a human, a giraffe <u>has</u> seven bones in its neck.
- Ⓐ simple subject
- Ⓑ complete subject
- Ⓒ simple predicate
- Ⓓ complete predicate

7 <u>Large hooves at the end of long legs</u> help a giraffe balance.
- Ⓐ simple subject
- Ⓑ complete subject
- Ⓒ simple predicate
- Ⓓ complete predicate

8 These <u>animals</u> can run quite fast.
- Ⓐ simple subject
- Ⓑ complete subject
- Ⓒ simple predicate
- Ⓓ complete predicate

Using the Parts of Speech

All the words in our language fit into eight groups. These word groups are called the **parts of speech**.

Nouns

A **noun** names a person, a place, a thing, or an idea.

classmate   Los Angeles   bottle   joy

Kinds of Nouns

Common Nouns	A **common noun** names any person, place, thing, or idea.

girl	building	team	day
dog	house	window	flower
boy	zoo	sidewalk	lake

Proper Nouns	A **proper noun** names a specific person, place, thing, or idea. Proper nouns are capitalized.

Ann	Sears Tower
Atlanta Braves	Thursday
Central Park	California
Thanksgiving Day	Lake Erie

Nouns 1

■ **Common and Proper Nouns**

For each sentence below, write one common noun and one proper noun.

Example: The special quarter for
New Jersey came out
in 1999.
quarter   New Jersey

1. A picture of George Washington is on it.

2. A great big oak tree is on the quarter for Connecticut.

3. Georgia has a peach on its coin.

4. Can you guess which quarter has the Statue of Liberty on it?

5. Maine, the state Mom was born in, has a lighthouse on its quarter.

Next Step: Write a sentence about any state. Include the state's name in your sentence.

Nouns . . .

Singular Nouns	A **singular noun** names one person, place, thing, or idea. kid town computer time
Plural Nouns	A **plural noun** names more than one person, place, thing, or idea. kids towns computers times

Possessive Nouns	A **possessive noun** shows ownership.
	
	  My school's colors are blue and white.
	  Both schools' teams played well.
	
	See page **474** for the rules on forming possessives.

Singular	Plural	Singular possessive	Plural possessive
one person	more than one person	belongs to one person	belongs to more than one person
neighbor	neighbors	neighbor's	neighbors'

Nouns 2

■ Singular and Plural Nouns

Fold your paper in half. Write "singular" on the left and "plural" on the right. Write each noun from the paragraph below in the correct column, like this:

Singular	Plural
Viking	boats

1   Vikings became famous for their ships. A

2   longship often had the head of a dragon carved

3   into its front end. Colorful sails and 10 oars helped

4   move the wooden ship. Painted shields decorated

5   its sides. What a sight it must have been!

Next Step: Write a sentence or two about any ship you've seen. Underline the singular nouns and circle the plural nouns.

Pronouns

A **pronoun** is a word that takes the place of a noun.

Karl climbed over the fence.

He could have been hurt.
(The pronoun *he* replaces the noun *Karl*.)

The lunchroom was a busy place.

It was very crowded.
(The pronoun *it* replaces the noun *lunchroom*.)

Kinds of Pronouns

Common Personal Pronouns	Singular Pronouns	Plural Pronouns
	I, me, my, mine, you, your, yours, he, him, his, she, her, hers, it, its	we, us, our, ours, you, your, yours, they, them, their, theirs

Possessive Pronouns

A **possessive pronoun** shows ownership.

Karl hurt his arm while climbing the fence.
(Karl's arm)

My desk was messy.
(the speaker's desk)

Kendra left her lunch on the table.
(Kendra's lunch)

Pronouns

■ Possessive Pronouns

▶ **For each sentence below, write a possessive pronoun to take the place of the underlined noun or nouns.**

Example: Leann kicked <u>Leann's</u> ball into the sky. *(his, her)*
her

1. Then Ralph brought <u>Ralph's</u> ball over. *(his, their)*

2. Leann and Ralph took turns kicking <u>Leann's and Ralph's</u> balls to each other. *(her, their)*

3. Marina and I want to learn how to play <u>Marina's and my</u> new flutes. *(their, our)*

4. Marina got <u>Marina's</u> flute from a cousin. *(his, her)*

5. The flute was missing one of <u>the flute's</u> keys. *(its, their)*

6. Marina's parents had one of <u>the parents'</u> friends repair it. *(their, its)*

Next Step: Write a sentence about a musical instrument. Use the possessive form of *you*.

Verbs

A **verb** shows action or links two ideas in a sentence.

The monkey eats a banana.   I am happy.

Types of Verbs

Action Verbs

An **action verb** tells what the subject is doing.

Lela eats lots of carrots.

Todd jumped like a kangaroo.

Linking Verbs

A **linking verb** links the subject to a word in the predicate part of a sentence. A linking verb tells something *about* the subject.

My teacher is helpful.
(The verb *is* links *teacher* to *helpful*.)

My friends are happy in our school.
(The verb *are* links *friends* to *happy*.)

Common Linking Verbs: is, are, was, were, am, be, been

Helping Verbs

A **helping verb** comes before the main verb, and it helps state when an action happens.

Pat had called two times.
(*Had* helps the main action verb *called*.)

Pat will be the butler in our play.
(*Will* helps the main linking verb *be*.)

Helping Verbs: has, have, had, will, can, could, should, would, do, did, does, may

Verbs 1

■ Action, Linking, and Helping Verbs

▶ **For each sentence, tell if the underlined verb is "linking," "action," or "helping."**

Example: My cat's name <u>is</u> Tiger.
  linking

1. He does not <u>growl</u> fiercely, though!

2. Tigers <u>are</u> the largest wild cats.

3. A tiger <u>can</u> weigh more than 700 pounds.

4. Tiger cubs <u>stay</u> with their mothers for two years.

5. They <u>live</u> in swamps, forests, and jungles.

6. In 2004, fewer than 5,000 tigers <u>were</u> alive.

7. Without help, they <u>could</u> become extinct.

Next Step: Write a sentence about another wild cat. Use a strong action verb.

Verbs . . .

Tenses of Verbs

The **tense** of a verb tells when the action takes place. Verb tense is often shown by a word's ending (play**s**, play**ed**) or with a helping verb (*will* play, *has* played).

Present Tense Verbs	**Present tense** means the action is happening now or that it happens as a regular event. Jackie plays on our soccer team. Our practices help us a lot.
Past Tense Verbs	**Past tense** means the action happened before the present time, or in the past. Yesterday Jackie played at Hope Field. Three girls scored goals.
Future Tense Verbs	**Future tense** means the action will take place at a later time, or in the future. Tomorrow Jackie will play goalie. We will see a soccer video.

 Some helping verbs describe the time of the action in more detail.

Jackie has played soccer for three years.

Our coach is planning a tournament.

The soccer field had been a pasture.

Verbs 2

■ Simple Tenses

► For each sentence, identify the tense of the underlined verb. Write "present," "past," or "future."

Example: Inspector Sawyer <u>looks</u> for clues.
present

1. Last year he <u>solved</u> most of his cases.

2. He <u>will retire</u> next year.

3. He <u>will spend</u> his time gardening, fishing, and relaxing.

4. Inspector Sawyer <u>lives</u> in the apartment next door to our family.

5. Usually he <u>walks</u> his dog after dinner.

6. Yesterday he <u>worked</u> late, so I walked his dog.

7. Maybe he <u>will offer</u> me one of his prize tomatoes as a thank-you.

Next Step: Write a sentence about a neighbor. Have a classmate identify the tense of the verb in your sentence.

Verbs . . .

Forms of Verbs

Singular Verbs	Use a **singular verb** when the subject is singular. (*Singular* means "one.") Kayla eats almonds. (*Eats* is a singular verb.) Most nouns ending in *s* are plural, but most *verbs* ending in *s* are singular.
Plural Verbs	Use a **plural verb** when the subject is plural. (*Plural* means "more than one.") The other girls love cashews. (*Love* is a plural verb.) Use a verb without an *s* ending for a plural subject.
Regular and Irregular Verbs	Many verbs in our language are **regular**. This means you add *-ed* to form the past tense. I play. Yesterday I played. He kicks. He has kicked. Some verbs in our language are **irregular**. You might use a different word to form the past tense, or you might use the same word. (See page **544**.) I see. I saw. I have seen. She writes. She wrote. She has written.

Verbs 3

■ **Singular and Plural Verbs**

▶ **Write the correct verb (in parentheses) to complete each sentence.**

Example: My family *(have, has)* a new computer.

has

1. I *(type, types)* on an old keyboard.

2. The keys *(stick, sticks)*.

3. My sister *(type, types)* fast on the new keyboard.

4. The new computer *(work, works)* much faster than our old computer did.

5. It *(hold, holds)* more memory, too.

6. My parents *(use, uses)* it more often than they used the old one.

7. Sometimes they *(ask, asks)* for my help!

Next Step: Write a sentence about using computers. Make sure the verb agrees with its subject.

Common Irregular Verbs

Present Tense	Past Tense	Past Tense with *has, have, had*
am, are, is	was, were	been
begin	began	begun
break	broke	broken
bring	brought	brought
catch	caught	caught
come	came	come
do	did	done
draw	drew	drawn
drive	drove	driven
eat	ate	eaten
fall	fell	fallen
fly	flew	flown
get	got	gotten
give	gave	given
go	went	gone
grow	grew	grown
hide	hid	hidden, hid
know	knew	known
put	put	put
ride	rode	ridden
run	ran	run
see	saw	seen
sing	sang, sung	sung
take	took	taken
throw	threw	thrown
write	wrote	written

Verbs 4

■ Irregular Verbs

▶ **For each pair of sentences, write the correct tense of the underlined verb to fill in the blank.**

Example: Sometimes we <u>eat</u> pancakes for dinner. Yesterday we __ate__ beef burritos for dinner.

1. Please <u>bring</u> your treat to school tomorrow.
Last week Tina _____ carrots for a treat.

2. I _____ sick over the weekend. Today I <u>am</u> fine.

3. My dad and I <u>go</u> to the zoo often in summer.
Last winter we _____ there twice.

4. The Jameson brothers <u>throw</u> snowballs.
Once Jerry _____ one at me, but it missed.

5. Terrell, can you <u>catch</u> this boomerang?
Lucy _____ it when she played with it.

Next Step: Write one or two sentences using the past tense of each of these verbs: *sing* and *write*.

Adjectives

An **adjective** is a word that describes a noun or a pronoun. Adjectives tell *what kind*, *how many*, or *which one*.

Some dogs have funny faces.
(An adjective usually comes before the word it describes.)

The fur on a sheepdog is fluffy.
(An adjective may come after a linking verb like *is* or *are*.)

Kinds of Adjectives

Articles

The articles *a*, *an*, and *the* are adjectives.

A pug is a small dog.
(*A* is used before words beginning with a consonant sound.)

An otterhound is a big dog with a long tail.
(*An* is used before words beginning with a vowel sound.)

Proper Adjectives

Some adjectives are formed from proper nouns. They are always capitalized.

The dingo is an Australian dog.

Compound Adjectives

Some adjectives are made up of more than one word. These adjectives are often hyphenated.

The bulldog is our football team mascot.

A dalmatian has a short-haired coat.

A dachshund has a sausage-shaped body.

Adjectives 1

■ **Proper, Common, and Compound Adjectives**

▶ **Write the adjectives found in each sentence below. Do not include articles.**

Example: The poor snowman melts.
   poor

1. It is a Texan snowman.

2. A sunbaked area doesn't work well for a snowman.

3. If it were an Alaskan snowman, it wouldn't melt so quickly.

4. In fact, a snowman could have a long life there.

5. The ice-cold air would keep it from melting.

6. Does a snowman take a July vacation at the North Pole?

7. A trip to Florida would be a short vacation for a snowman!

Next Step: Write the two compound adjectives you found in the sentences above.

Adjectives . . .

Forms of Adjectives

Positive Adjectives	An adjective describes a noun. A pug has a small face.
Comparative Adjectives	Some adjectives compare two nouns. A bulldog is smaller than a dalmatian. (Many comparative adjectives use the ending -*er*.) Bulldogs are more muscular than poodles. (*More* is used before some comparative adjectives with two or more syllables.)
Superlative Adjectives	Some adjectives compare three or more nouns. That Chihuahua is the smallest dog I have ever seen. (Many superlative adjectives use the ending -*est*.) This golden retriever is the most beautiful dog here. (*Most* is used before some superlative adjectives with two or more syllables.)
Irregular Forms of Adjectives	The following adjectives use different words to make comparisons.

Positive	Comparative	Superlative
good	better	best
bad	worse	worst
many	more	most

Adjectives 2

■ Comparative and Superlative Adjectives

▶ **Choose the comparative or the superlative form of the underlined adjectives to fill in the blanks.**

Example: The delivery truck is large, but the garbage truck is ___larger___ .
(larger, largest)

1. A garbage truck is bigger than a pickup truck. Mining trucks are the _____ trucks in the world. *(big, biggest)*

2. Although all trucks are powerful, mining trucks with their two engines are _____ than most trucks. *(more powerful, most powerful)*

3. Mining trucks perform important work, but fire trucks and ambulances perform the _____ work of all. *(more important, most important)*

4. Fire trucks can be fast. However, the _____ vehicle on the road is a car. *(faster, fastest)*

5. A good car uses little fuel. A _____ car will protect the people in it, too. *(better, best)*

Next Step: Write one or two sentences comparing cars and trucks. Use a comparative or superlative adjective in each sentence.

Adverbs

An **adverb** is a word that describes a verb. It tells *how, where,* or *when* an action is done.

Desert temperatures drop quickly as the sun goes down.
Desert animals hunt for food nightly.

Kinds of Adverbs

Adverbs of Manner (How)	Adverbs often tell *how* something is done. The desert sun shines brightly. The horned viper moves silently.
Adverbs of Place (Where)	Some adverbs tell *where* something happens. One scientist works nearby. She stays outside for a long time.
Adverbs of Time (When)	Some adverbs tell *how often* or *when* an action is done. Sand dunes often change their shape. A group of scientists explored the desert yesterday.

 Adverbs often end with *ly,* but not always. Words like *not, never, very,* and *always* are common adverbs.

Adverbs

► Write the adverb that you find in each sentence below. The clue (word) will help you find the adverb.

Example: Alvin said softly, "I have a secret." *(How?)*
softly

1. Then he asked, "Do you want to hear it?" *(When?)*

2. "No," Cedric said, "I'm leaving now." *(When?)*

3. "Are you going far?" Alvin asked. *(Where?)*

4. "No, I'll return soon," Cedric replied as he opened the door. *(When?)*

5. Alvin sadly watched his older brother leave. *(How?)*

6. Cedric called to Alvin, "Tell me your secret later, Al!" *(When?)*

7. "I'll tell you as soon as you get back," he said. *(Where?)*

8. Alvin walked slowly into the kitchen. *(How?)*

Next Step: Write a sentence about a secret. Use an adverb and underline it.

Prepositions

A **preposition** is a word that introduces a prepositional phrase.

Todd slept under the covers. (*Under* is a preposition.)

Teddy slept on the chair. (*On* is a preposition.)

Prepositional Phrases

A prepositional phrase begins with a preposition, and it ends with a noun or a pronoun.

Teddy sleeps on his side.

Todd has a stuffed animal, and he always sleeps with it.

Common Prepositions

about	below	near	to
above	beneath	of	toward
across	between	off	under
after	by	on	underneath
against	during	onto	until
along	for	out of	up
among	from	outside	with
around	in	over	within
at	inside	past	without
before	into	since	
behind	like	through	

Prepositions

▶ **Write the prepositions you find in each sentence.**

Example: The candle flame danced in a warm draft of air.

in, of

1. It was 1889, and Pau read an old book by candlelight.

2. The light formed strange shadows on the ceiling.

3. Pau's cat hid behind the drapes.

4. A spider climbed up a silky thread into its web.

5. The quiet inside his room was scary.

6. Suddenly, there was a knock at the door.

7. "It's time for bed," Pau's dad called to him.

8. As Pau's dad put out the flame, smoke drifted toward the open window.

9. With a sigh, Pau crawled under his covers and went to sleep.

Next Step: Write two sentences about being alone in a quiet room. How many prepositions did you use?

Conjunctions

A **conjunction** connects words or groups of words.

Coordinating Conjunctions	The most common conjunctions are listed here. They are called **coordinating conjunctions**. and but or for so yet We could use <u>skateboards</u> or <u>bikes</u>. (*Or* connects two words.) Maya <u>wrote a poem</u> and <u>sang a song</u>. (*And* connects two phrases.) <u>We ate early,</u> but <u>we still missed the bus.</u> (*But* connects two simple sentences.)
Other Conjunctions	Other conjunctions connect ideas in specific ways. Here are some of these conjunctions: after because when before since I like to skateboard when it is hot. After I saw the lightning, I heard the thunder.

Interjections

An **interjection** is a word or phrase used to express strong emotion or surprise.

Interjections	An interjection is followed by an exclamation point or by a comma. Hey! Slow down! Wow, look at him go!

Conjunctions

▶ Write a coordinating conjunction (and, but, or, for, so, yet) to complete each sentence.

Example: The solar system is made up of nine planets _and_ the sun.

1. Is Mercury ____ Pluto the smallest planet?

2. There may have been water on Mars once, ____ there isn't any now.

3. Rock and metal make up some planets, ____ they are called the rocky planets.

4. The gas planets move quickly ____ have many moons.

5. Jupiter has rings, ____ they are lighter rings than Saturn's rings are.

6. Neptune looks blue, ____ the Romans named Neptune after the god of the sea.

Next Step: Write a sentence comparing two of the planets. Use a coordinating conjunction.

Practice Test

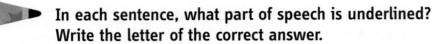

In each sentence, what part of speech is underlined? Write the letter of the correct answer.

1 Do <u>you</u> know who works in your neighborhood?
- Ⓐ pronoun
- Ⓒ preposition
- Ⓑ interjection
- Ⓓ verb

2 You will <u>soon</u> notice many workers.
- Ⓐ pronoun
- Ⓒ adverb
- Ⓑ noun
- Ⓓ conjunction

3 A letter carrier puts mail <u>in</u> your mailbox.
- Ⓐ pronoun
- Ⓒ preposition
- Ⓑ interjection
- Ⓓ verb

4 Waiters or waitresses serve <u>food</u> in restaurants.
- Ⓐ pronoun
- Ⓒ adverb
- Ⓑ noun
- Ⓓ verb

5 A police officer <u>helps</u> if you are lost.
- Ⓐ pronoun
- Ⓒ adverb
- Ⓑ noun
- Ⓓ verb

6 If you are hurt, a nurse <u>quickly</u> takes care of you.
- Ⓐ pronoun
- Ⓒ adverb
- Ⓑ adjective
- Ⓓ verb

7 <u>At</u> the pool, a lifeguard keeps you safe.
- Ⓐ noun
- Ⓑ pronoun
- Ⓒ preposition
- Ⓓ conjunction

8 <u>Wow</u>, there are so many things I can do when I grow up!
- Ⓐ pronoun
- Ⓑ interjection
- Ⓒ preposition
- Ⓓ conjunction

9 I would really like to be a <u>pilot</u>.
- Ⓐ pronoun
- Ⓑ noun
- Ⓒ adverb
- Ⓓ verb

10 Then I could fly a <u>large</u> jet.
- Ⓐ verb
- Ⓑ adjective
- Ⓒ preposition
- Ⓓ pronoun

11 Maybe I could visit Hawaii <u>and</u> Alaska.
- Ⓐ conjunction
- Ⓑ adverb
- Ⓒ pronoun
- Ⓓ interjection

12 Those would be some <u>long</u> trips!
- Ⓐ adverb
- Ⓑ noun
- Ⓒ pronoun
- Ⓓ adjective

Quick Guide: Parts of Speech

Nouns Words that name a person, a place, a thing, or an idea (**Anna, park, scooter, fun**)

Pronouns Words that take the place of nouns (**I, me, you, her, them, ours, theirs**)

Verbs Words that show action or link ideas (**run, jump, is, are**)

Adjectives Words that describe a noun or a pronoun (**old, beautiful, five, the, funny**)

Adverbs Words that describe a verb (**gently, easily, often, nearby**)

Prepositions Words that introduce prepositional phrases (**in, near, under, on top of**)

Conjunctions Words that connect words or groups of words (**and, or, but, when, after**)

Interjections Words (set off by commas or exclamation points) that show emotion or surprise (**Wow, Look out!**)

Credits

Dictionary page: page 303

Copyright © 2007 by Houghton Mifflin Company. Adapted and reproduced by permission from *The American Heritage Children's Dictionary*.

Getty Images: page 300

Acknowledgements

We are grateful to many people who helped bring Write Source to life. First, we must thank all the teachers and students from across the country who contributed writing models and ideas.

In addition, we want to thank our Write Source/Great Source team for all their help:

Steven J. Augustyn, Laura Bachman, Ron Bachman, William Baughn, Heather Bazata, Colleen Belmont, Evelyn Curley, Sandra Easton, Chris Erickson, Mark Fairweather, Jean Fischer, Hillary Gammons, Mariellen Hanrahan, Tammy Hintz, Rob King, Lois Krenzke, Joyce Becker Lee, Mark Lalumondier, Ellen Leitheusser, Dian Lynch, Colleen McCarthy, Sheryl Mendicino, Pat Moore, Kevin Nelson, Sue Paro, Mike Ramczyk, Pat Reigel, Jason C. Reynolds, Christine Rieker, Susan Rogalski, Chip Rosenthal, Janae Sebranek, Lester Smith, Richard Spencer, Julie Spicuzza, Thomas Spicuzza, Barbara Stratton, Stephen D. Sullivan, Jean Varley, and Claire Ziffer.

Index

The index will help you find specific information in this book. Words that are in italics are from the "Using the Right Word" section. The colored boxes contain information you will use often.

A

Abbreviations,
Acronyms, 496
Address, 498
Capitalization of, 205, 488
Initialisms, 496
Punctuation of, 463
State, 498
Academic writing, see
Writing, academic
Acronyms, 496

Across the curriculum writing,
Art, 116–117
Health, 218–219
Music, 168–169
Practical, 118–119, 170–171, 220–221
Science, 215–217
Social studies, 113–115, 165–167

Action, in a story, 275, 280–281
Action verbs, 100, 383, 538
Address,
Abbreviations, 498
Envelope, 212
Inside, 186, 211
Punctuation of, 468

Adjectives, 389–390, 546–549, 558
Articles, 389, 546
Comparative, 390, 548
Compound, 546
Forms of, 390, 548
Irregular, 548
Positive, 390, 548
Proper, 486, 546
Punctuation of, 470
Superlative, 390, 548
Adverbs, kinds of, 391, 550, 558
Agreement,
Antecedent-pronoun, 381
Subject-verb, 388, 406
Alphabet book, 448
Alphabet poem, 293
Ant / aunt, 510
Antecedent, 381
Antonym, 304
Apostrophes, 472–475
Article,
Nonfiction response to an, 264–266
Summarizing an, 308–311, 428–429
Articles, 389, 546

Assessment,
Grammar tests,
Editing for mechanics, 500–501
Parts of speech, 556–557
Punctuation, 484–485
Sentences, 530–531
Using the right word, 524–525
Peer response, 16–19, 93, 145, 193, 330–331
Rubrics, 26–33
Expository, 28–33, 160–161
Narrative, 108–109
Persuasive, 208–209
Writing prompts,
Descriptive, 68–70
Expository, 172–174
Narrative, 120–122
Persuasive, 222–224
Response to literature, 264–266

Ate / eight, 510
Aunt / ant, 510
Autobiography, see
Personal narrative

B

Bar graph, 460
Bare/bear, 510
Basics-of-life list, 434
Beginning, 22, 53, 83, 135, 223, 238, 247, 252, 253, 257, 259, 262, 265, 272, 281, 324, 325
  MODELS 22, 52, 82, 110, 113, 121, 134, 162, 165, 170, 173, 223, 235, 244, 247, 251, 253, 257, 259, 263, 265, 272, 325
Biographical writing, 113–115
Blew/blue, 510
Body, also see *Middle paragraphs*
  Of a letter, 187, 210, 445
  Of a paragraph, 44, 47, 74, 77, 126, 129, 178, 181, 228, 231, 311, 416, 420–421
Book review,
  Comparison, 255–257
  Fiction, 234–235
  Nonfiction, 246–247
Books,
  Capitalizing titles of, 488
  Parts of, 301
  Punctuation of titles, 476, 478
  Reference, 297, 301
Brake/break, 512
Business letter, 185–213, 480
By/buy, 512

C

Call numbers, 297, 299
Capitalization, 486–491
  Abbreviations, 488
  Geographic names, 490
  Proper adjectives, 205, 486
  Proper nouns, 375, 486
  Sentences, 402, 488
Captions, 301
Card catalog, 298–299
Cent/scent/sent, 512
Characters, 271, 280
Charts,
  Five W's, 11, 166, 442
  Gathering, 11, 84
  Ideas, 180
  Plot, 281
  Sensory, 46, 443
  T-chart, 94, 188, 254, 284
  Three-two-one, 249
  Topic, 114, 136–137

Checklists,
  Editing for conventions, 25, 79, 106, 158, 206, 243, 334
  Expository writing, 158
  Listening, 363
  Narrative writing, 106
  Persuasive writing, 206
  Response to literature, 243

Choosing a subject, see *Topics, selecting*

Chronological order, 96, 422
Classroom portfolio, 39–40
Clerihew poem, 291
Climax, see *High point*
Close/clothes, 512
Closing, also see *Ending*
  Letter, 187, 210, 445, 466
  Sentences, 44, 47, 74, 126, 129, 178, 181, 228, 231, 417, 419
Clustering, 128, 316, 424, 436
Colons, 480–481
Combining sentences, 102, 154, 202, 395, 408–409
Commas, 466–471
  In a series, 157, 466
  With introductory word groups, 470
  With quotations, 470
Commercials, viewing, 360
Common noun, 375, 532
Commonly misused words, 510–523
Comparative form adjectives, 390, 548
Complete,
  Predicate, 399, 528
  Sentence, 397–402
  Subject, 398, 526
Compound,
  Adjective, 546
  Predicate, 102, 401, 409, 528
  Sentence, 395, 410, 468
  Subject, 102, 401, 409, 526

Computer,
  Catalog, 300
  Lab, 297
  Multimedia
    presentation,
    338–341
  Research on a, 305
  Web sites, viewing,
    307, 361
  Writing with a, 37
Conflict, 271, 280
Conjunctions,
  coordinating, 394–395,
    554, 558
Context (vocabulary),
  450–451
Contractions, 472

Conventions, 14, 25
  Descriptive writing,
    49, 64, 71
  Expository writing,
    131, 157, 158, 160–
    161, 167, 175
  Multimedia presenta-
    tion, 341
  Narrative writing, 79,
    105, 106, 108–109,
    115, 123
  Paragraphs, 49, 79,
    131, 183, 233, 311
  Persuasive writing,
    183, 205, 206, 208–
    209, 217, 225
  Research writing, 334
  Response to literature,
    233, 243, 250, 256,
    262
  Stories, 277
  Summary paragraph,
    311

Coordinating conjunctions,
  394–395, 554
Copyright page, 301
Correction marks,
  see *Editing and
    proofreading marks*
Creak / creek, 512
Creative writing,
  Poems, 282–293
  Stories, 270–281

Dates, punctuation of,
  468
Days of the week,
  Abbreviations, 496
  Capitalization of, 488
Dear / deer, 512
Declarative sentences,
  411, 463
Delivering a speech,
  344–349
Describing wheel, 436
Description, see
    Descriptive writing

Descriptive writing,
  42–71
  Assessment, writing
    for, 68–70
  Essay, 50–67
  MODELS 45, 52, 66, 69
  Paragraph, 44–49
  Process of, 71
    Editing, 49, 64–65
    Prewriting, 46, 54–55
    Revising, 48, 62–63
    Writing, 47, 56–57
  Prompts, 68–70

Sample topics, 435
Sensory details, 46, 71
Starting points, 56
Voice, 446

Design, page, 36–37
Details,
  Clustering (web), 128,
    316, 424, 436
  Five W's, 11, 166, 442
  Gathering, 46, 55, 85,
    114, 189, 216, 237,
    249, 261, 285, 318–
    319, 424
  Organizing, 422–423
  Sensory, 46, 146, 443
  Time line, 76, 85, 439
  T-Chart, 94
  Types of, 436
Dew / do / due, 512
Dewey decimal system,
  297
Diagrams, see *Graphic
    organizers*
Dialogue, 88, 278–280,
  476
Dictionary, using, 302–
  303, 450
Direct quotation,
  punctuation of, 476
Dividing words, 453–457,
  482
Do / dew / due, 512
Dollars and cents,
  punctuation of 463
Draft, first, see *Writing,
    first draft*

E

Editing,
Conventions, see
Conventions
Descriptive writing,
64–65
Expository writing,
157–158
Narrative writing,
105–107
One writer's process,
14
Paragraph, 49, 53, 79,
131, 183, 233, 311,
425
Persuasive writing,
205–207
Poems, 289
Research writing, 334,
335, 341
Response to literature,
233, 243, 250, 256,
262
Stories, 277
Summary paragraph,
311
**Editing and proofreading
marks**, inside back
cover
Educational programs,
viewing, 358
Eight/ate, 510
Electronic sources, 305
Elements of fiction, 280
E-mail message,
220–221
Encyclopedias, 305

Ending, 22, 53, 61, 83, 91,
135, 143, 223, 241,
247, 253, 257, 259,
263, 273, 281, 328,
329
<u>MODELS</u> 22, 52, 82, 110,
113, 134, 162, 170,
173, 191, 223, 235,
244, 247, 251, 253,
257, 259, 263, 265,
329
Envelope, addressing,
212
Essay tests, 370
Assessment, 68–70,
120–122, 172–174,
222–224, 264–266

Essays,
Assessment, 68–70,
120–122, 172–174,
222–224, 264–266
Book review, 234–257
Descriptive, 50–62
Expository, 32–33,
132–163
Personal narrative,
80–111
Response to literature,
234–257

Event, 280
Exaggeration, 198
Exclamation points, 464
Exclamatory sentence,
411, 464
Experiences, writing
about, 74–121
Explanation, 421

Expository writing,
124–175
Across the curriculum,
Practical, 170–171
Social studies, 165–167
Assessment, writing
for, 172–174
Book reviews, 234–257
Business letter, 186
Essay, 132–163
How-to essay, 170–171
Interviews, 320–321
Learning logs, 354–355
<u>MODELS</u> 32, 127, 134,
162, 165, 170, 173
Paragraphs, 126–131
Process of, 175
Editing, 131, 157–161
Prewriting, 128,
136–137
Publishing, 162
Revising, 130, 144–
156, 167, 175
Writing, 129, 138–
143, 167, 175
Prompts, 172–174
Research reports,
312–341
Response to literature,
226–267
Rubric, 28–33, 160–161
Speeches, 344–349
Summaries, 308–311,
428–429
Test taking, 68–70,
120–122, 172–174,
222–224, 264–266
Topics, 128, 136, 435
Voice, 447

Eye/I, 514

Fact, 182
Family stories, 448
Fantasy time travel, 448
Fiction, 234–245, 252
  Elements of, 280
Fiction book, review of,
  234–245
Fill-in-the-blank test, 369
Final copy, 36–37, 66,
  110, 162, 244, 251,
  257, 263, 336
First draft, see *Writing,
  first draft*
First words, capitalizing,
  402, 488
Five W's, 11, 442
  Poem, 260, 292
Flash cards, 371
Fluency, sentence, see
  *Sentence fluency
  (writing trait)*
For / four, 514

Forms of writing,
  Across the curriculum,
    see *Practical
    writing, Science,
    Social studies*
  Autobiography, see
    Personal narrative
  Book review,
  Business letter, 184–
    213
  Descriptive, see
    Descriptive writing
  Essay, see *Essay*
  Evaluating, see
    Assessment

Expository, see
  Expository writing
Friendly letter, 118–119
Journals, 351–353
Learning logs, 354–355
Narrative, see
  Narrative writing
Persuasive, see
  Persuasive writing
Poems, 282–293
Research, see *Research
  writing*
Response to literature,
  see *Response to
  literature*
Speeches, 344–349
Stories, 270–281
Summary, 308–311,
  428–429

Fragment sentence, 403
Free-verse poem, 448
Friendly letter, 118–119,
  445
Future tense, 387, 540

Gathering details, see
  Details, gathering
Gathering grid, 318–319
Gathering wheel, 84
General noun, 152, 378
Geographic names,
  capitalization of, 490
Glossary, 301
Goals, understanding
  your, 51, 81, 133, 185
Grammar,
  Parts of speech, 532–558
  Sentences, 526–531

Graphic organizers,
  Bar graph, 460
  Basics-of-life list, 434
  Clustering, 128, 316,
    436
  Describing wheel, 436
  Diagram,
    Picture, 55
    Table, 222, 429
    Venn, 255, 438
    Five W's, 11, 442
  Gathering grid, 318–
    319
  Gathering wheel, 84
  Idea map, 371
  Ideas chart, 180
  Plot chart, 281
  Sensory details, 46,
    285, 443
  Storyboard, 340
  T-chart, 94, 188, 254,
    284
  Three-two-one chart,
    249
  Time line, 76, 85, 439
  Topic chart, 114, 136–
    137
  Web, see *Clustering*

Graphs, 460
Greeting, letter, 187, 210,
  445, 466, 480
Grid, gathering, 318–319
Group skills, advising,
  see *Peer responding*
Growth portfolio, 39
Guide words, 302, 303
Guidelines,
  Modeling, 412
  Paragraphs, 424–425

Haiku, 260
Hare/hair, 514
Heading, letter, 187, 210, 445
Heal/heel, 514
Hear/here, 514
Heard/herd, 514
Helping verbs, 200, 385, 538
High point, 273, 281
Hole/whole, 514
Holidays, 488
Homonyms, 510
Homophones, 105, 510
Hour/our, 514
How-to essay, 170–171
Hyphens, 482

Ideas,
Descriptive writing, 45, 51, 54, 69
Expository writing, 127, 133, 135, 140, 145, 146, 156, 160–161, 173
Narrative writing, 75, 81, 83, 92, 94, 104, 108–109, 121
Persuasive writing, 179, 185, 192, 204, 208–209, 223
Research writing, 315
Response to literature, 229, 230, 235, 247, 253, 259, 265
Summary paragraph, 309

Ideas chart, 180
Ideas cluster, 128, 316, 436
Ideas list, 172, 216
Ideas, writing, 9, 434
Imperative sentences, 411, 463
Importance, organization by, 422–423
Index, 301
Information, finding, 296–307
Initialisms, 496
Initials, punctuation of, 463
Inside address, 186–211
Interjection, 554, 558
Internet,
Encyclopedia, 305
Using, 307
World Wide Web, 361
Interrogative, sentence, 411, 464
Interviews, 320–321
Introductory words, punctuation of, 470
Irregular,
Adjective, 548
Noun, 492
Verb, 542, 544
Italics, 478
Its/it's, 516

Journal,
Learning log, 354–355
Personal, 350, 351, 448
Reading, 352–353
Response, 359

Key words, sentence combining, 408
Keywords, computer catalog, 300, 305
Knew/new, 516
Knight/night, 516
Know/no, 516

L

Learning log, 354–355
Legend, map, 304
Letters,
Business, 186–213
Friendly, 118–119, 445
Parts of, 187, 210, 445, 466, 480
Persuasive, 186–213
Library, using, 297–307
Call numbers, 297, 299
Card catalog, 298–299
Computer catalog, 300
Reference materials, 302–307
Life map, 441
Limerick, 290
Linking verbs, 384, 538
Linking words, see *Transitions*
Listening skills, 18, 362–363
Listing, 436, 448
Literature,
Elements of fiction, 280
Response to, 226–267
Location,
Organization by, 422–423

M

Made/maid, 516
Magazine articles, citing as sources, 306
Main/mane, 516
Map,
　Atlas, 304
　Legend, 304
　Life, 441
　Story 440
Margins, page, 37
Marking paragraphs, 426–427
Matching test, 367
Math, log 354
Meaning, 302, 450, 451
Meat/meet, 516
Media grid, 339
Media section, library, 297
Memory trick, 371
Methods of organization, 422–423
Middle paragraphs, 53, 58–59, 83, 88–89, 135, 140–141, 223, 235, 240, 246, 252, 253, 257, 259, 263, 326
　MODELS 52, 82, 110, 113, 121, 134, 162, 170, 173, 191, 223, 235, 244, 246, 251, 253, 257, 259, 263, 265, 326, 327
Modeling sentences, 412–413
Modes of writing, see
　Descriptive writing

Expository writing
Narrative writing
Persuasive writing
Money, punctuation of, 463
Months,
　Abbreviations, 496
　Capitalization of, 488
Moral, 280
Multimedia, presentation, 338–341
Multiple-choice test, 368

N

Names of people, capitalization of, 486

Narrative writing, 72–123
　Across the curriculum,
　　Practical, 118–119
　　Social studies, 115–117
　Assessment, writing for, 120–122
　Biographical, 115–117
　Essay, 80–111
　MODELS 75, 82, 110, 113, 121
　Organization, 83
　Paragraphs, 74–79
　Personal narrative, 80–111
　Process of, 123
　　Editing, 79, 105–107, 115
　　Prewriting, 76, 84–85
　　Publishing, 110

　Revising, 78, 92–104, 115, 123
　Writing, 77, 86–91, 115
　Prompts, 120–122
　Reflecting on, 111
　Rubrics, 108–109
　Topics, 84, 435
　Voice, 446

Narrator, 280
New/knew, 516
News programs, viewing, 357
News report, 165–167
Newspaper stories, 448
Night/knight, 516
No/know, 516
Nonfiction, 226, 246–251, 252–257, 297
　Article, response to, 264–266
　Book review of, 246–251
Note cards, speech, 347
Notebook,
　New-word, 449
　Writer's, 432–433
Nouns, 375–378, 532–535, 558
　Common, 375, 532
　General, 152, 378
　Plurals of, 376–377, 492, 534
　Possessives, 377, 474, 534
　Proper, 375, 486, 532
　Singular, 376, 534
　Specific, 152, 378
Numbers,
　Punctuating, 466
　Using numerals for, 494

Object pronoun, 379
One / won, 516
One writer's process, 10–15
Opinion, 182
  Sentence, 189
  Supporting an, 194
Oral presentations, 336–339, 342–347
Organization,
  Checklist, 196
  Location, by, 58, 422
  Methods of, 422–423
  Order of importance, by, 422
  Time order, by, 96, 422

Organization, 22
  Descriptive writing, 45, 51, 53, 69
  Expository writing, 127, 133, 135, 144, 149, 156, 160–161, 173
  Narrative writing, 75, 81, 83, 92, 96, 104, 108–109, 121
  Paragraph, 422–423
  Persuasive writing, 179, 185, 187, 192, 196, 204, 208–209, 223
  Poems, 283
  Research writing, 315
  Response to literature, 229, 235, 247, 253, 255, 259, 265
  Stories, 273
  Summary paragraph, 309

Organizers, graphic, see *Graphic organizers*
Our / hour, 514
Outline,
  Sentence, 322–323
  Topic, 444
Ownership, see *Possessives*

Page design, 37
Pair / pare / pear, 518
Paragraphs, 416–429
  Basic parts, 416–417
  Beginning, see *Topic sentences*
  Body, 44, 47, 74, 77, 126, 129, 179, 181, 228, 231, 416, 420
    MODELS, 45, 75, 127, 179, 228, 417
  Closing sentence, 44, 47, 74, 77, 126, 129, 179, 181, 228, 231, 416, 419
    MODELS, 45, 75, 127, 179, 228, 417
  Descriptive, 44–49
  Details, 46, 76, 420–421
  Expository, 126–131
  Marking, 426–427
  Narrative, 74–79
  Organizing, 422–423
  Parts of, 416–417
  Persuasive, 178–183
  Response to literature, 228–233
  Summary, 308–311, 428–429

Topic sentence, 418
  Transitions in, 96, 458–459
  Writing guidelines, 424–425
Parentheses, 482
Partners, working with, 16-19
Parts of a book, nonfiction, 301
Parts of speech, 532–555
  Adjectives, 389–390, 546–549, 558
  Adverbs, 391–392, 550, 558
  Conjunctions, 393–395, 554, 558
  Interjections, 554, 558
  Nouns, 375–378, 532–535, 558
  Prepositions, 393, 552, 558
  Pronouns, 379–382, 536, 558
  Quick guide, 558
  Verbs, 100, 383–388, 538–545, 558
Past tense, 386, 540
Peace / piece, 518
Peer responding, see *Working with partners*
  Response sheet, 19, 93, 145, 193, 331
Periodicals, 297, 306
Periods, 397, 463
Personal,
  Journal, 351, 448
  Narrative, 80–111
  Portfolio, 38
  Pronouns, 379, 536

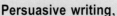

Persuasive writing,
176–225
Across the curriculum,
Practical, 220–221
Science, 215–217
Assessment, writing
for, 222–224
Checklist, 196, 206
E-mail message, 220–
221
Evaluating, 193
Letter, 185–213
MODELS 179, 186, 211
Opinion sentence, 189
Paragraph, 178–183
Poster, 215–217
Process of, 225
Editing, 183, 205–
207
Prewriting, 180,
188–189
Publishing, 210–212
Revising, 182, 192–
204
Writing, 181, 190–191
Prompts, 222–224
Reflecting on, 213
Rubric, 208–209
Sample topics, 435
Supporting an opinion,
194
Traits of, 185
Voice, 447

Photo essay, 448
Phrase poem, 261
Picture diagrams, 55
Places, names of, 490
Plain / plane, 518
Play, 278–279
Plot (story) line, 271, 275,

280, 281
Plural nouns, 376, 492,
534
Plural pronouns, 382, 536
Plural verbs, 542
Poems, 258–263,
282–293
Alphabet, 293
Clerihew, 291
Five W's, 260, 292
Free-verse, 448
Haiku, 260
Limerick, 290
Phrase, 261
Responding to, 258–263
Rhyming, 283
Techniques, 286
Writing, 282–293
Portfolios, 38–41
Positive form, adjectives,
390, 548
Possessive nouns, 377,
474, 534
Possessive pronouns,
380, 536
Possessives, forming,
474
Poster, persuasive,
215–217

Practical writing,
Business letter, 185–213
E-mail message, 220–
221
Friendly letter, 118–
119
How-to essay, 170–171
Persuasive letter,
185–213

Predicate of a sentence,
233
Complete, 399, 528
Compound, 102, 409,
528
Simple, 400, 528
Prefixes, 453–454
Prepositional phrases,
393, 552
Prepositions, 393, 552,
558
Present tense, 386, 540

Presentation,
Multimedia, 338–341
Oral, 344–349

Prewriting, 6, 11
Descriptive writing, 46,
54–55
Expository writing,
128, 136–137
Multimedia report, 339
Narrative writing, 76,
84–85
Paragraph, 46, 76, 128,
180, 230, 424
Persuasive writing,
180, 188–189
Poems, 284–285
Research writing,
310, 316–323, 339
Response to literature,
236–237, 248–249,
254–255, 260–261
Stories, 274–275
Summary paragraph,
310
Process,
One writer's, 10–15
Writing, using the, 2–9

Prompts for assessment,
Classroom tests, 370
Descriptive, 68–70
Expository, 172–174
Narrative, 120–122
Persuasive, 222–224
Response to literature,
264–266
Pronouns, 379–382,
536, 558
Agreement, 381
Antecedent, 381
Object, 379
Personal, 379, 536
Plural, 382, 536
Possessive, 380, 536
Singular, 380
Subject, 379
Pronunciation, 302,
450–451
Proofreader's guide,
462–558
Editing for mechanics,
486–501
Parts of speech,
532–558
Punctuation, 463–485
Spelling, 502–509
Understanding
sentences, 526–531
Using the right word,
510–525
Proofreading marks,
inside back cover
Proper adjective, 486,
546
Proper noun, 375, 486,
532
Publishing, 7, 15, 34–37
Descriptive writing, 66
Expository writing, 162

Narrative writing, 110
Persuasive writing,
210–212
Research writing, 336
Punctuation,
463–485
Apostrophes, 472–475
Colons, 480
Commas, 167, 466–471
Exclamation points,
464
Hyphens, 482
Italics and
underlining, 478
Parentheses, 482
Periods, 402, 463
Question marks, 464
Quotation marks, 476
Underlining, as italics,
478

Q

Question mark, 402, 464
Quotation marks, 476
Quotations, punctuation
of, 470, 476

R

Rambling sentence, 405
Read/red, 518
Reading journal, 352–353
Red/read, 518
Reasons, 436
Reference books, 297,
302–305
Reflecting on your
writing, 67, 111, 163,
213, 245, 337
Regular verbs, 542
Repetition, 286

Research writing,
312–341
Internet, using the, 307
Library, using the,
297–307
MODELS 313–315
Process of,
Editing, 334–335,
341
Prewriting, 316–323,
339
Publishing, 336
Revising, 330–333,
341
Writing, 324–329,
340
Reference materials,
302–307
Reflecting on your
writing, 337
Research report, 312–
337
Summary paragraph,
308–311

Responding, peer, 16–19

Response to literature,
226–267
Assessment, writing
for, 264–266
Book review, 234–257
MODELS 229, 235, 244,
247, 251, 253, 257,
259, 263, 265
Nonfiction article,
264–266
Paragraph, 228–233
Poem, 258–263
Process of, 267
Editing, 233, 243,
250, 256, 262
Prewriting, 230, 236,
248, 254, 260–261
Revising, 232, 242,
250, 256, 262
Writing, 231, 238–
241, 250, 256, 262
Prompts, 264–266
Reflecting on your
writing, 245

Review, book,
Comparison, 252–257
Fiction, 234–245
Nonfiction, 246–251
Revising, 6, 13
Descriptive writing, 48,
62–63
Expository writing,
130, 144–156
Multimedia
presentation, 341
Narrative writing, 78,
92–104
Paragraph, 48, 78, 130,
182, 232, 311, 425
Persuasive writing,

182, 192–204
Poems, 289
Research writing,
330–333
Response to literature,
232, 242, 256, 262
Stories, 277
Summary paragraph,
311
Rhyme, 286
Rhythm, 286
Right / write, 518
Rising action, 272, 281
Road / rode / rowed, 518
Roots, 456–457

Rubrics,
Expository writing,
28–33, 160–161
Narrative writing,
108–109
Persuasive writing,
208–209
Using, 26–33

Run-on sentence, 404

Salutation, 187, 210, 445,
466, 480
Scene / seen, 518
Scent / cent / sent, 512

Science,
E-mail message, 220–
221
Log, 355
Persuasive poster,
215–217

Sea / see, 520
Selecting a topic, see
Topics, selecting
Sending letters, 210–212
Sensory details, 46, 146,
443
Sent / cent / scent, 512

Sentence fluency, 24
Expository writing,
133, 154–155, 160–
161
Narrative writing,
81, 92, 102–103,
108–109
Persuasive writing,
185, 202, 208–209

Sentences, 396–415,
526–531
Basic parts of, 398–
401, 526, 528
Beginnings, 494
Choppy, 154, 202
Closing, 44, 47, 74, 77,
126, 127, 178, 181,
228, 231, 309, 311,
417, 419
Combining, 102, 154,
202, 395, 408–409
Complete, 397–402
Compound, 395, 410,
468
Declarative, 411, 463
Exclamatory, 411, 464
Fragment, 403
Imperative, 411, 463
Interrogative, 411, 464
Kinds of, 411
Length, 102
Modeling, 412–413

Outline, 322–323
Parts, 526–529
Practice test, 414–415, 530–531
Problems, 403–406
Punctuation of, 402, 463, 464, 466, 468, 470
Rambling, 405
Run-on, 166, 404
Style, 407–413
Subject-verb agreement, 388, 406
Topic, 44, 47, 74, 77, 126, 129, 178, 181, 228, 231, 416, 419
Series,
Punctuation of, 157, 466
Of words and phrases, combining, 102, 394, 408
Setting, 271, 274, 278–280
Sew/so/sow, 520
Showcase portfolio, 39
Signature (letter), 187, 210, 445
Simple,
Predicate, 400, 528
Subject, 400, 526
Tenses, 386–387
Singular nouns, 376, 534
Singular pronouns, 380
Singular verbs, 542
Soar/sore, 520

Social studies,
Biographical narrative, 113–115
Log, 354
News report, 165–167

Some/sum, 520
Son/sun, 520
Sources, library, 302–307
Speaking skills, 344–349
Specific nouns, 152, 378
Speech, parts of, 302, 374–395, 532–555
Speech skills, 344–349
Spelling,
Commonly misspelled words, 503–507
Dictionary, 302, 450
Irregular plurals, 492
Rules, 502–503
State abbreviations, 498
State or district writing tests, taking, see *Tests*
Step-by-step organization, see *Chronological order*
Story map, 440
Story (plot) line, 271, 275, 280, 281
Story writing, 280–281
MODEL 272–273
Plays, 278–279
Plot chart, 281
Plot line, 271, 275, 280, 281
Storyboard, 340
Student-response sheet, see *Working with partners*

Study skills,
Listening, 362–363
Test taking, 364–371
Vocabulary, 449–457

Style, sentence, 407–413

Subject cards/entries, 298–299
Subject, of a sentence, 233
Complete, 398, 526
Compound, 102, 401, 409, 526
Simple, 400, 526
Subject pronoun, 379
Subject-verb agreement, 388, 406
Subjects, choosing, see *Topics, selecting*
Suffixes, 454–455
Sum/some, 520
Summary paragraph, 428–429
Superlative form, adjectives, 390, 548
Support, for an opinion, 194
Supporting, details, see *Details*
Syllable divisions, 302, 450, 451
Symbols, correction, see *Editing and Proofreading Marks,* inside back cover
Synonym, 302–303, 304, 450, 451, 452

T

Table diagram, 222, 429
Table of contents, 301
Tables, 461
Tail / tale, 520
Tall tale, 448
T-chart, 94, 188, 284
Technical writing, see
　Practical writing
Techniques,
　Poetry, 286
　Vocabulary building,
　　449–457
Television viewing skills,
　356–361
Tense of verbs, 386–387,
　540

Test prep,
　Editing for mechanics,
　　500–501
　Marking punctuation,
　　484–485
　Spelling, 508–509
　Understanding
　　sentences, 414–415,
　　530–531
　Using the parts of
　　speech, 556–557
　Using the right word,
　　524–525

　Tests, taking, 364–371
　Responding to
　　prompts, 370
　Summary, 428–429
　Types, 366–369
Their / there / they're, 520
Theme, 241, 280
Thesaurus, 304, 450

Threw / through, 520
Time line, 76, 85, 439
Time order, 96
Time, organized by,
　422–423
Time, punctuation of, 480
Time-travel fantasy, 448
Title cards/entries, 298–299
Title page, 301
Titles,
　Adding, 289, 334
　Capitalization of, 488
　Punctuation of, 476, 478
Titles of people,
　Capitalization of, 488
　Punctuation of, 463
To / too / two, 522
Topic,
　Chart, 114, 136
　Outlines, 444
　Sentences, 44, 46, 74,
　　77, 126, 129, 178,
　　181, 228, 231, 416,
　　419, 418, 437
　　MODELS 45, 75, 127,
　　　179, 229, 417, 437
Topics,
　Sample, 434–435
　Selecting, 11, 432–435
　　Descriptive writing,
　　　54
　　Expository writing,
　　　128, 136, 166
　　Multimedia
　　　presentation, 339
　　Narrative writing,
　　　84, 114
　　Paragraph, 424
　　Persuasive writing,
　　　180, 188, 216
　　Poems, 284

Research writing,
　316
Response to
　literature, 236,
　248, 254, 260
Speech, 345
Stories, 274–275

Traits of writing, 5, 20–25
　Conventions, 25, also
　　see *Conventions*
　Ideas, 21, also see
　　Ideas
　Organization, 22, also
　　see *Organization*
　Publishing, 34–41
　Sentence fluency, 24,
　　also see *Sentence
　　fluency*
　Voice, 23, also see
　　Voice
　Word choice, 24, also
　　see *Word choice*

Transitions, 96, 458–459
True/false test, 366
Two / to / too, 522

U

Underlining, as italics,
　478–479
Understanding,
　Rubrics, 26–33
　The writing process,
　　4–9
Using the right word,
　510–523

Venn diagram, 255, 438
Verbs, 383–388, 538–
    545, 558
  Action, 100, 383, 538
  Agreement with
    subject, 388–406
  Compound, 102
  Helping, 200, 385, 538
  Irregular, 542, 544
  Linking, 384, 538
  Plural, 542
  Predicate in a
    sentence, 102, 233,
    399–401, 409, 528
  Regular, 542
  Simple tense, 386, 540
  Singular, 542
  Tense, 386–387, 540
Viewing skills, 356–361
Vocabulary,
  Building techniques,
    449–457
  Homophones, 105
  Notebook, 449
  Prefixes, suffixes,
    roots, 453–457
  Using a dictionary,
    302–303, 450

Voice, 23
  Descriptive writing,
    45, 51, 53, 446
  Expository writing,
    133, 150, 160–161,
    447
  Narrative writing, 81,
    98, 108–109, 446

Persuasive writing,
    185, 198, 208–209,
    447
  Revising for, 98, 150,
    198
  Stories, 273
  Summaries, 309

W

Waist / waste, 522
Wait / weight, 522
Way / weigh, 522
Weak / week, 522
Wear / where, 522
Web diagram, see
    Clustering
Web sites, viewing, 307,
    361
Which / witch, 522
Whole / hole, 514
Why write?, 1
Won / one, 516
Wood / would, 522

Word choice, 24
  Descriptive writing, 51,
    53, 69
  Expository writing,
    127, 133, 135, 152,
    160–161, 173
  Narrative writing, 75,
    81, 83, 100, 108–109,
    121
  Persuasive writing,
    179, 185, 187, 200,
    208–209, 223
  Poems, 283
  Research writing, 315,
    332–333

Response to literature,
    229, 235, 247, 253,
    259, 265
  Stories, 273

Word history, 302, 450,
    451
Words,
  Division of, 482, 453–
    457
  Linking, see
    Transitions
  Parts of, 453–457
  Series of, 157, 466
  Using the right, 510–
    525
Working with partners,
    16-19
Workplace writing,
  Business letters, 184–
    212, 480
  E-mail message, 220–
    221
Write / right, 518
Writer's notebook, 432
Writing,
  Assessment prompts,
    Class tests, 370
  Descriptive, 68–70
  Expository, 172–174
  Narrative, 120–122
  Persuasive, 222–224
  Response to
    literature, 264–266
  Beginnings, see
    Beginning
  Endings, see *Ending*
  Essays, see *Essays*
  Forms of, see *Forms of
    writing*

Middles, see *Middle paragraphs*
Paragraphs, see *Paragraphs*
Publishing, 7, 15, 34–37
Selecting a topic,
  Descriptive writing, 54
  Expository writing, 128, 136, 166
  Narrative writing, 84, 114
  Persuasive writing, 180, 188, 216
  Poems, 284
  Research writing, 316
  Response to literature, 236, 248, 254, 260
  Stories, 274–275
Sentences, see *Sentences*
Topics, see *Topics*
Traits of writing, 5, 20–25 (also see each individual entry)
  Conventions, 14, 25
  Ideas, 21
  Organization, 22
  Sentence fluency, 24
  Voice, 23
  Word choice, 24

Writing, academic
  Assessment, responding to a prompt, 264–266
  Book reviews, 234–257
  Literature response paragraph, 228–233

Nonfictional article, response to a, 264–266
Poetry, response to, 258–263
Research report, 312–337
Summary paragraph, 308–311, 428–429
Test prompts, 68–70, 120–122, 172–174, 222–224, 264–266

Writing across the curriculum,
  see *Across the curriculum writing*
Writing a first draft, 6, 12
  Descriptive writing, 47, 56–61
  Expository writing, 129, 138–143
  Multimedia presentation, 340
  Narrative writing, 77, 86–91, 115
  Paragraph, 311, 425
  Persuasive writing, 181, 190–191, 217
  Poems, 288
  Research writing, 324–329
  Response to literature, 231, 238–241, 250, 256, 262
  Stories, 276
  Summary paragraph, 311

Writing, modes of, see
  Descriptive writing
  Expository writing
  Narrative writing
  Persuasive writing
Writing, practical,
  see *Practical writing*

Writing process, using, 2–41
  Editing, 7, 14
  One writer's process, 10–15
  Prewriting, 6, 11
  Publishing, 7, 15, 34–37
  Revising, 6, 13
  Understanding the, 4–9
  Writing, 6, 12

Writing tests, see *Tests, taking*
Writing with partners, 16–19

Your / you're, 522